# 100 ENGLISH LESSONS

## Terms and conditions

### IMPORTANT – PERMITTED USE AND WARNINGS – READ CAREFULLY BEFORE USING

Recommended system requirements:

- Windows: XP (Service Pack 3), Vista (Service Pack 2), Windows 7 or Windows 8 with 2.33GHz processor
- Mac: OS 10.6 to 10.8 with Intel Core™ Duo processor
- 1GB RAM (recommended)
- 1024 x 768 Screen resolution
- CD-ROM drive (24x speed recommended)
- 16-bit sound card
- Adobe Reader (version 9 recommended for Mac users)
- Broadband internet connections (for installation and updates)

For all technical support queries, please phone Scholastic Customer Services on 0845 6039091.

Book End, Range Road, Witney, Oxfordshire, OX29 0YD
www.scholastic.co.uk

© 2014, Scholastic Ltd

1 2 3 4 5 6 7 8 9   4 5 6 7 8 9 0 1 2 3

British Library Cataloguing-in-Publication Data
A catalogue record for this book is available from the
British Library.

ISBN 978-1407-12761-3
Printed by Bell & Bain Ltd, Glasgow

Extracts from *The National Curriculum in English*, *English
Programme of Study* © Crown Copyright. Reproduced
under the terms of the Open Government Licence
(OGL). http://www.nationalarchives.gov.uk/doc/open-
government-licence/open-government-licence.htm

**Author**
Paul Hollin

**Editorial team**
Rachel Morgan, Melissa Somers, Sarah Sodhi,
Gemma Cary

**Cover Design**
Andrea Lewis

**Design Team**
Sarah Garbett, Shelley Best and Andrea Lewis

**CD-ROM development**
Hannah Barnett, Phil Crothers, MWA Technologies
Private Ltd

**Typesetting**
Brian Melville

**Illustrations**
Jim Peacock

**Acknowledgements**
The publishers gratefully acknowledge permission
to reproduce the following copyright material:
**Moira Andrew** for the use of 'King Midas and the
Golden Touch' by Moira Andrew, first published in
*Child Education Topics* December 2005. Text © Moira
Andrew, (2005, Scholastic Ltd). **Clare Bevan** for the
use of the story 'Sleeping Beauty' by Clare Bevan,
first published in *Child Education Plus* in December
2008. Text © 2008, Clare Bevan (2008, Scholastic
Ltd). **Paul Cookson** for the use of 'Rejected names
found in a superhero's bin' by Paul Cookson first
published in *Pants on Fire* by Paul Cookson. Poem
© 2005 Paul Cookson (2005, Macmillan Children's
Books) and for the use of the poem 'Superman's
dog' by Paul Cookson first published in *The very
Best of Paul Cookson* by Paul Cookson. Poem © 2001
Paul Cookson (2001, Macmillan Children's Books).
**David Higham Associates** for the use of an extract
from *The Twits* by Roald Dahl. Text © 1980, Roald
Dahl Nominee Ltd (1980, Jonathan Cape); for the
use of an extract from *Charlie and the Chocolate
Factory* by Roald Dahl. Text © 1964, Roald Dahl
Nominee Ltd (1964, Jonathan Cape); for the use of
an extract from *George's Marvellous Medicine* by
Roald Dahl. Text © 1981, Roald Dahl Nominee Ltd
(1981, Jonathan Cape); for the use of an extract
from *The Twits: Plays for Children* by Roald Dahl
adapted by David Wood. Text © 2003, Roald Dahl
Nominee Ltd and David Wood (2003, Puffin Books)
and for the use of extracts from *Revolting Rhymes*
by Roald Dahl. Text © 1982, Roald Dahl Nominee
Ltd (1982, Jonathan Cape). **Egmont** for the use
of an extract from *King of the Cloud Forests* by
Michael Morpurgo. Text © 1987, Michael Morpurgo.
(1987, William Heinemann Ltd). **Gillian Howell** for
the use of 'Princess and the Pea' by Gillian Howell,
first published in *100 Literacy Assessment Lessons
Year 1* by Gillian Howell. Text © 2010, Gillian Howell
(2010, Scholastic Ltd). **Brian Moses** for the use of
the poem 'Aliens stole my underpants' by Brian
Moses from *Behind The Staffroom Door – The
Very Best of Brian Moses* by Brian Moses. Poem ©
2007, Brian Moses (2007, Macmillan). **Scholastic
Inc** for the use of a spread from *The Adventures
of Captain Underpants* by Dav Pilkey. Text © 1997,
Dav Pilkey (1997, Scholastic Inc). **Sourcebooks** for
the use of the poem 'Steve the Superhero' by Kenn
Nesbitt first published in *Hippo has the Hiccups* by
Kenn Nesbitt. Poem © 2009, Kenn Nesbitt (2009,
Sourcebooks www.sourcebooks.com). **Wade &
Doherty Literary Agency Ltd** for the use of the
poem 'Auntie Betty thinks she's a batgirl' by Andrea
Shavick. Poem © 2005, Andrea Shavick. **Celia
Warren** for the use of five poems: 'Pick'n'Mix Zoo'
by Celia Warren, first published in *First Verses* by
John Foster. Poem © 1996 Celia Warren (1996, OUP);
'Gingerbread Man' by Celia Warren, first published
in *More First Verses* by John Foster. Poem © 1999,
Celia Warren (1999, OUP); 'Chocolate Box', 'I'd do
anything for chocolate' and 'An Easter wish' by
Celia Warren. Poems © 2014, Celia Warren (2014,
Scholastic Ltd).
Every effort has been made to trace copyright
holders for the works reproduced in this book,
and the publishers apologise for any inadvertent
omissions.

# Contents

# Introduction

## About the series

The *100 English Lessons* series is designed to meet the requirements of the 2014 Curriculum, English Programmes of Study. There are six books in the series, Years 1–6, and each book contains lesson plans, resources and ideas matched to the new curriculum. It can be a complex task to ensure that a progressive and appropriate curriculum is followed in all year groups; this series has been carefully structured to ensure that a progressive and appropriate curriculum is followed throughout.

## About the new curriculum

The curriculum documentation for English provides a single-year programme of study for Year 1 and Year 2, but joint programmes of study for Years 3–4 and Years 5–6.

There is a much greater focus on the technical aspects of language – including grammar, punctuation, spelling, handwriting and phonics. These are the building blocks to help children to read and write. It has been perceived that these aspects have to be taught discretely, however the approach encouraged in this series is to embed these elements into existing learning. For example, using a focus text to identify the use of punctuation and using that as a springboard to practise it.

There is a spoken language Programme of Study which outlines statutory requirements across Years 1–6. Within the English curriculum there are also attainment targets that involve 'discussion', 'talking', 'participating' and 'listening'. The aims of speaking and listening are below:

> *The National Curriculum for English reflects the importance of spoken language in children's development across the whole curriculum – cognitively, socially and linguistically. The quality and variety of language that children hear and speak are vital for developing their vocabulary, grammar and their understanding for reading and writing. Teachers should therefore ensure the continual development of children's confidence and competence in spoken language. Children should develop a capacity to explain their understanding of books and other reading, and to prepare their ideas before they write. They must be assisted in making their thinking clear to themselves as well as to others and teachers should ensure that children build secure foundations by using discussion to probe and remedy their misconceptions. Children should also be taught to understand and use the conventions for discussion and debate.*
>
> *Statutory requirements which underpin all aspects of speaking and listening across the six years of primary education form part of the National Curriculum. These are contextualised within the reading and writing domains which follow.*

## Terminology

The curriculum terminology has changed; the main terms used are:

- **Domains:** The area of the subject, for English the domains are 'Reading' and 'Writing'.
- **Sub-domains:** The next level down to the domains. In English, Reading's sub-domains are 'Word reading' and 'Comprehension' and Writing's sub-domains are 'Transcription' and 'Composition'.
- **Curriculum objectives:** These are the statutory programme of study statements or objectives.
- **Appendix:** Any reference to an appendix refers to an appendix of the National Curriculum for English document. There are two appendices – one for spelling (Appendix 1) and one for vocabulary, grammar and punctuation (Appendix 2).

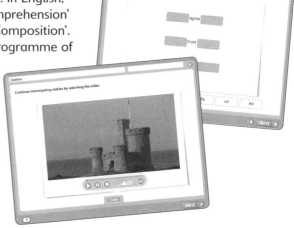

■SCHOLASTIC

# About the book

This book is divided into six chapters; each chapter contains a half-term's work and is based around a topic or theme. Each chapter follows the same structure:

## Chapter introduction

At the start of each chapter there is a summary of what is covered. This includes:

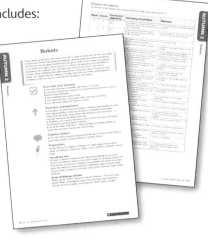

- **Introduction:** A description of what is covered in the chapter.
- **Expected prior learning:** What the children are expected to know before starting the work in the chapter.
- **Overview of progression:** A brief explanation of how the children progress through the chapter.
- **Creative context:** How the chapter could link to other curriculum areas.
- **Preparation:** Any resources required for the teaching of the chapter, including things that need to be sourced or prepared and the content that can be located on the CD-ROM.
- **Chapter at a glance:** This is a table that summarises the content of each lesson, including: the curriculum objectives (using a code system, please see pages 8–10), a summary of the activities and the outcome.
- **Background knowledge:** A section explaining grammatical terms and suchlike to enhance your subject knowledge, where required.

## Lessons

Each chapter contains six weeks' of lessons, each week contains five lessons. At the start of each week there is an introduction about what is covered and the expected outcomes. The lesson plans then include the relevant combination of headings from below.

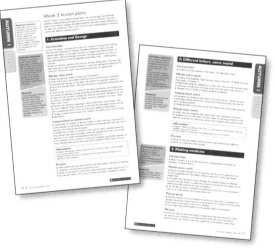

- **Curriculum objectives:** A list of the relevant objectives from the Programme of Study.
- **Resources:** What you require to teach the lesson.
- **Introduction:** A short and engaging activity to begin the lesson.
- **Whole-class work:** Working together as a class.
- **Group/Paired/Independent work:** Children working independently of the teacher in pairs, groups or alone.
- **Differentiation:** Ideas for how to support children who are struggling with a concept or how to extend those children who understand a concept without taking them onto new work.
- **Review:** A chance to review the children's learning and ensure the outcomes of the lesson have been achieved.

## Assess and review

At the end of each chapter are activities for assessing and reviewing the children's understanding. These can be conducted during the course of the chapter's work or saved until the end of the chapter or done at a later date. There are four focuses for assess and review activities in each chapter:

- Grammar and punctuation
- Spelling
- Reading
- Writing

Elements of speaking and listening will be included where relevant within these four areas.

All four focuses follow the same format:

- **Curriculum objectives:** These are the areas of focus for the assess and review activity. There may be one focus or more than one depending on the activity.
- **Resources:** What you require to conduct the activities.
- **Revise:** A series of short activities or one longer activity to revise and consolidate the children's learning and ensure they understand the concept(s).
- **Assess:** An assessment activity to provide a chance for the children to demonstrate their understanding and for you to check this.
- **Further practice:** Ideas for further practice on the focus, whether children are insecure in their learning or you want to provide extra practice or challenge.

## Photocopiable pages

At the end of each chapter are some photocopiable pages that will have been referred to in the lesson plans. These sheets are for the children to use; there is generally a title, an instruction, an activity and an 'I can' statement at the bottom. These sheets are also provided on the CD-ROM alongside additional pages as referenced in the lessons (see page 7 About the CD-ROM). The children should be encouraged to complete the 'I can' statements by colouring in the traffic lights to say how they think they have done (red – not very well, amber – ok, green – very well).

## English starter activities

At the beginning of the book there is a bank of English starter activities (pages 11–14). These are games and activities that will help children familiarise and consolidate their knowledge of grammar, punctuation and spelling. The use of these will be suggested throughout the chapters, but they are also flexible and therefore could be used at any time.

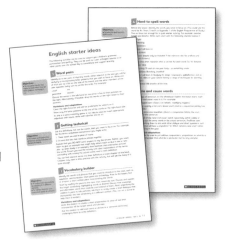

■**SCHOLASTIC**

# About the CD-ROM

The CD-ROM contains:
- Printable versions of the photocopiable sheets from the book and additional photocopiable sheets as referenced in the lesson plans.
- Interactive activities for children to complete or to use on the whiteboard.
- Media resources to display.
- Printable versions of the lesson plans.
- Digital versions of the lesson plans with the relevant resources linked to them.

## Getting started
- Put the CD-ROM into your CD-ROM drive.
  - For Windows users, the install wizard should autorun, if it fails to do so then navigate to your CD-ROM drive. Then follow the installation process.
  - For Mac users, copy the disk image file to your hard drive. After it has finished copying double-click it to mount the disk image. Navigate to the mounted disk image and run the installer. After installation the disk image can be unmounted and the DMG can be deleted from the hard drive.
- To complete the installation of the program you need to open the program and click 'Update' in the pop-up. Please note – this CD-ROM is web-enabled and the content will be downloaded from the internet to your hard-drive to populate the CD-ROM with the relevant resources. This only needs to be done on first use, after this you will be able to use the CD-ROM without an internet connection. If at any point any content is updated you will receive another pop-up upon start up with an internet connection.

## Navigating the CD-ROM
There are two options to navigate the CD-ROM either as a Child or as a Teacher.

### Child
- Click on the 'Child' button on the first menu screen.
- In the second menu click on the relevant class (please note only the books installed on the machine or network will be accessible. You can also rename year groups to match your school's naming conventions via the Teacher > Settings > Rename books area).
- A list of interactive activities will be displayed, children need to locate the correct one and click 'Go' to launch it.
- There is the opportunity to print or save a PDF of the activity at the end.

### Teacher
- Click on the Teacher button on the first menu screen and you will be taken to a screen showing which of the *100 English* books you have purchased. From here, you can also access information about getting started and the credits.
- To enter the product click 'Next' in the bottom right.
- You then need to enter a password (the password is: login).
- On first use:
  - Enter as a Guest by clicking on the 'Guest' button.
  - If desired, create a profile for yourself by adding your name to the list of users. Profiles allow you to save favourites and to specify which year group(s) you wish to be able to view.
  - Go to 'Settings' to create a profile for yourself – click 'Add user' and enter your name. Then choose the year groups you wish to have access to (you can return to this screen to change this at any time). Click on 'Login' at the top of the screen to re-enter the disk under your new profile.
- On subsequent uses you can choose your name from the drop-down list. The 'Guest' option will always be available if you, or a colleague, wish to use this.
- You can search the CD-ROM using the tools or save favourites.

For more information about how to use the CD-ROM, please refer to the help file which can be found in the teacher area of the CD-ROM. It is a red button with a question mark on it on the right-hand side of the screen just underneath the 'Settings' tab.

# Curriculum grid

This grid shows the full curriculum objectives for Year 3. The codes are referenced in the chapter introductions. Additional information is provided in italics, this includes the statutory information from the appendices and information about when certain objectives are introduced.

| Domain | Code | Curriculum objective |
|---|---|---|
| Reading: Word reading | RWR1 | To apply their growing knowledge of root words, prefixes and suffixes (etymology and morphology) as listed in English Appendix 1, both to read aloud and to understand the meaning of new words they meet. |
| Reading: Comprehension | RWR2 | To read further exception words, noting the unusual correspondences between spelling and sound, and where these occur in the word. |
| | RC1 | To develop positive attitudes to reading and understanding of what they read by listening to and discussing a wide range of fiction, poetry, plays, non-fiction and reference books or textbooks. |
| | RC2 | To develop positive attitudes to reading and understanding of what they read by reading books that are structured in different ways and reading for a range of purposes. |
| | RC3 | To develop positive attitudes to reading and understanding of what they read by using dictionaries to check the meaning of words that they have read. |
| | RC4 | To develop positive attitudes to reading and understanding of what they read by increasing their familiarity with a wide range of books, including fairy stories, myths and legends, and retelling some of these orally. |
| | RC5 | To develop positive attitudes to reading and understanding of what they read by identifying themes and conventions in a wide range of books. |
| | RC6 | To develop positive attitudes to reading and understanding of what they read by preparing poems and playscripts to read aloud and to perform, showing understanding through intonation, tone, volume and action. |
| | RC7 | To develop positive attitudes to reading and understanding of what they read by discussing words and phrases that capture the reader's interest and imagination. |
| | RC8 | To develop positive attitudes to reading and understanding of what they read by recognising some different forms of poetry. |
| | RC9 | To understand what they read, in books they can read independently, by checking that the text makes sense to them, discussing their understanding and explaining the meaning of words in context. |
| | RC10 | To understand what they read, in books they can read independently, by asking questions to improve their understanding of a text. |
| | RC11 | To understand what they read, in books they can read independently, by drawing inferences such as inferring characters' feelings, thoughts and motives from their actions, and justifying inferences with evidence. |
| | RC12 | To understand what they read, in books they can read independently, by predicting what might happen from details stated and implied. |
| | RC13 | To understand what they read, in books they can read independently, by identifying main ideas drawn from more than one paragraph and summarising these. |
| | RC14 | To understand what they read, in books they can read independently, by identifying how language, structure, and presentation contribute to meaning. |
| | RC15 | To retrieve and record information from non-fiction. |
| | RC16 | To participate in discussion about both books that are read to them and those they can read for themselves, taking turns and listening to what others say. |

| Domain | Code | Curriculum objective |
|---|---|---|
| Writing: Transcription | WT1 | To use further prefixes and suffixes and understand how to add them (English Appendix 1). |
| | WT2 | To spell further homophones. |
| | WT3 | To spell words that are often misspelled (English Appendix 1). |
| | WT4 | To place the possessive apostrophe accurately in words with regular plurals and in words with irregular plurals. |
| | WT5 | To use the first two or three letters of a word to check its spelling in a dictionary. |
| | WT6 | To write from memory simple sentences, dictated by the teacher, that include words and punctuation taught so far. |
| | WT7 | To use the diagonal and horizontal strokes that are needed to join letters and understand which letters, when adjacent to one another, are best left unjoined. |
| | WT8 | To increase the legibility, consistency and quality of their handwriting. |
| Writing: Composition | WC1 | To plan their writing by discussing writing similar to that which they are planning to write in order to understand and learn from its structure, grammar and vocabulary. |
| | WC2 | To plan their writing by discussing and recording ideas. |
| | WC3 | To draft and write by composing and rehearsing sentences orally (including dialogue), progressively building a varied and rich vocabulary and an increasing range of sentence structures (English Appendix 2). |
| | WC4 | To draft and write by organising paragraphs around a theme. |
| | WC5 | To draft and write by, in narratives, creating settings, characters and plot. |
| | WC6 | To draft and write by, in non-narrative material, using simple organisational devices such as headings and subheadings. |
| | WC7 | To evaluate and edit by assessing the effectiveness of their own and others' writing and suggesting improvements. |
| | WC8 | To evaluate and edit by proposing changes to grammar and vocabulary to improve consistency and accuracy, including the accurate use of pronouns in sentences. |
| | WC9 | To proofread for spelling and punctuation errors. |
| | WC10 | To read aloud their own writing, to a group or the whole class, using appropriate intonation and controlling the tone and volume so that the meaning is clear. |
| | WC11 | To develop their understanding of the concepts set out in English Appendix 2 by extending the range of sentences with more than one clause by using a wider range of conjunctions, including *when, if, because, although*. |
| | WC12 | To develop their understanding of the concepts set out in English Appendix 2 by using the present perfect form of verbs in contrast to the past tense. |
| | WC13 | To develop their understanding of the concepts set out in English Appendix 2 by choosing nouns or pronouns appropriately for clarity and cohesion and to avoid repetition.<br><br>*Using pronouns to avoid repetition is the focus in Year 3. Using pronouns for clarity and cohesion is taught in Year 4.* |
| | WC14 | To develop their understanding of the concepts set out in English Appendix 2 by using conjunctions, adverbs and prepositions to express time and cause. |

| Domain | Code | Curriculum objective |
|---|---|---|
| Writing: Composition | WC15 | To develop their understanding of the concepts set out in English Appendix 2 by using fronted adverbials.<br><br>*This is introduced in Year 4, not Year 3* |
| | WC16 | To develop their understanding of the concepts set out in English Appendix 2 by learning the grammar for Years 3 and 4 in English Appendix 2. |
| | WC17 | To indicate grammatical and other features by using commas after fronted adverbials.<br><br>*This is introduced in Year 4, not Year 3.* |
| | WC18 | To indicate grammatical and other features by indicating possession by using the possessive apostrophe with singular and plural nouns. |
| | WC19 | To indicate grammatical and other features by using and punctuating direct speech. |
| | WC20 | To draft and write by, in non-narrative material, using simple organisational devices such as headings and subheadings. |
| | WC20 | To use and understand the grammatical terminology in English Appendix 2 accurately and appropriately when discussing their writing and reading. |

# English starter ideas

The following activities can be used to support your children's grammar, punctuation and spelling. They can be used as a part of English lessons or at other points over the school day to consolidate and support learning.

##  Word pairs

**Objectives**
- To recognise words that relate to each other through letter pattern, meaning or use.

Identify six to ten pairs of rhyming words, either relevant to the text you will be studying or incorporating letter patterns that you wish to focus on. Write one of each pair as a list on one side of the board, and the other members of the pair opposite, being sure to jumble the order. For example:

coach                  me

guarantee          brooch

Discuss the words in the left-hand list and draw a line to their partners on the right. Alternatively, if feasible, drag the words on the right closer to their partners.

### Variations and adaptations
Cover the right-hand list and ask for predictions for what is on it.

Show only the letter patterns at the end of the words on the right-hand side.

As this is a word-matching game, it can also be used to match appropriate adjectives with nouns, verbs with adverbs, and so on.

## 2 Getting technical

**Objectives**
- To better understand the grammar and punctuation of Standard English.

List the definitions, but not the words, that you want to focus on. For example, for the terms *conjunction* and *pronoun* you might write:

1. These words are used in place of nouns.

2. A word that links two words or phrases together.

Explain that you DO NOT want anyone to say the answer. Rather, you want them to give an example that might help others (such as *blue is one* or *slow plus '-ly' gives slowly is an example*), then facilitate class interaction around the words. Ensure you end the activity with clear explanations of the terms, concluding with writing the actual words next to each definition.

You can find relevant terms and their definitions in each chapter of this book. Children may need a little practice with this activity, but will get the hang of it soon enough.

## 3 Vocabulary builder

**Objectives**
- To embed new vocabulary by applying it in different contexts.
- To initiate ideas for new, connected words or phrases.

Identify the words and phrases that you want to introduce to the class, such as *telephone, communication, interruption* and *technology*. Prior to the lesson, find or prepare a short written piece incorporating the words.

Start by reading the piece to the class, then reveal the text. Discuss and explain the target vocabulary, highlighting words as desired. Discuss their meanings and alternative words that could be used instead of them. Next, organising the children in pairs as talk partners, ask them to orally create a brief dialogue that incorporates the new vocabulary in a different context. (You can set a scene to help them if needed.)

### Variations and adaptations
Invite the children to create a short presentation or piece of text that incorporates all the target words and phrases.

Ask the children to add each word or phrase to a 'personal dictionary', challenging them to write definitions.

# 4 Hard-to-spell words

**Objectives**
● To learn to spell hard-to-spell words.

Before the lesson, identify the words you want to focus on. (You could use the word list for Years 3 and 4 in Appendix 1 of the English Programme of Study.) Two or three are enough for a quick starter activity. For example, *exercise*, *breath* and *breathe*. Write each word with the following checklist below it:

● *Type:*
● *Meaning:*
● *Variations:*
● *How I will learn it:*
● *In context:*

('Variations' should only be included if the relevant rules for prefixes and suffixes are known.)

Children must then research what is correct for each word. So, for *breathe*:

● *Type: Verb*
● *Meaning: To suck air into your body – or something similar*
● *Variations: Breathing, breathed*
● *How I will learn it: Studying the shape, mnemonics, syllabification, and so on. (This relies on your school having a range of techniques for learning spellings.)*
● *In context: We breathe all the time.*

# 5 Time and cause words

**Objectives**
● To show how 'time and cause' words (adverbs, prepositions or conjunctions used to give an indication of time or cause) modify or clarify meaning.

Write a range of sentences on the whiteboard before the lesson starts, each with a 'time and cause' word in it. For example:

● *It will happen soon.* (*Soon* is an adverb, modifying *happen*.)
● *Jane was wearing a hat and a brown scarf.* (*And* is a conjunction joining two equal words.)
● *I haven't eaten since breakfast.* (*Since* is a preposition linking the noun *breakfast* to the sentence.)

Write down all of the 'time and cause' words separately (either visible or not), then rub out the same words in the actual sentences. Facilitate class discussions, inviting them to ask each other oblique and direct questions, such as *Which sentence will have a preposition?* or *Which sentence uses* since? rather than simply filling in the gaps.

**Variations and adaptations**
This activity can be used to just address conjunctions, prepositions or adverbs in isolation. Do remember that adverbs in particular can be very complex.

## 6 Adverbs

**Objectives**
● To engage thinking about the use of adverbs at an analytical level.

Start by recapping the meaning of an adverb, which is: adverbs modify verbs. (In fact they are much more complicated than this, but for this age group this fact is enough.)

You might also point out that very often, but not always, adverbs can be made by taking an adjective and adding the suffix '-ly'. For example, *slow* becomes *slowly*, and *easy* becomes *easily*.

Write six adjectives on the board and say a sentence for each. Next, ask the class to look at the adjectives and consider whether they could be converted into adverbs.

Ask for volunteers to think of one of the adverbs, but not to say it, and then to say a verb that would make sense if used in a sentence alongside the adverb they are thinking of. For example, if they are looking at the adjective *slow* and thinking of the adverb *slowly*, they might say the verb *eat*.

Next, challenge the class to say which adverb the volunteer is thinking of, and give a sentence to illustrate this, incorporating the verb given.

### Variations and adaptations
Try using adjectives that cannot be converted so easily, such as *fast*.

The same principles can also be used for an activity on comparative and superlative adjectives.

## 7 Conjunction challenge

**Objectives**
● To increase children's awareness of conjunction words and how they affect sentences.

Start by recapping the meaning of conjunction: conjunctions join words together. (This is a simplification, but it captures the essence of their use.) Select as many of the main conjunctions as you wish (a maximum of five is suggested). For example, *and*, *because*, *but*, *if*, *for*, *never*, *or*, *since*, *so*, *that*, *until*, *when*, *while* and *yet*.

List these vertically down the middle of the board. Divide the class into teams of around six and ask each team to choose a conjunction and create a sentence around it, such as *I like tea and coffee*. The sentence can be as long or short as they wish. If you want to avoid skulduggery they should write it down. Next, invite a group to state the start of their sentence, stopping before the conjunction. In the example given this would be *I like tea...* Challenge the other teams to identify the conjunction they have in mind and complete a sentence for it. Allow teams to discuss and write down their responses. Score each team as follows:

● If a team chooses a conjunction and completes a sentence that is grammatically correct they score one point (at the teacher's discretion).
● If they choose the same conjunction as the original sentence they score an additional point.
● If they create an identical sentence they score five points.

Circulate until each team has issued a conjunction challenge.

### Variations and adaptations
Play this individually, or within groups of six challenging each other.

This activity is also suitable for focused work on clauses.

## 8 Prepositions

**Objectives**
● To increase children's awareness of prepositions and how they affect sentences.

Start by recapping the meaning of *preposition*: prepositions join nouns to sentences. (This is a simplification, but it captures the essence of their use.) Write the main prepositions you wish to look at on the board. You may wish to focus on positional prepositions, for example *across*, *between*, *beside*, *in front of*, *on*, *over*, *under* and so on.

Challenge the children to choose three prepositions and then state a chain of events for a particular animal that has entered your classroom. For example, *A spider crawled along the ruler, then went over the edge of the desk, then hid under the carpet*. Repeat this until all the main prepositions have been used. Focus on a couple of examples to explain how the preposition links the other words.

## 9 The perfect form

**Objectives**
● To exemplify how the perfect form is used to mark relationships of time and cause.

Prior to the lesson write two or three sentences on the board, such as:

● ***I have ordered lots of paint*** because the living room needs decorating.
● ***He has eaten a good lunch*** so he won't be hungry.
● ***They have played this team*** before and they lost ten–nil!
● ***You have been unhappy*** since that new teacher arrived.

Then, before the children see it, rub out either the first phrase (bold) or the second, noting these down for reference if necessary.

Gather the children in front of the remaining parts of the sentences, and ask them (individually or in pairs) to consider what the missing phrase could be for each. Elicit suggestions and discuss them, drawing attention to correct sentences and use of the perfect form where appropriate. If desired, highlight the conjunction linking the consequence of the initial statements.

**Variations and adaptations**
This activity can also be used to focus on the conjunctions that join phrases and clauses.

## 10 Being descriptive

**Objectives**
● To encourage effective use of evocative, sensory, and descriptive language.

Prior to the lesson find (or write) a brief passage for display on the board. For example:

*The room smelled of vinegar; she wrinkled her nose in disgust. The bright red walls glistened, and a small dab of her finger proved they were still wet – freshly painted. She quickly made her way to the kitchen: a cold, dark room where she suddenly remembered how long it was since she had eaten – two whole days! She grabbed at a loaf and bit off two huge chunks – it tasted of air and sawdust, but she chewed it furiously. The doorbell suddenly chimed; it was as loud as a church bell in the silence of the house. She jumped in alarm, dropping the loaf, and quickly opened the back door. Its handle was like ice in her sweating palm.*

Before revealing the text, ask the class to write these five words, each on a separate line:

● *See*
● *Hear*
● *Smell*
● *Taste*
● *Touch*

Looking at the text with the class, ask them to read it to themselves and note down which words or phrases belong to which sense.

## 11 Direct speech

Use the children's speech to practise writing using inverted commas. Throughout the day, pause the class occasionally after someone has spoken to discuss how you would represent that as direct speech using inverted commas. For example, *Julia said "Can you pass me the scissors, please?"*

### Variations and adaptations
You can also use this activity to discuss alternatives for *said*. This could stem from a discussion about how the phrase was said in the first place.

## 12 Word displays

**Objectives**
● To collect new vocabulary and improve spelling.

Set up a word wall area. Focus on a specific area of language, for example words with the prefixes 'auto-', 'super-' or 'anti'; or words ending in '-sure' or '-ture'. Encourage the children to add any words and their definitions of the words when they come across them in their reading or writing. Change the focus of the wall regularly.

## 13 A or an?

**Objectives**
● To use the forms 'a' or 'an' according to whether the next word begins with a consonant or a vowel.

Produce a set of cards with nouns on them starting with a mixture of vowels and consonants. Ask the children to sort the words into two sets, those that would use 'a' and those that would use 'an' before them. Compare the children's sets. Use this exercise to reinforce the terms *vowel* and *consonant* and ensure the children know, through investigation, that 'an' is used before a vowel.

### Variations and adaptations
You may wish to add nouns beginning with 'h' as often it feels correct to add 'an' to these words even though it should usually be 'a'.

# Roald Dahl

The focus of this chapter is the expressive use of rich language to convey characters, stories, rhymes and humour, and what better author to introduce this to Year 3 with than Roald Dahl.
Using his shorter stories and rhymes – namely, *The Enormous Crocodile*, *George's Marvellous Medicine*, *The Twits* (the book and the play), and *Revolting Rhymes* – the chapter focuses strongly on creative writing and expressive speech, with many opportunities for children to discuss Dahl's rich characters and plots, and also present their own variations.

## Expected prior learning
● Can understand and is familiar with non-fiction.
● Can understand the basic features of instructions.
● Can understand the basic features of organising texts and story maps.
● Know that we can find out about characters from what they say.
● Can locate direct speech in a text.
● Can talk about poems.

## Overview of progression
● Through this chapter children will enhance their awareness of Roald Dahl, his work and his style, as well as developing their understanding of organising texts, descriptive language, inverted commas, time and cause words (adverbs, prepositions and conjunctions).
● Children will also study rhyming and exception words. They will examine extracts of the texts to gain an understanding of these features, before developing their own variations, and creating and performing their own plays and poems in the same vein.

## Creative context
● The chapter carefully develops children's confidence in creating and performing interesting language. As such, dramatic techniques could also be investigated alongside the work.
● There is a strong cross-curricular link to PSHE, with children being given several opportunities to consider and debate Dahl's theme of greedy and unpleasant people getting their comeuppance, often in nasty ways.

## Preparation
With the chapter having a focus on a specific author (Roald Dahl) you will need to ensure you have the relevant books to hand: *The Enormous Crocodile*, *George's Marvellous Medicine*, *The Twits* (the book and the play), and *Revolting Rhymes*. Multiple copies would be helpful, but are not essential. The main preparation is to familiarise yourself thoroughly with the texts involved (they are all fairly quick reads), and with the relevant background knowledge (see page 18).

### You will also need:
Optional resources include audio recordings of the books, internet access, storyboard or story map templates, clothes and props for creating a revolting character (week 4, lesson 2), and props for performing short plays (week 5).

### On the CD-ROM you will find:
Media resources 'Making a cake', 'Mr and Mrs Twit'; interactive activities 'Hard-to-spell words', 'Affixes', 'Time and cause words'; photocopiable pages 'Roald Dahl biography', 'Queen Victoria fact file', 'George's rhyme', 'How to make a pizza', 'Sample police report', 'The Wormy Spaghetti', '*The Twits* playscript', '*Revolting Rhymes* extracts'

■ SCHOLASTIC

# Chapter at a glance

An overview of the chapter. For curriculum objective codes, please see pages 8–10.

| Week | Lesson | Curriculum objectives | Summary of activities | Outcome |
|---|---|---|---|---|
| 1 | 1 | RC: 15 | Discuss and research the life of Roald Dahl. | • Can research and find out about an author. |
|  | 2 | RC: 15 | Look at Roald Dahl's bibliography and consider interesting aspects of it. | • Can research and find out about an author. |
|  | 3 | RC: 15 | Create a fact file about Roald Dahl and his life. | • Can write a simple fact file. |
|  | 4 | RC: 1 | Read The Enormous Crocodile. Create a story list/board/map. | • Can identify effective language in stories. |
|  | 5 | RC: 4 | Orally retell the story of The Enormous Crocodile in the children's own words. | • Can retell stories using intonation and appropriate language. |
| 2 | 1 | RC: 1, 11, 12 | Read the opening of George's Marvellous Medicine and focus on characterisation. | • Can appreciate the intent of the book and the use of a specific letter pattern ('gr') for alliteration. |
|  | 2 | RWR: 2 WT: 3, 6 | Identify rhymes from a text and develop knowledge of spelling patterns. | • Can increase knowledge and understanding of spelling patterns. |
|  | 3 | RC: 7 WC: 6 | Structure texts using headings and bullet points. | • Can understand the conventions for writing instructions. |
|  | 4 | WC: 14, 20 | Introduce time and cause conjunctions, adverbs and prepositions to help write instructions. | • Can appreciate the use of rich and varied vocabulary and the purpose of time and cause words. |
|  | 5 | WC: 3 | Write own recipe by composing orally and using text-level features such as headings and numbered points. | • Can write a clear set of instructions. |
| 3 | 1 | RWR: 2 RC: 6, 7 | Consider rhythm and rhyme and prepare a performance. | • Can appreciate rhyme and interesting words. |
|  | 2 | WC: 6, 14 | Create a list of changes that happened to Grandma, making suggestions as to what caused each one. | • Can create a clear list of events, attempting to use 'time and cause' words. |
|  | 3 | RC: 11, 16 | Prepare reasoned arguments as a group and participate in a whole-class discussion about Mr Kranky's personality. | • Can infer meaning from a text and debate it. |
|  | 4 | RC: 11 | Write brief character profiles for all the characters using suitable vocabulary. | • Can infer meaning from a text. |
|  | 5 | RC: 11, 12 | Write a police report summarising what children believe happened and suggesting what should happen next. | • Can offer opinions on characters' personalities and attitudes based on inference. |
| 4 | 1 | RC: 13 | Introduce The Twits and consider descriptive techniques. | • Can appreciate the use of rich and varied vocabulary in creating characters. |
|  | 2 | WC: 5 | Orally create a truly horrid Dahl-esque character. | • Can use literary techniques for their own work. |
|  | 3 | RC: 4, 5, 10 | Complete the reading of the book and consider the Twits' fate. | • Can refer to texts to develop ideas and arguments. |
|  | 4 | WC: 19, 20 | Introduce or recap the key aspects of recording direct speech. | • Can understand what inverted commas are. |
|  | 5 | WC: 3, 19, 20 | Focus on the use of direct speech in the book. | • Can understand what inverted commas are and begin to use them in writing. |
| 5 | 1 | RC: 1, 2 | Look at a playscript of The Twits and consider its variation from the original book. | • Can understand the different features of a playscript. |
|  | 2 | RWR: 1 | Introduce the suffix '-y' to help understand morphology and new words. | • Can develop knowledge and understanding of words. |
|  | 3 | RC: 6 | Read and prepare a performance from The Twits playscript. | • Can read and interpret playscripts. |
|  | 4 | WC: 3 | Collaboratively write an original playscript based on a new situation for the Twits. | • Can write playscripts. |
|  | 5 | RC: 6 | Perform and evaluate part of a playscript, using dramatic techniques and controlled voice for impact and clarity. | • Can perform a small section of a playscript. |

## Chapter at a glance

| Week | Lesson | Curriculum objectives | Summary of activities | Outcome |
|---|---|---|---|---|
| **6** | 1 | RC: 1, 8 | Look at Roald Dahl's poetic technique and consider the variation from the traditional tales. | • Can appreciate rhyming verse, and that existing stories can be used as starting points for new work. |
| | 2 | RWR: 2 | Look in detail at a section of *Revolting Rhymes*, in particular the rhyming words. | • Can increase knowledge and understanding of homophones and exception words. |
| | 3 | RC: 6 | Perform an excerpt from *Revolting Rhymes*. | • Can perform poems using intonation and movement. |
| | 4 | RC: 6 | Create their own revolting rhyme based on a traditional nursery rhyme. | • Can write a poem in a specific style (rhyming couplets). |
| | 5 | RC: 6 | Refine and present their own revolting rhymes. | • Can perform poems using intonation and movement. |

## Background knowledge

**Alliteration**: A literary technique where every word in a phrase starts with the same letter(s).

**Biography**: A work about a person, written by someone else. Contrast with *autobiography*.

**Bullet point**: Organisational feature for writing lists.

**Conjunction**: A word that links two phrases together, suggesting time or cause.

**Exception word**: A word that needs to be learned rather than using rules or strategies to decode it.

**Narrative poetry**: Poetry that tells a story.

**Onomatopoeia**: A word that sounds like the thing it represents.

**Preposition**: The link between a noun or pronoun to another word in the sentence.

**Rhyming couplet**: A form of poetry where lines are written in rhyming pairs.

**Synonym**: A word that means the same thing as another word, even though they are spelled differently.

■SCHOLASTIC

# Week 1 lesson plans

The focus for this week is Roald Dahl and the sort of author he was. Through investigating non-fiction texts children will develop their understanding of his life and literature, then write a small fact-file about him and his books. This is followed by listening to and discussing *The Enormous Crocodile*, then retelling sections of the text using children's own actions and language.

## 1: Meet Roald Dahl

### Introduction

● Display the photograph of Roald Dahl from photocopiable page 'Roald Dahl biography' from the CD-ROM. Ask the children to describe his face and consider what sort of person he might be (whether they know him or not). Write interesting words to describe him around the photograph.
● Explain that in this lesson everyone will be finding out about Roald Dahl's life and his work.
● Read Dahl's motto to the class (it can be found in the back of some of his books):

> My candle burns at both ends
> It gives a lovely light
> But ah my foes and oh my friends
> It will not last the night

● Ask for ideas about what this little rhyme tells us about Dahl – both his attitude to life and his style of writing. Note down interesting ideas.

### Whole-class work

● Keeping the photo displayed, discuss what the children already know about him and his work.
  ● Have they read any of his books?
  ● Have they seen any of the animations or films?
  ● Do they know anything about him as a person?
● Choosing one or two books, read and discuss the information about Roald Dahl in them.
● Display photocopiable page 'Roald Dahl biography', or distribute photocopies of the text. Discuss what sort of text it is (biography, non-fiction), and what makes it different from stories and other texts.
● Ask what we might expect to find in a biography. Model and reinforce appropriate language, such as *information*, *true*, *real* and *factual*.
● Look at the first paragraph together, asking the children what the main facts are. Highlight these as appropriate.

### Independent or paired work

● Distribute photocopiable page 40 'Roald Dahl quiz' and ask the class to complete it by referring to the biography text, either displayed on the board or also distributed.

---

**Differentiation**
● Support less confident writers by allowing them to highlight or cut out the answers.
● Extend learning by encouraging children to research further information using the Roald Dahl books and the Internet (such as www.roalddahl.com).

---

### Review

● Gather the class together again and review their answers, focusing particularly on children who have used additional sources.
● Ask the class to consider what questions they would have liked to ask Roald Dahl if they could have had the chance to meet him, using any interesting ideas to discuss aspects of his life and work further.

---

**Expected outcomes**
● All children will encounter and produce non-fiction texts and retell a small section of a story.
● Most children will incorporate aspects of non-fiction text into their own writing, and use their own language to retell parts of a story.
● Some children will create non-fiction texts and effectively retell a story.

**Curriculum objectives**
● To retrieve and record information from non-fiction.

**Resources**
Photocopiable page 'Roald Dahl biography' from the CD-ROM; photocopiable page 40 'Roald Dahl quiz'; a selection of Roald Dahl books; internet access (optional)

**Curriculum objectives**
● To retrieve and record information from non-fiction.

**Resources**
Selection of Roald Dahl books; photocopiable page 41 'Roald Dahl bibliography'; internet access (optional)

# 2: What Roald wrote

## Introduction
● Start the lesson with a large pile of books in front of you, some by Roald Dahl, and ask the children to identify whether each is a Roald Dahl book or not. Filter the books into separate piles.
● Discuss the style of illustration, and why Quentin Blake's and Dahl's styles suit each other so well.

## Whole-class work
● Briefly recap the main aspects of lesson 1. Explain that in this lesson you will be reviewing a bibliography and discuss what this means.
● Display photocopiable page 41 'Roald Dahl bibliography' and discuss what sort of quiz questions might arise from looking at the information in it.

## Independent, paired or group work
● Arrange the class as preferred, displaying or distributing copies of the Roald Dahl bibliography.
● Ask the children to identify suitable information, and create five or so interesting quiz questions, such as *How many books did he write?*

> **Differentiation**
> ● Support learning by demonstrating that highlighting a fact to start with can make it easier to form questions.
> ● Extend learning by asking children to research what else Roald Dahl wrote, including his output for adults.

## Review
● Gather the class together and share questions with each other, using the opportunity to consolidate knowledge of his books and his themes.

**Curriculum objectives**
● To retrieve and record information from non-fiction.

**Resources**
Photocopiable page 'Queen Victoria fact file' from the CD-ROM; photocopiable page 'Roald Dahl biography' from the CD-ROM; selection of Roald Dahl books; internet access (optional)

# 3: A Roald Dahl fact file

## Introduction
● Display photocopiable page 'Queen Victoria fact file' from the CD-ROM and read through it together.
● Discuss the use of headings and punctuation to list information, and the language used. How does it differ from the other non-fiction texts?

## Whole-class work
● Recap the previous two lessons, stressing the focus on non-fiction texts.
● Explain that in this lesson children must use the main pieces of information that interest them to create their own Roald Dahl fact file.
● Recap on what makes a good fact file, and how to order the information.

## Independent or paired work
● Ensuring that all children have access to the biography and bibliography from previous lessons, ask them to create a simple fact file on Roald Dahl.
● Stress that it is entirely up to them what they want to focus on.

> **Differentiation**
> ● Support children by allowing them to cut out and stick pieces of text.
> ● Extend learning by allowing children access to Roald Dahl books and the Internet.

## Review
● Gather the class together and compare work, reinforcing good use of genre and language.

## Curriculum objectives
● To listen to and discuss a wide range of fiction, poetry, plays, non-fiction and reference books or textbooks.

## Resources
*The Enormous Crocodile* by Roald Dahl (book, video or audio); storyboard and story map templates (optional, not provided)

# 4: Meet the Enormous Crocodile

## Introduction
● If possible, play an audio recording or video animation of *The Enormous Crocodile*. If this is not possible, read the story to the class, showing the pictures and using varied voices for the different characters.

## Whole-class work
● Invite the children to discuss the story together and their feelings about it. Ask: *Is what happened to the crocodile fair? Is there a moral to the story?*
● Recap the first few pages of the story together as a class, listing key events and characters for everyone to see. You can do this with text and/or simple pictures – the main purpose is for the children to see this as a simple way of remembering the story. Stress the need to keep it simple.

## Paired or group work
● Organising the children in pairs or small groups, as desired, ask them to create a list of events, a storyboard or story map for *The Enormous Crocodile*.

> **Differentiation**
> ● Support learning by providing children with a timeline support sheet, dividing the story into sections.
> ● Extend learning by modelling how to make third-person notes on key events and encourage children to use this style.

## Review
● Bring the class together again and share work as appropriate.
● Recap the story and ask the children to check and amend their own work.

## Curriculum objectives
● To increase their familiarity with a wide range of books, including fairy stories, myths and legends, and retell some of these orally.

## Resources
*The Enormous Crocodile* by Roald Dahl (book, video or audio); children's story lists, story maps or storyboards from the previous lesson

# 5: In our own words

## Introduction
● Start the lesson by retelling the class a (brief) story of your choice (for example, 'The Hare and the Tortoise'), modelling effective intonation and gesture to dramatise the story.

## Whole-class work
● Discuss and recap *The Enormous Crocodile* as desired, asking children to identify particular words and phrases that they enjoy.
● Stress the importance of language and expression in Roald Dahl's writing.

## Paired or group work
● Ask the children to create a retelling of *The Enormous Crocodile* using their story lists, story maps or storyboards. They should also try to use Roald Dahl's descriptive language or substitute their own words as they see fit.
● Encourage the children to retell the story in their own way, perhaps with different members taking the parts of characters or each narrating a section.

> **Differentiation**
> ● Provide structured story maps for those who need support.
> ● Allow children to retell different amounts, from a single scene up to a complete retelling for the more confident.
> ● Consider carefully how children are grouped and the order in which they speak, so that they support each other.

## Review
● Ask the children to perform all or part of their retellings for the rest of the class.

**Curriculum objectives**
● To listen to and discuss a wide range of fiction, poetry, plays, non-fiction and reference books or textbooks.
● To draw inferences such as inferring characters' feelings, thoughts and motives from their actions, and justify inferences with evidence.
● To predict what might happen from details stated and implied.

**Resources**
*George's Marvellous Medicine* by Roald Dahl (ideally the book and an audio version); clothing props for the introductory activity (optional); drawing materials; vocabulary banks for facial features – factual and descriptive (optional, not provided)

# Week 2 lesson plans

Week 2 looks in more detail at Roald Dahl's use of language, and develops children's understanding and ability to write instructions correctly. They will listen to and discuss *George's Marvellous Medicine*, and then create instructions for their own medicines. There is also a focus on the understanding of rhyming words with different spelling patterns.

## 1: Grandma and George

### Introduction
● Start the lesson with yourself in role as an unusual character (but nothing like the main characters in *George's Marvellous Medicine*), such as an old colonel-type figure, an arrogant rock star or a hyperactive fitness-freak – in other words, a Roald-Dahl-type character. The main purpose is to create a noticeable appearance and exaggerated personality traits – clothing props will help.
● Interact with the class for a few minutes, perhaps letting them 'hot-seat' you. Then step out of role to briefly brainstorm words and phrases that describe the character. Model and explain new words and phrases as appropriate.

### Whole-class work
● Read the opening chapter of the book ('Grandma').
● Draw a line down the middle of the board and write the word 'Grandma' on one side and 'George' on the other. Ask children to volunteer words or phrases that describe them – their age and status, appearance, personality and situation.
● Focus on the recurring 'gr' words for describing Grandma's personality (*she was always complaining, grousing, grouching, grumbling, griping about something or other*) and discuss their meaning. Are they all real words? Reinforce the use of commas, and discuss why the author uses four synonyms in a row – what effect does it have?
● Mention the meaning of synonyms and of alliteration, and consider why this line is effective. (You may wish to note that the description starts with the word *complaining*, which is not a 'gr' word but explains all the others.)
● Finally, consider how the text so far confirms thoughts on the sort of author Roald Dahl is.

### Independent or paired work
● Organising the children as desired, explain to them that you want them to create sketches of what they think Grandma and George both look like, and to describe what they are like as people.
● Explain that as well as a picture of each person's face (labelled if desired), they should write some descriptive sentences beneath each one, and should feel free to use words and expressions from the text.
● To conclude, ask the children to write two sentences, giving their opinions on what George thinks of Grandma, and what Grandma thinks about George.

---

**Differentiation**
● Support learning by providing vocabulary banks relevant to faces – both biological terms and descriptive words.
● Extend children's learning by challenging them to write using synonyms and/or alliteration where possible.

---

### Review
● Invite children to share their sketches and descriptions, focusing particularly on adjectives and descriptive expressions used.
● Recap on the opening of the story, discussing what might happen next. To finish, remind children not to try and make any kind of medicine at home!

## Curriculum objectives
- To read further exception words, noting the unusual correspondences between spelling and sound, and where these occur in the word.
- To write from memory simple sentences, dictated by the teacher, that include words and punctuation taught so far.
- To spell words that are often misspelled (Appendix 1).

## Resources
*George's Marvellous Medicine* by Roald Dahl (ideally the book and an audio version); photocopiable page 'George's rhyme' from the CD-ROM

# 2: Different letters, same sound

## Introduction
- Read the second chapter of the book ('The Marvellous Plan').

## Whole-class work
- Display photocopiable page 'George's rhyme' from the CD-ROM (from the final pages of Chapter 2).
- Read/chant/sing this together as a class. Then focus on the rhyming words, in particular noting which rhyming words have the same letter patterns.
- Develop lists of words and letter patterns as desired.

## Independent work
- Distribute the photocopiable sheet to the class and ask children to work individually, finding words that rhyme even though they may not have the same spelling patterns.
- Challenge them to list other words that share some of the letter patterns.

## Whole-class work
- Gather the class together and review their work, focusing in particular on spellings and pronunciation. To help assess the learning, dictate a small selection of sentences containing some of the irregular letter patterns used.

> **Differentiation**
> - Support children by writing all the words on cards and then breaking them down by syllables or by onset and rime.
> - Extend children's learning by encouraging them to write new rhymes.

## Review
- Recap on the main letter patterns covered and reinforce that different patterns can make the same sounds.

## Curriculum objectives
- To discuss words and phrases that capture the reader's interest and imagination.
- In non-narrative material, to use simple organisational devices.

## Resources
*George's Marvellous Medicine* by Roald Dahl (ideally the book and an audio version)

# 3: Making medicine

## Introduction
- Read Chapters 3 to 6 of the book (from 'George Begins to Make the Medicine' to 'Brown Paint').

## Whole-class work
- Discuss George's thoughts on the possible effects of each ingredient, and ask for suggestions for what effect children think some of the ingredients might have.
- Through class discussion, recap through the chapters listing the different locations George visited, in order. Write these on the board and explain to the children that the locations list acts as headings.
- For the first location, underline the heading and list one or two ingredients under it as bullet points, and explain these also.

## Paired work
- Ask the children to try to remember and list as many items as possible that George discovered in each location, using locations as headings and then using bullet points to list them in the correct location.
- They might also add thoughts on the possible effects of ingredients.

## Review
- Invite the class to share their work, writing down the best answers to show the correct use of headings and bullet points. Model the use of numbered points to show the correct order that ingredients were added in each room.

**Curriculum objectives**
● To use conjunctions, adverbs and prepositions to express time and cause.
● To use and understand the grammatical terminology in Appendix 2 accurately and appropriately when discussing their writing and reading.

**Resources**
Photocopiable page 'How to make a pizza' from the CD-ROM; photocopiable page 42 'How to make a chocolate cake'

# 4: Writing instructions

## Introduction
● Recap yesterday's list of places that George visited and the ingredients he found in each, reinforcing the use of headings and bulleted or numbered lists.

## Whole-class work
● Read through photocopiable page 'How to make a pizza' from the CD-ROM. Next, hide the text and ask children to recount the steps involved.
● Look at the instructions again, highlighting conjunctions, adverbs and prepositions (you do not need to explain these terms at this stage) and explain how these words are used to express time and cause.

## Independent or paired work
● Distribute photocopiable page 42 'How to make a chocolate cake' and ask children to go through it highlighting any time and cause words.
● Challenge them to rewrite the instructions as a clear and helpful list.

## Review
● Invite the children to share their work, and recap on the use of time and cause words to help clarify instructions.
● Introduce the terms *adverb*, *preposition* and *conjunction* only if you feel children will be receptive to them.

**Curriculum objectives**
● To compose and rehearse sentences orally (including dialogue), progressively building a varied and rich vocabulary and an increasing range of sentence structures (see Appendix 2).

**Resources**
Small cake; media resource 'Making a cake' on the CD-ROM; instructions writing frame and vocabulary banks (optional, not provided)

# 5: George's cool cakes

## Introduction
● If possible, have a small cake in your hand for the start of the lesson. Ask the children to suggest what ingredients might be in it.
● Suggesting that everyone keeps it to themselves, ask the class to imagine that it may have been made by George. If so, what would he have put in it and what would it do to you if you ate it.
● Show the video 'Making a cake' on the CD-ROM – as well as instructions, there may be language that 'embellishes' the process, which may be interesting to note.

## Independent, paired or group work
● Recap (and ideally display) the ingredients and instructions vocabulary from lessons 3 and 4 as necessary. Challenge the children to write their own special cake recipes, including cooking instructions, especially for George.
● Explain that it is fine for them to compose this orally, making notes and jottings to support their work if they need to.

> **Differentiation**
> ● Support learners by grouping children appropriately and providing an instructions writing frame that includes suitable vocabulary banks.
> ● Extend learning by encouraging the use of the appropriate conjunctions, adverbs and prepositions to help build stronger sentences and smoother prose.

## Review
● Ask for volunteers to read/present their recipes to the class.
● Reinforce effective vocabulary, especially appropriately used conjunctions and adverbs.

# Week 3 lesson plans

This week's lessons conclude the work on *George's Marvellous Medicine*. Lesson 1 recaps and extends children's knowledge of interesting words and rhymes, focusing on real versus imaginary words and introducing onomatopoeia. Lesson 2 further develops children's understanding and ability to structure texts using lists and time and cause words (conjunctions, adverbs and prepositions), although it does not aim to explain these terms (they are covered in later chapters). The final three lessons focus on inferring the personalities and attitudes of the characters, culminating in an imaginary police report.

## 1: Casting spells

### Introduction

● Open the interactive activity 'Hard-to-spell words' on the CD-ROM. Work through it with the class, discussing how some words have irregular or unusual letter patterns with non-phonetic pronunciations.

### Whole-class work

● Re-read the 'spell' that George chants in Chapter 5 ('The Cook-up'), including the paragraph that precedes it. Use gestures and exaggerated pronunciation to emphasise the language.
● Display the spell, and chant it to your directions as a whole class. If classroom space permits allow the children to stand and mimic your gestures.
● Discuss some of the words in the chant – are they real or invented?
● Build lists of real or invented words from the rhyme on the board – discuss and explain their meanings.
● Talk about onomatopoeia (words that sound like what they mean) – do any of the real or imagined words do this?

### Group work

● Distributing photocopiable page 'George's rhyme' from the CD-ROM to groups of four to six children (they will be familiar with this from last week), ask them to do two things:
  ● Decide on an approach for presenting some or all of this rhyme aloud, using actions and varied pronunciation. Will they all recite the whole rhyme, or will they each do different sections? How can they make their version unique, fun and memorable?
  ● Replace or add words wherever they see fit, especially imaginary words that will give the rhyme more mystery and excitement (remind the children of the 'spell' from the introduction).
● Explain that each group will present their work to their peers.
● As the children develop their pieces, circulate and guide them towards slow, clear pronunciation, varied tone and gestures to match their words.
● Ideally, take the class to a large space, such as the school hall, and have groups practise performing to each other from one end of the hall to the other – this is a good way of helping them to understand the need for clear diction.

> **Differentiation**
> Ensure that less confident children have the opportunity to perform lines alongside or after others, organising groups appropriately.

### Review

● Ask for volunteers to perform all or part of their rhyme to the whole class. Note particularly effective delivery and interesting new words. Are there any examples of onomatopoeia?
● Recap new vocabulary and focus on the pronunciation and spelling of the real words. Are any of these exception words?

## Expected outcomes

● All children will develop their understanding of exception words, organising their writing and inferring meaning from texts.
● Most children will produce well-written lists and character profiles.
● Some children will produce writing that incorporates more complex words and whole-text structures.

## Curriculum objectives

● To read further exception words, noting the unusual correspondences between spelling and sound, and where these occur in the word.
● To discuss words and phrases that capture the reader's interest and imagination.
● To prepare poems and playscripts to read aloud and to perform, showing understanding through intonation, tone, volume and action.

## Resources

Interactive activity 'Hard-to-spell words' on the CD-ROM; *George's Marvellous Medicine* by Roald Dahl (ideally the book and an audio version); photocopiable page 'George's rhyme' from the CD-ROM

**Curriculum objectives**
● In non-narrative material, to use simple organisational devices.
● To use conjunctions, adverbs and prepositions to express time and cause.

**Resources**
*George's Marvellous Medicine* by Roald Dahl (ideally the book and an audio version)

# 2: What happened to Grandma?

## Introduction
● Prepare a list on the board about your day so far – getting breakfast, having breakfast, and so on. Recap that this is a way of summarising events. Briefly discuss why each thing was done and model the use of time and cause words as appropriate.

## Whole-class work
● Read Chapters 7 and 8 to the class ('Grandma Gets the Medicine' and 'The Brown Hen').
● Write *1. Grandma took the medicine and her body immediately shot up into the air.* as a bullet point on the board. This will be the first item in everyone's list.

## Independent or paired work
● Invite the children to write a list for everything that happened to Grandma. As they work, encourage them to use bullets or numbers for the sequence of events, as well as time and cause words where appropriate.

> **Differentiation**
> ● Have a list of time and cause words, such as *because, then, after* and so on, displayed clearly in the classroom or on children's desks. Direct children to reference this list as necessary.
> ● Extend children's thinking further by asking them to write why they think each thing happened to Grandma.

## Review
● Gather the class and discuss their work, using the opportunity to model and discuss effective use of time and cause words.

**Curriculum objectives**
● To participate in discussion about both books that are read to them and those they can read for themselves, taking turns and listening to what others say.
● To draw inferences such as inferring characters' feelings, thoughts and motives from their actions, and justifying inferences with evidence.

**Resources**
*George's Marvellous Medicine* by Roald Dahl (ideally the book and an audio version)

# 3: Mr Kranky

## Introduction
● Read Chapters 9 to 11 (*The Pig, the Bullocks...* to *Mr Kranky's Great Idea*). If possible, during Chapter 9 allow children to look at the illustrations, which in places show events that the text does not mention.

## Group work
● Explain that today's focus is on the personality of Mr Kranky.
● Write *Mr Kranky* at the top of the board and draw two vertical lines below this to divide the board into three columns. Write the words *Ingenious*, *Crazy* and *Greedy* as headings for each column.
● Arranging the children in six roughly equal groups, assign one of the three words to any two of the groups, so that every group has a word.
● Ask the groups to discuss and justify why their word is the most appropriate.
● After five to ten minutes, ask for suggestions, writing down key points in each column as they crop up. Allow groups to counter each other's points with reasoned and polite questioning and debate.

## Review
● Recap on the events that took place in the chapters and the points made by the groups for and against which word best sums up Mr Kranky.
● To conclude, have a vote to choose the favoured word to best describe him.

**Curriculum objectives**
● To draw inferences such as inferring characters' feelings, thoughts and motives from their actions, and justifying inferences with evidence.

**Resources**
*George's Marvellous Medicine* by Roald Dahl (ideally the book and an audio version); photocopiable page 43 'Character profiles'

# 4: Character profiles

## Introduction

● Finish reading the book (you may need to do some of this in advance of this lesson). Note that the ending may be shocking to some children.

## Whole-class work

● Explain that part of creating good stories is having good characters – something Roald Dahl excelled at. Invite the children to consider what made each of these characters interesting (not likeable, but interesting).
● Display photocopiable page 43 'Character profiles' and discuss one of the characters together, modelling how to award 'ratings' as well as requesting suggestions for key words and sentences.

## Independent work or paired work

● Distribute the photocopiable sheet and ask children to complete this for the four characters of the story.
● Encourage them to refer to specific incidents and quotes wherever possible.

> **Differentiation**
> ● Support children by providing vocabulary lists and allow some to work orally.
> ● Extend children's learning by encouraging them to reference specific pages that justify their descriptions.

## Review

● Gather the class together and ask for volunteers to share their work. Discuss sentence structure and vocabulary choices and consider improvements.
● Reinforce the way character is often inferred rather than stated, and pose hypothetical questions, such as: *What would character X do if the house was on fire?*

**Curriculum objectives**
● To draw inferences such as inferring characters' feelings, thoughts and motives from their actions, and justifying inferences with evidence.
● To predict what might happen from details stated and implied.

**Resources**
Photocopiable page 'Sample police report' from the CD-ROM

# 5: A police report

## Introduction

● Display photocopiable page 'Sample police report' from the CD-ROM and read it through with the class. Discuss the content, and then look carefully at the structure of the report and the style of writing.

## Independent work

● Explain to the children that a neighbour has heard lots of noise from George's house and has called the police.
● Ask children to imagine they are a police officer arriving at George's house shortly after Grandma has vanished. Tell them that they have had a chance to look around and talk with George, his mother and his father, and ask them to write a report to be sent to the chief constable. The style of the report can either be serious, or in the humorous and surreal tone of the actual book.
● Circulate and support children, encouraging them to use headings to categorise their report and to use time and cause words as appropriate.

> **Differentiation**
> ● Ensure that suitable vocabulary lists are available to support children's writing.
> ● Allow some children to write about just one of the characters.
> ● Extend children's learning by asking them to add recommendations for next steps to the end of their report.

## Review

● If time permits (or preferably in a separate session), ask for volunteers to read their reports to the class, focusing on an appropriate style of delivery.

## Expected outcomes
● All children will use rich vocabulary and inverted commas to create interesting characters and dialogue.
● Most children will develop effective characterisation and dialogue.
● Some children will make good use of alliteration and a wide range of punctuation to enhance their writing and when reading aloud.

## Curriculum objectives
● To identify main ideas drawn from more than one paragraph and summarise these.

## Resources
*The Twits* by Roald Dahl (ideally the book and an audio version); media resource 'Mr and Mrs Twit' on the CD-ROM; photocopiable page 44 'Who's worse?'; vocabulary support sheets (optional, not provided)

# Week 4 lesson plans

The chapter now moves on to one of Roald Dahl's best-loved short books: *The Twits*. The book is a masterclass in how to create rich, engaging characters with a minimum of words, and lends itself well to re-enactment of scenes and exaggerated characterisation. (There is a superb audio recording by Simon Callow, and playing this to your class will reap rich rewards.) The first three lessons cover a complete reading of the book, with opportunities for children to create their own revolting characters and to consider style and content, moving on to learning about the use of inverted commas for recording direct speech, both writing and reading it.

## 1: Meet the Twits

### Introduction
● Hiding the book and any other clues, explain to the class that they will shortly be meeting the most awful characters they have ever met.
● Ask for names of other awful characters or creatures that the class might know of from books, stories, films or animations, and ask for words or phrases to explain why the characters are unpleasant. Write these on the whiteboard in categories such as: *Name*, *Appearance*, *Habits*, *Diet*, *Sayings*, and so on.
● Build up expectations by diminishing these characters' awfulness in comparison to the Twits.

### Whole-class work
● Explain that this week you will be looking at another Roald Dahl short masterpiece: *The Twits*.
● Display the illustration 'Mr and Mrs Twit' from the CD-ROM .
● Explain that Roald Dahl did not like beards, and that the idea for *The Twits* originated in trying to do 'something against beards'.
● Read the opening half of the book, up to and including 'The House, the Tree, and the Monkey Cage', or play an audio version to the class.
● Discuss the relationship between Mr and Mrs Twit. Recap on their pasts and ask for ideas as to how they might have met, how long they might have been together, and so on. Wherever possible, model how to refer to (but not necessarily quote) the book when making points.

### Group work
● Explain that children will be working in groups to discuss and debate a given view. This may not necessarily be a view they agree with, but nevertheless groups must try to create a compelling statement to support their view.
● Arrange the class roughly into six groups and distribute photocopiable page 44 'Who's worse?'.
● Assign a 'Who's worse?' view to each group – *Mr Twit*, *Mrs Twit*, or *As bad as each other* (with two groups having each view) – and clarify how to use the photocopiable sheet to support group discussion.

---

#### Differentiation
● Support less confident learners by grouping them appropriately with clear rules for group interaction and contribution.
● Extend children's learning by challenging them to draft opinion pieces arguing their case. Such pieces would need to reference both characters and list arguments.

---

### Review
● Gather the class together and facilitate a discussion on different groups' views, starting with each group reading their statement. To conclude, decide who is worse with a whole-class vote. For interest, ask how many children changed from their own group's argument, and why (or indeed why not).

## Curriculum objectives
● In narratives, to create settings, characters and plot.

## Resources
Media resource 'Mr and Mrs Twit' on the CD-ROM; clothes and props for creating a revolting character (optional)

# 2: A revolting character of my own

## Introduction
● If possible, using simple props either yourself or with a volunteer, create a real-life revolting character at the front of the class (a simple hat, old jacket and a few bits and pieces will suffice).
● As with lesson I, ask children to provide details about your character and write these on the whiteboard in categories such as: *Name*, *Appearance*, *Habits*, *Diet*, *Sayings*, and so on.
● Briefly request one or two questions from the class, then answer these in role as the new character.

## Whole-class work
● Display the illustration 'Mr and Mrs Twit' on the CD-ROM and remind children of the Twits' characters, and how Roald Dahl gives a strong impression of them through description, behaviour and speech.
● Using the list of categories from the above Introduction, recap some of the words and phrases used to describe the Twits from lesson I.

## Independent work
● Challenge the children to develop and sketch their own awful character, and write a paragraph introducing them.

### Differentiation
● Support children's learning by providing a writing frame to help categorise the description in the categories mentioned above.
● Extend children's learning by suggesting a scenario and inviting them to write about how their characters behave and interact in it.

## Review
● Ask for volunteers to describe their characters to the class. If appropriate, have children present information in role as their character.

## Curriculum objectives
● To identify themes and conventions in a wide range of books.
● To increase their familiarity with a wide range of books, including fairy stories, myths and legends, and retell some of these orally.
● To ask questions to improve their understanding of a text.

## Resources
*The Twits* by Roald Dahl (ideally the actual book and an audio version); media resource 'Mr and Mrs Twit' on the CD-ROM

# 3: What happened to the Twits?

## Introduction
● Complete the reading of the book and discuss the elements of the story: *Who was the worst character? What was the worst thing the Twits did? Did they deserve to die?*
● Compare the story to *George's Marvellous Medicine*: *Are there any common aspects? How do they compare?*
● Discuss Roald Dahl's frequent theme of comeuppance: *Is it fair? Is it justified?*

## Whole-class and group work
● Display the illustration 'Mr and Mrs Twit' from the CD-ROM and explain that as a class you are going to consider whether what happened to the Twits was justified or not.
● Recap on the plot of the second half of the book as needs be (using the chapter list can help aid this), then arrange the class in groups of four to six.
● Ensuring that everyone understands the usual rules for group work in your classroom, ask groups to discuss the key events of the second half of the book using the following questions as prompts: *What did the Twits do, and why did they do it? What happened to the Twits, and why did it happen? Was it fair?*
● Consensus reached, the group must record their verdict for each event.

## Review
● Gather the class together and debate each point in turn, with yourself moderating, then take a vote – did the Twits get their just desserts or not?

## Curriculum objectives
● To use and punctuate direct speech.
● To use and understand the grammatical terminology in Appendix 2 accurately and appropriately when discussing their writing and reading.

## Resources
Comic with speech bubbles; photocopiable page 45 'Twit-talk'

# 4: Twit-talk

## Introduction
● Display a comic. Discuss the speech bubbles and what they represent.

## Whole-class work
● Draw two heads with a speech bubble for each on the board, ensuring the bubbles are large enough for you to write in.
● Write a joke question in the first speech bubble, such as *Why did the chicken cross the road?* Then ask for a suitable answer for the other speech bubble.
● Next, demonstrate how this can be represented as lines of text with inverted commas to represent spoken words, with correct punctuation and a new paragraph for a new speaker. Repeat and vary as appropriate. Introduce the terms *direct speech* and *inverted commas*.

## Independent or paired work
● Ask the children to work alone or with a partner to create a short conversation by completing the speech bubbles on photocopiable page 45 'Twit-talk'. Then invite them to convert the contents of the speech bubbles into a written conversation, using inverted commas as demonstrated.

### Differentiation
● Support children's learning by asking them to just complete the speech bubbles and then narrate their conversation to you or a partner.
● Extend children's learning by asking them to choose strong adverbs to describe how characters are talking, or choose verbs other than *said*.

## Review
● Share children's work and reinforce the correct use of punctuation.

## Curriculum objectives
● To use and punctuate direct speech.
● To compose and rehearse sentences orally (including dialogue), progressively building a varied and rich vocabulary and an increasing range of sentence structures (see Appendix 2).
● To use and understand the grammatical terminology in Appendix 2 accurately and appropriately when discussing their writing and reading.

## Resources
Photocopiable page 'The Wormy Spaghetti' from the CD-ROM

# 5: Direct speech

## Introduction
● Read photocopiable page 'The Wormy Spaghetti' from the CD-ROM to the class. Exaggerate the voices and use suitable expression to represent disgust, delight, and so on. Discuss how Roald Dahl has captured the Twits' speech.

## Whole-class work
● Display and work through the photocopiable sheet with the class, highlighting the direct speech and reinforcing the conventions used.
● Demonstrate how to write the speech and any essential supporting words from the text, starting with:
  "Hey, my spaghetti's moving!" cried Mr Twit.
  "It's a new kind," Mrs Twit said.

## Paired work
● Ask the children to work with a partner to copy the opening two lines, then continue writing down the speech for as much of the extract as possible.
● With any time remaining, ask pairs to perform snippets of the dialogue they have created, using intonation and expression.

### Differentiation
● Allow less confident writers to highlight the text on the photocopiable sheet.
● Challenging children to continue the dialogue with their own ideas.

## Review
● Gather the class together to share their work, reinforcing the key aspects of direct speech and effective reading.

## Expected outcomes
● All children will use and create playscripts, and be involved in performing plays.
● Most children will develop their understanding of playscripts as a genre.
● Some children will create and re-enact high-quality dialogues using strong vocabulary.

## Curriculum objectives
● To listen to and discuss a wide range of fiction, poetry, plays, non-fiction and reference books or textbooks.
● To read books that are structured in different ways and reading for a range of purposes.

## Resources
Photocopiable page 'The Twits playscript' from the CD-ROM; photocopiable page 'The Wormy Spaghetti' from the CD-ROM

# Week 5 lesson plans

This week's lessons focus on playscripts as a genre, based around David Wood's adaptation of *The Twits*. Initial lessons are based around understanding playscripts and approaches to new words encountered. Lesson 3 moves on to reading and rehearsing a section of the script, before children work collaboratively to produce their own playscripts. The week culminates in small performances using dramatic techniques for clear and engaging delivery.

## 1: The play of *The Twits*

### Introduction
● Explain that this week you will be developing and acting out short plays, which will involve the whole class using their voices clearly and effectively.
● Writing the following lyrics on the board, start the lesson with a quick sing-along, explaining that this verse is the ideal song for Mr Twit:

*Nobody likes me, everybody hates me*
*I'm going down the garden to eat worms.*
*Long thin slimy ones, short fat fuzzy ones*
*Squirmy, squiggly, squishy, squashy worms.*

● Repeat two or three times (the melody is available on the Internet if you do not know it), working on the clarity and accuracy of the class's renditions.

### Whole-class work
● Explain how plays tell stories, not just through dialogue but also by how the actors present themselves and deliver their lines. Discuss who decides this.
● Briefly, ask if any children have been to see a play. Explain how many more people will be involved in creating the play – probably many more than were actually on the stage. Brainstorm who these people might be.
● Display photocopiable page 'The Twits playscript' from the CD-ROM, and look at its features: the use of a narrator, capital letters to identify speakers, square brackets to separate directions, and so on.
● Consider how the majority of the text is, in effect, non-fiction – it is instructions for how the actors should move and talk.

### Paired work
● Distributing photocopiable pages 'The Wormy Spaghetti' and 'The Twits playscript' from the CD-ROM (or leaving this displayed on the board), ask pairs of children to consider differences in the dialogues.

### Whole-class work
● Gather the class together again and review their work so far. Discuss why the play is different to the original story and whether children feel these changes are beneficial or not.
● Splitting the class in half, with one half taking the part of Mr Twit, the other Mrs Twit, and the teacher reading the directions, model the use of the script to develop a short piece of drama.
● If space is limited, have only two children acting the parts, with the rest of the class collectively taking the role of director, contributing suggestions for changes either as you go or after the first reading.
● To conclude, focus just on one or two lines and talk in greater depth about different ways that these lines might be delivered for greater effect.

> **Differentiation**
> ● Support less confident learners by pairing them with children they can work alongside.

### Review
● Recap the main features of a playscript and how it differs from fiction texts.

**Curriculum objectives**
● To apply their growing knowledge of root words, prefixes and suffixes (etymology and morphology) as listed in Appendix 1, both to read aloud and to understand the meaning of new words they meet.

**Resources**
Interactive activity 'Affixes' on the CD-ROM; photocopiable page 46 'The '-y' suffix'

## 2: Simple suffixes

### Introduction

● Introduce the lesson with interactive activity 'Affixes' on the CD-ROM.
● Clearly explain the meaning of *prefix* and *suffix*.

### Whole-class work

● Start the lesson with yesterday's verse written on the board: *Nobody likes me...* Focus attention on the last line, which contains alliteration.
● Ask what sort of words *squirmy, squiggly, squishy* and *squashy* are (adjectives), and point out that they all have a 'y' at the end.
● Show that removing the 'y' shows the root words: *squirm, squiggle, squish* and *squash*, and note that these four words become adjectives when the suffix '-y' is added.
● Point out that this comes from Old English, hundreds of years ago, when it sounded very different from how it does now. Also explain that it means 'made up of' or 'characterised'.
● Note which of the words has had its spelling altered.

### Independent or paired work

● Distribute photocopiable page 46 'The '-y' suffix' and ask children to complete as much as they can.

> **Differentiation**
> ● Extend children's learning by asking them to identify words ending in 'y' that do not belong to this category (such as '-ly' adverbs).

### Review

● Discuss children's work and address confusion or difficulties, recapping the key vocabulary involved and how the '-y' suffix works.

**Curriculum objectives**
● To prepare poems and playscripts to read aloud and to perform, showing understanding through intonation, tone, volume and action.

**Resources**
Photocopiable page 'The Twits playscript' from the CD-ROM; *The Twits: Plays for children* (optional)

## 3: Let's be Twits

### Introduction

● Start the lesson by speaking to the class in as many different volumes and tones as possible, using a phrase such as: *Okay everyone, you need to listen carefully.* Start simply with a whisper, and ask the class to identify how you have spoken. As well as covering whispering, screaming, gasping, and so on, move on to implying your mood through tone, such as threatening, welcoming, happy, sad, uncertain, confident, and so on.
● After each utterance ask the class to say what you conveyed, and build up banks of words on the board.

### Paired work

● Reminding them about clear pronunciation, distribute photocopiable page 'The Twits playscript' from the CD-ROM and ask the children to work with their partners to discuss, rehearse and enact the scene on the sheet (either of them, or indeed the teacher, can deliver the narrator's line at the start).

> **Differentiation**
> ● Children who find performing difficult can 'understudy' other children. So, in a group of four there might be two Mr Twits and two Mrs Twits, with lines being narrated in unison or alternately.
> ● Challenge pairs to use the book to look at new scenes and create them independently.

### Review

● Ask for volunteers to perform all or part of their interpretations, asking the audience to consider how well they used intonation.

## Curriculum objectives
● To compose and rehearse sentences orally (including dialogue), progressively building a varied and rich vocabulary and an increasing range of sentence structures (see Appendix 2).

## Resources
Photocopiable page 'The Twits playscript' from the CD-ROM

# 4: A brand new scene

## Introduction
● Play starter activity 3 'Vocabulary builder', focusing on terms of endearment from the playscript in lesson 3, such as *dearest*, *little dumpling*, *dreamboat* and *angel-puss*. As well as asking children to use these expressions in new sentences, consider negative expressions too.

## Whole-class work
● Use the photocopiable sheet to remind the children of the play, and ask for ideas for brand new scenes. Collate suggestions and build up a list of possible scenarios for Twit-like tricks on the board, such as filling shoes with slugs, using dandruff for salt, shaving off hair in the night, and so on.

## Group or paired work
● Ask children to work collaboratively to build up a small scene of their own, involving interaction between the Twits. They should work orally initially and then draft in rough.
● Remind them about the exaggerated dialogue between Mr and Mrs Twit from lesson 3, showing the love–hate nature of their relationship, as well as relevant playscript conventions.

> **Differentiation**
> ● Children who find oral composition difficult can understudy other children.

## Review
● Do not perform the scripts at this stage. Instead, discuss difficulties encountered and allow for suggestions as to how to overcome them.

## Curriculum objectives
● To prepare poems and playscripts to read aloud and to perform, showing understanding through intonation, tone, volume and action.

## Resources
Ideally, a good-sized performance space; scripts drafted in lesson 4

# 5: Performance time

## Introduction
● Briefly recap on effective dramatic techniques for clarity and expression when speaking, and the importance of these for creating interesting characters on stage. Using simple sentences of your choice model variations in tone, volume and style, combining facial expression, body posture and hand gestures to emphasise this.

## Group or paired work
● Ask the pairs and groups to continue working to refine their scripts, from lesson 4, and include rough directions and notes as appropriate.
● Allow them a reasonable amount of time to rehearse.

> **Differentiation**
> ● Support learners by allowing them to perform 'script in hand', with their lines highlighted if need be.
> ● Extend children's learning by asking children who have created good, clear scripts to swap with other pairs or groups and try to perform each other's work.

## Review
● Allow plenty of time for children to perform their work to the rest of the class. Try to set up a space that will encourage attentive audience behaviour, and clear strong speaking in performers. If possible and appropriate, video the performances.
● To conclude, encourage the children to review their work, giving themselves ratings for the quality of their script and the quality of their delivery, considering how they could improve them both.

# Week 6 lesson plans

The final week of this chapter moves on to poetry, looking at traditional rhymes and tales and considering how Roald Dahl changes these in his *Revolting Rhymes*. Dahl's rhyming technique is also a focus, with the chapter providing lots of opportunities for children to hear, read, create and perform existing rhymes, as well as their own. There is also work looking at letter patterns in irregular rhyming words. Note that the *Revolting Rhymes* sometimes contain vocabulary that will probably be new to the children – some is not relevant to the learning and tasks involved, but some may need discussion and explanation. Also be aware that some of the rhymes are quite gruesome and shocking, as was Dahl's way, and consider if they are all suitable for your whole class.

## 1: *Revolting Rhymes*

### Introduction
- Write the following rhyme on the board:
   *Thank goodness it is Saturday,*
   *Now we can all go out to play.*
- Use this example to introduce, explain and discuss these key terms: *rhyming couplets*, *syllables* (clap these) and *rhythm*.

### Whole-class work
- Explain that the focus for this week's work is using rhyme to retell stories. Read one of the *Revolting Rhymes* to the class – *Jack and the Beanstalk* or *Goldilocks and the Three Bears* are suggested, but not essential.
- Briefly explain how the rhyme uses syllables, rhyming couplets and rhythm.
- Also introduce the term *narrative poetry*, meaning poetry that tells stories.
- Write the title of the rhyme that you have read across the top of the whiteboard, and draw a line underneath to create two columns. At the top of one column write *Traditional tale* and above the other *Revolting rhyme*.
- In discussion, consider the characteristics of the original and the rhyme, writing them for comparison in each column. Use the headings *Plot*, *Character*, *Tone* and *Setting* to help give structure and guide thinking.
- Consider how much the two have in common, and where the main changes have occurred. Also, consider if there is any change in moral from the original to the Dahl version.

### Paired or group work
- Read a second rhyme at least once to the class. Ask them to work in small groups, each with a scribe or two, to perform the same exercise, comparing the original plot, character, tone and setting to the rhymed version.

### Whole-class work
- Ask groups to share their work with the class, and focus on the way Dahl has changed the essence of the stories. Discuss his motives and aspects that are common to other books already covered (naughty and greedy people getting their comeuppance).
- Discuss the benefits and shortcomings of using rhyme (for example it is often more engaging, but is much harder to write).

> **Differentiation**
> - Challenge children by accessing rhyming dictionaries to find new words.

### Review
- To conclude, re-read the rhyme and reinforce the vocabulary introduced earlier: *narrative poetry*, *syllables*, *rhyming couplets* and *rhythm*.

# 2: Words that rhyme

**Curriculum objectives**
● To read further exception words, noting the unusual correspondences between spelling and sound and where these occur in the word.

**Resources**
*Revolting Rhymes* by Roald Dahl (the book and if possible an audio version); photocopiable page '*Revolting Rhymes* extracts' from the CD-ROM

## Introduction
● Choose around six to ten pairs of rhyming words, either of your choice, from week 2, or from *Revolting Rhymes*. Use these to work through starter activity 1 'Word pairs', with 'partner' words in separate lists but not next to each other.

## Whole-class work
● Read a new rhyme from *Revolting Rhymes* to the class and briefly discuss the variation on the original story.
● Explain that in this lesson you will be looking at rhyming words, and that sometimes their rhyming letter patterns look the same, but sometimes not (as in week 2, lesson 2).
● Display photocopiable page '*Revolting Rhymes* extracts' from the CD-ROM, then highlight and discuss a selection of rhyming words, modelling pronunciation and discussing exception words where appropriate.

## Independent work
● Closing down the photocopiable sheet, explain that you are going to dictate some of the lines from it. Use this as an opportunity for children to practise their handwriting skills too. You can add some focus by omitting the second rhyming word from each couplet and asking children to insert it from memory.

**Differentiation**
● Support learning of difficult spellings by writing these on cue cards and keeping them visible.

## Review
● Recap on the dictated lines and allow children to check their own work, focusing on any exception words covered.

# 3: Revolting recitals

**Curriculum objectives**
● To prepare poems and playscripts to read aloud and to perform, showing understanding through intonation, tone, volume and action.

**Resources**
*Revolting Rhymes* by Roald Dahl (the book and if possible an audio version); photocopiable page '*Revolting Rhymes* extracts' from the CD-ROM

## Introduction
● Randomly call out a word used in yesterday's lesson, writing it on the board. Ask the children to write a rhyming word for it.
● After six or so words, recap and ask for contributions, writing the correct rhymes on the board and drawing attention to common spelling patterns and exception words.

## Group or paired work
● Read another rhyme from *Revolting Rhymes* to the class.
● Organising the children as desired, distribute photocopiable page '*Revolting Rhymes* extracts' from the CD-ROM. Explain that you would like each group to choose an excerpt that they will then present to the class.
● As children develop their work, circulate and reinforce that effective presentation is about their voice, their face and their body.
● Focus on syllables. Most of the lines (apart from where Dahl deliberately alters the format) have eight syllables. Use clapping to reinforce this.

**Differentiation**
● Allow children who are not confident with public speaking to act along with the words of others. This will keep them included, while still reinforcing the language for them.

## Review
● Ask for volunteers to perform their pieces to the class, using the opportunity to reinforce the rhyming words encountered.

**Curriculum objectives**
● To prepare poems and playscripts to read aloud and to perform, showing understanding through intonation, tone, volume and action.

**Resources**
Selection and/or listing of traditional nursery rhymes; photocopiable page 47 'A rhyme of my own'; internet access (optional)

# 4: A rhyme of my own

## Introduction
● Read a further rhyme from *Revolting Rhymes* to the class and, if desired, discuss and consider the variation from the original story.
● Recap once more the pattern of syllables used by Roald Dahl.

## Whole-class work
● Show the class a selection of traditional rhymes, such as 'Humpty Dumpty'. Explain that the challenge for the next two lessons is to prepare and perform a new version of one of these traditional rhymes in the style of Roald Dahl.
● Using any one rhyme, work with the class to model how you might plan a variation. List the key elements of the original (character, location, plot or theme, outcome) and then collectively brainstorm to devise variations on these aspects as the basis of a new version.

## Independent or paired work
● Hand out photocopiable page 47 'A rhyme of my own'. Ask the children to choose a traditional rhyme and plan their work, thinking about key elements of the original and how they will reinterpret it.
● Ensure children do not dwell too long on the pacing of the original rhyme – this will be differ from Roald Dahl's style and may confuse them.

> **Differentiation**
> ● Extend learning by letting children access an online rhyming dictionary to find new words.

## Review
● Allow the class to offer constructive help to others.

**Curriculum objectives**
● To prepare poems and playscripts to read aloud and to perform, showing understanding through intonation, tone, volume and action.

**Resources**
Selection and/or listing of traditional nursery rhymes; preparation work from lesson 4; internet access (optional)

# 5: Performing rhymes

## Introduction
● Use starter activity 2 'Getting technical', recapping on the meanings of *rhyming couplets*, *rhythm* and *syllables*.

## Whole-class work
● Read a final rhyme from *Revolting Rhymes* to the class, using expressive intonation and gestures and, if desired, cover variations on the original.
● Discuss the aspects of performing such a piece – the use of voice, expression, gesture and pacing.
● Explain and recap the terms *syllable*, *rhyming couplets* and *rhythm*, noting once more the pattern of eight syllables per line used by Roald Dahl.

## Independent or paired work
● Continue with the previous lesson's work on a rhyming retelling of a traditional nursery rhyme. Encourage children to complete their rhymes and then retell them using oral and physical techniques they have been practising.

> **Differentiation**
> ● Rhyming couplets and not essential. The main purpose is to ensure that everyone completes at least part of a rhyme that they are then able to perform to the class.

## Review
● Ask the children to perform their work to each other, and then for volunteers to perform to the class. Pick out successes and use these as opportunities to model and recap effective use of language, reviewing technical terms such as *rhythm* where appropriate.

## Curriculum objectives
● To use conjunctions, adverbs and prepositions to express time and cause.

## Resources
Interactive activity 'Time and cause words' on the CD-ROM; highlighter pens; photocopiable page 42 'How to make a chocolate cake' (optional)

# Grammar and punctuation: Identifying time and cause words

## Revise
● If you wish to revise the grammatical language, use starter activity 2 'Getting technical'.
● Use starter activity 5 'Time and cause words' and the interactive activity 'Time and cause words' on the CD-ROM.
● Look at texts from the chapter and identify words as appropriate, discussing why they are called time and cause words.

## Assess
● Using an appropriate passage of text, such as photocopiable page 42 'How to make a chocolate cake', ask children to identify any time and cause words.
● Next, ask them to redraft the passage without these words, typically as a set of numbered instructions.

## Further practice
● Look at lists of instructions and convert them into flowing prose, adding time and cause words wherever possible.
● Reverse this approach, sourcing suitable texts and converting the prose to lists by removing the time and cause words where possible.
● Ask the children to write a piece reviewing and commenting on the children's books written by Roald Dahl, commenting on the order written and offering thoughts on why he wrote certain books.

## Curriculum objectives
● To spell words that are often misspelled (Appendix 1).

## Resources
Appropriate wordlists; dictionaries

# Spelling: Hard-to-spell words

## Revise
● Select the words you wish to focus on and use starter activity 4 'Hard-to-spell words'.
● Display the words clearly in the classroom and discuss letter patterns, irregularities and rhyming words, presenting the best strategies for children to practise and learn the spellings.

## Assess
● Dictate a passage or sentences with the words in, ensuring that the other vocabulary is within the children's repertoire.
● Examine children's work for common or unusual errors and deal with these as per school policy.

## Further practice
● Ask the children to write sentences containing the words.
● Use dictionaries to check spellings and reinforce usage by writing down relevant information and meanings.
● Play a range of memory games with the words.
● Break down words into their parts, or consider other words that can be formed with each word.

**Curriculum objectives**
● To draw inferences such as inferring characters' feelings, thoughts and motives from their actions, and justify inferences with evidence.
● To identify main ideas drawn from more than one paragraph and summarise these.

**Resources**
*The Twits* by Roald Dahl; *George's Marvellous Medicine* by Roald Dahl; photocopiable page 44 'Who's worse?' (blank or already completed); photocopiable page 43 'Character profiles' (blank or already completed); selection of Roald Dahl novels

# Reading: Inferring and identifying from fiction

## Revise

● Revisit photocopiable page 44 'Who's worse?' (week 4, lesson 1), discussing why decisions were reached about each character. Re-read the opening chapters describing Mr Twit and Mrs Twit, and discuss how to summarise each paragraph, listing points on the board.

● Also revisit the character profiles (ideally already completed) from *George's Marvellous Medicine* (week 3, lesson 4) and review why different comments were made and ratings given, discussing freely without using the book. When specific points are made, ask whether they are direct quotes or inferences, exploring what words or information lead us to make assumptions about characters.

● Separately discuss both books and consider what makes an effective summary, listing the main events and ideas from each chapter.

## Assess

● The most effective assessments are usually done with reference to different texts and contexts. As such you should assess the Curriculum objectives on this page with reference to other class readers or books that the children have already read and are familiar with. Because the assessments are of reading, it can be beneficial to avoid children having to write too much to provide evidence. It is difficult, but comprehension can often be more efficiently assessed via discussion, ideally with small groups based around the same books.

● Ask the class to prepare brief presentations about characters in the books they are reading, offering them a template to structure their thoughts around if necessary.

● By adapting photocopiable page 43 'Character profiles', invite children to complete them for characters in the books they are currently reading.

● Similarly, ask children to summarise a chapter of a class reader or a book they are currently reading. Look for work (written or oral) that states the gist of the book in the child's own words.

## Further practice

● Create a Roald Dahl character wall in your classroom and, starting with characters from the books already covered in this chapter, ask the children to draw illustrations of different characters, and write key words or phrases from the text that best describe the character.

● Move on to reading other short novels by Dahl, such as *The Giraffe and the Pelly and Me*, *The Magic Finger* and *Esio Trot*, focusing on the characters in those books and creating ratings cards for them as per *George's Marvellous Medicine*.

● If time permits, pick out sections from his longer stories, such as *Matilda* and *The Witches*, and continue focusing on what is inferred and what is clearly stated about each character.

● Similarly, identify key sections from these books and work through them with the class, discussing and agreeing on the main ideas and summarising them.

## Curriculum objectives
● To use and punctuate direct speech.
● To proofread for spelling and punctuation errors.
● To assess the effectiveness of their own and others' writing and suggest improvements.

## Resources
Photocopiable page 'The Wormy Spaghetti' from the CD-ROM

# Writing: Punctuating direct speech and checking work

## Revise
● Look at photocopiable page 'The Wormy Spaghetti' from the CD-ROM and discuss the use of inverted commas to denote spoken words. Focus also on punctuation within the inverted commas and language after them. Consider how (and why) this is different in a playscript.
● Re-read 'The Wormy Spaghetti' to the class, exaggerating the voices for the characters. Discuss how the inverted commas help with this. Ask the children to find a section in their current reading book that contains inverted commas
and practise reading it aloud, using intonation and expression to show characters' voices.
● Draw two speech bubbles on the board and work with the class to create quick 'question and answer' style conversations. Ask the class to rewrite these as a brief dialogue.
● Distribute the sentences of a dialogue on strips of paper. Invite the children to arrange these in a sensible order, adding appropriate punctuation and other text around the given words.
● Display texts with known errors in and have the class consider them. Ask for volunteers to give clues as to where the errors are and challenge their peers to find them.
● Be sure to develop consistent conventions for self- and peer-marking of writing, distinguishing between spelling, punctuation and grammatical errors and considering improvements. Help them to distinguish between words they should know and words that are hard to spell.

## Assess
● Provide short texts that include dialogue but with all the punctuation missing. Ask the children to add all the punctuation, including inverted commas, paying particular attention to punctuation that lies inside the inverted commas.
● Provide texts that have a range of technical issues and ask children to highlight and correct errors according to set conventions.
● Similarly, provide draft texts that children will be able to reshape, and ask them to write about what they would change and why.
● To assess children's ability to proofread their own work, focus on a piece that is not too large and lends itself to such an exercise, including varied punctuation and interesting vocabulary.

## Further practice
● Continue looking at comic books, choosing a small number of frames and changing the speech bubbles into a dialogue.
● Devise small dramatic vignettes, composing orally, and then enacting them. Ask children to rewrite these as simple dialogues, punctuated as direct speech.
● Introduce different words for *said*, such as *whispered*, *screamed*, *shouted*, and so on, and ask the children to write sentences containing direct speech appropriate to each verb.
● Provide children with draft texts with a range of deliberate errors. Show them how reading aloud often helps to spot errors as the brain auto-corrects less when doing this. Children should then mark up the texts for errors, as well as suggest improvements.
● Show the class sample texts written in advance, showing first and second drafts, discussing the improvements made and considering the author's rationale for the changes.
● Use starter activity 11 'Direct speech'.

## Roald Dahl quiz

- How much do you know about Roald Dahl? Take the quiz below and find out.

**1.** Where was Roald Dahl born? _____

_____

**2.** Where were his parents from? _____

_____

**3.** Why did he not like his school? _____

_____

**4.** Where did he write most of his books? _____

_____

**5.** Which book has a horrible headteacher called Miss Trunchbull?

_____

**6.** Did he only write children's books? _____

_____

**7.** Can you name a screenplay that he wrote?

_____

**8.** How old was Roald Dahl when he died? _____

**9.** Roald Dahl said he could only write because he had children. Why do you think

he said this? _____

_____

**10.** What is the strangest thing you know about Roald Dahl?

_____

_____

I can find information in a non-fiction text.

How did you do?

# Roald Dahl bibliography

■ This is a list of the books Roald Dahl wrote for children. (It does not include his autobiographical books.) How many have *you* read?

*James and the Giant Peach* (1961): A crazy adventure with talking insects, cloud men and, of course, a giant peach.

*Charlie and the Chocolate Factory* (1964): Charlie Bucket wins the trip of a lifetime to the strange chocolate factory.

*The Magic Finger* (1966): A girl discovers magic powers to stop cruelty to animals.

*Fantastic Mr Fox* (1970): Mr Fox fights the awful farmers to save his family.

*Charlie and the Great Glass Elevator* (1972): The sequel to *Charlie and the Chocolate Factory*. Charlie goes into space.

*Danny, the Champion of the World* (1975): Danny's dad loves his son (and poaching) more than anything else, but soon needs his help.

*The Enormous Crocodile* (1978): Join Crocky in his hunt for a tasty child for lunch. Can the other jungle animals save the children?

*The Twits* (1980): Two horrible people who were made for each other.

*George's Marvellous Medicine* (1981): George's plans have bigger effects than he had expected.

*The BFG* (1982): Everyone's favourite giant, even the Queen's.

*Revolting Rhymes* (1982 poetry): Nasty versions of traditional tales.

*The Witches* (1983): A truly scary tale of evil doings.

*Dirty Beasts* (1984 poetry): Animals as you have never imagined them before.

*The Giraffe and the Pelly and Me* (1985): A wonderful, wacky tale about a ladderless window cleaning company.

*Matilda* (1988): A girl genius from an awful family is sent to a terrible school.

*Esio Trot* (1989): Mr Hoppy loves Mrs Silver but is too shy to let her know. Could tortoises help him?

*The Vicar of Nibbleswicke* (1990): A vicar who gets all his words muddled up. Written to raise money for dyslexia.

*The Minpins* (1991): Something big and scary is in the woods where the tiny Minpins live.

## How to make a chocolate cake

### Ingredients

**For the cake:**

100g plain flour; 150g caster sugar; 40g cocoa powder; 1 teaspoon baking powder; 1 teaspoon bicarbonate of soda; 1 free-range egg; 100ml milk; 50ml vegetable oil; 1 teaspoon vanilla extract; 100ml boiling water.

**For the chocolate icing:**

100g plain chocolate; 100ml double cream.

**Oven temperature:** 180°C/350°F/Gas mark 4

### Method

Turn on the oven to heat it up, then put all of the cake ingredients except the boiling water into a large mixing bowl, and use a whisk to beat the mixture until it is smooth and well mixed. Next, add the boiling water to the mixture, a little at a time, stirring until it is smooth and runny. Finally, pour the mixture into a round cake tin and place it in the oven.

While the cake is baking, prepare the icing. Put the chocolate and cream in a saucepan over a low heat until the chocolate melts. Remove the pan from the heat and whisk the mixture until it is smooth and shiny, then leave it to settle so that it will get thicker.

After 25 minutes, check that the cake is ready, then remove it from the oven and let it cool completely. When it has cooled, remove the cake from the tin by moving a blunt knife around the inside of the cake tin to loosen it, and then carefully tip it out.

When the icing is thick enough, spread it on the cake using a blunt knife, then share and enjoy your cake.

## Character profiles

■ Complete the profiles for each of the characters from *George's Marvellous Medicine*. Colour in the stars to show your ratings.

| Name: **George** | Name: **Grandma** |
|---|---|
| Appearance: _____ | Appearance: _____ |
| _____ | _____ |
| Pleasantness rating: ☆☆☆☆☆ | Pleasantness rating: ☆☆☆☆☆ |
| Intelligence rating: ☆☆☆☆☆ | Intelligence rating: ☆☆☆☆☆ |
| Mischief rating: ☆☆☆☆☆ | Mischief rating: ☆☆☆☆☆ |
| Important notes: _____ | Important notes: _____ |
| _____ | _____ |
| _____ | _____ |
| _____ | _____ |
| Name: **Mr Kranky** | Name: **Mrs Kranky** |
| Appearance: _____ | Appearance: _____ |
| _____ | _____ |
| Pleasantness rating: ☆☆☆☆☆ | Pleasantness rating: ☆☆☆☆☆ |
| Intelligence rating: ☆☆☆☆☆ | Intelligence rating: ☆☆☆☆☆ |
| Mischief rating: ☆☆☆☆☆ | Mischief rating: ☆☆☆☆☆ |
| Important notes: _____ | Important notes: _____ |
| _____ | _____ |
| _____ | _____ |
| _____ | _____ |

I can identify aspects of characters in a book.

How did you do?

## Who's worse?

■ You will be given a point of view as to who is the worst Twit: Mr Twit, Mrs Twit, or they are as bad as each other. Draw a circle round the one your group is given.

| | | |
|---|---|---|
| **I.** Mr Twit | **2.** Mrs Twit | **3.** They are as bad as each other |

■ Thinking about everything that has happened so far, your group should discuss why your point of view is true AND why the other two are false. One of your group should make notes when you have all agreed.

■ Here are some of the chapter titles to help you remember what happened:

| | | |
|---|---|---|
| Dirty Beards | The Glass Eye | The Frog |
| The Wormy Spaghetti | Mrs Twit Gets a Stretching | |

| Mr Twit is the worst | Mrs Twit is the worst | They are as bad as each other |
|---|---|---|
| | | |

I can develop ideas and arguments by referring to a text.

How did you do?

**PHOTOCOPIABLE**     ■SCHOLASTIC
www.scholastic.co.uk

## Twit-talk

■ Can you write funny or revolting speech? Decide what the Twits are saying to each other and write it in the speech bubbles below. Then rewrite their conversation on the lines beneath using inverted commas.

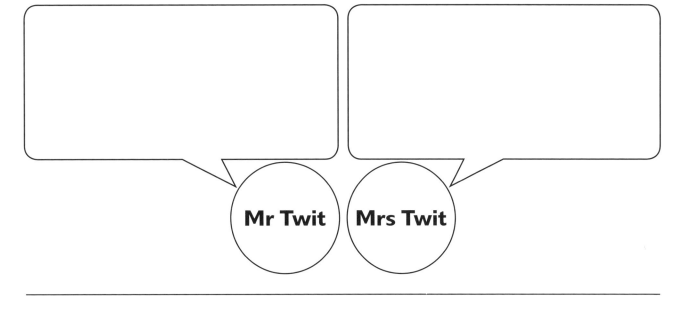

_____

_____

_____

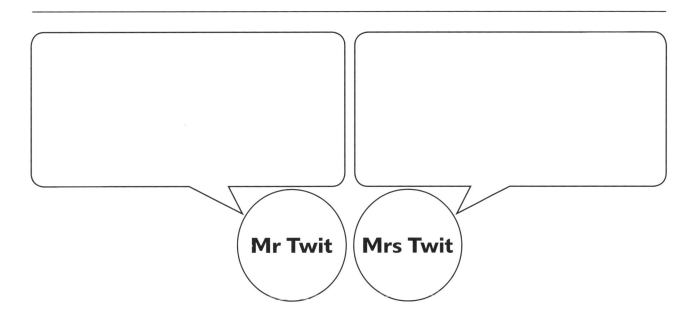

_____

_____

I can use inverted commas when writing reported speech.

How did you do?

## The '-y' suffix

■ Some words can have a 'y' added to them to make them into adjectives. Sometimes this changes their spelling; sometimes it does not. Which of these words change to adjectives with the '-y' suffix?

| Root word | Add '-y' to make an adjective | Is it a real word? | Spelling change for root word? |
|---|---|---|---|
| bag | baggy | yes | add a 'g' |
| cart | carty | no | |
| chew | chewy | yes | no |
| dirt | | | |
| fun | | | |
| house | | | |
| ice | | | |
| luck | | | |
| man | | | |
| mud | | | |
| noise | | | |
| rock | | | |

■ Can you think of any other words that change with the '-y' suffix?

| | | | |
|---|---|---|---|
| | | | |
| | | | |
| | | | |

■ Can you spot any rules to say why some words change their spelling when '-y' is added to the end?

_____

_____

I can use simple suffixes correctly.

How did you do?

# A rhyme of my own

■ Think about the characters that are going to be in your story. Work on character sketches for them.

■ Choose a traditional rhyme and write it here.

Title: _____

■ Note down the different features of the rhyme:

Characters: _____

Location: _____

What happens: _____

How does it end? _____

■ Now it's time for your version. How will you change the story in the rhyme? What will you keep the same?

Characters: _____

Location: _____

What happens: _____

How does it end? _____

■ Write your version. You may find it easier not to worry about rhyming words for your first draft.

_____

_____

_____

_____

_____

_____

I can create new versions of stories in a similar style to *Revolting Rhymes*.

How did you do?

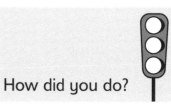

# Robots

Taking robots as its theme, this chapter starts with a range of lessons over the first two weeks based around *The Iron Man*, looking at language, characterisation and themes, considering how the book sits alongside traditional fairy-tale genre stories. It then moves on to looking at non-fiction texts about robots, using this as a stimulus for developing new and effective vocabulary and in children's own non-fiction texts. The final two weeks move back to creative writing, facilitating the careful production of a story and a poem around the robot theme, with opportunities for children to critically review their own work, consolidating the vocabulary, grammar and punctuation learned throughout the chapter.

## Expected prior learning
- Can understand and recall events and themes from fiction.
- Can understand the basic structure of a non-fiction book and how to use its features to find information.
- Can confidently locate nouns in texts.
- Can understand that a story needs a plot, character and setting.
- Can talk about rhythm and rhyme in a poem.

## Overview of progression
- Throughout this work there are activities to develop understanding of words with irregular spellings, correct use of pronouns, possessive apostrophes, constructing new words using prefixes, and using time and cause words – in particular adverbs for describing movement.
- Dictionary use is covered, and there is also a review of previous learning on structuring text and using inverted commas.
- For all the written work there is advice and ideas on helping children to review their own work critically and constructively.

## Creative context
- The robot theme provides many opportunities for non-fiction-based research and writing, as well as environmental and scientific themes.

## Preparation
*The Iron Man* by Ted Hughes; a collection of a good range of books about robots and robotics is essential for weeks 3 to 6; a selection of children's poetry books.

### You will also need:
A3 paper; a selection of coloured pens; dictionaries (ideally one per child); access to the internet is optional, but could be useful for extending research for some learners; one lesson (on adverbs) would benefit from access to a larger space that children can move around in; handwriting paper and pens; copies of your school's prospectus; structured writing frames (optional); video camera (optional).

### On the CD-ROM you will find:
Media resource 'Robots'; interactive activities 'Pronouns', 'Time and cause words', 'Affixes'; photocopiable pages 'Time and cause words sentences', 'Sample contents and index', 'Correcting text', 'Robot poetry samples'

# Chapter at a glance

An overview of the chapter. For curriculum objective codes, please see pages 8–10.

| Week | Lesson | Curriculum objectives | Summary of activities | Outcome |
|---|---|---|---|---|
| 1 | 1 | RC: 9<br>WC: 7 | Read Chapter 1 of *The Iron Man* and discuss the language. Describe the scene and work to improve vocabulary. | • Can appreciate and use descriptive language in context. |
| | 2 | RC: 11<br>WC: 13 | Introduce pronouns and read Chapter 2. Focus on the characters and consider their thoughts and actions. | • Can infer aspects of character by referring to the text and can use pronouns correctly. |
| | 3 | RC: 12 | Read Chapters 3, 4 and 5 and summarise and explain the remainder of the book. | • Can summarise a text. |
| | 4 | RC: 10, 16 | Discuss the themes of the book in groups. | • Can discuss a story with a partner, referring to details. |
| | 5 | RC: 3<br>WT: 5 | Introduce dictionaries, show how to use them and practise finding words from the text. | • Can use a dictionary to check spellings and locate the meanings of words they know. |
| 2 | 1 | WC: 14 | Identify time and cause words in a summary of the first three chapters, then write a summary for the final chapters. | • Can begin to use time words to connect words and phrases to extend sentences. |
| | 2 | RWR: 2<br>WT: 6<br>WC: 20 | Introduce the terms *adverb*, *conjunction* and *preposition* and embed the spelling of certain time and cause words. | • Can begin to use time and cause words to connect words and phrases to extend sentences. |
| | 3 | WT: 4<br>WC: 18 | Revise the use of the possessive apostrophe and introduce its use with plurals. | • Can use the apostrophe with some confidence to show possession. |
| | 4 | RC: 1 | Draw graphs of good vs. bad for *The Iron Man* and the dragon, annotated with attitudes to the characters at each point. | • Can interpret a story and offer opinions on its meaning. |
| | 5 | RC: 4, 5 | Compare *The Iron Man* to a well-known fairy tale by looking at its component parts. | • Can recognise the conventions of fairy tales. |
| 3 | 1 | RC: 2 | Discuss contents and index pages and how to use these effectively. Discuss what they want to find out about robots. | • Can understand the use of non-fiction reference books. |
| | 2 | RC: 2, 15 | Use a range of non-fiction sources to investigate the world of robots. | • Can use non-fiction sources to gather information. |
| | 3 | RC: 10<br>WC: 2, 6 | Work in groups to share and organise information about robots. | • Can use headings to organise information. |
| | 4 | WC: 4, 6 | Write a short non-fiction piece on robots in a well-structured text. | • Can understand the concept of a paragraph. |
| | 5 | WC: 7, 8, 9 | Proofread, edit and improve their non-fiction robot texts. | • Can review own work and correct fundamental grammar, punctuation and spelling. |
| 4 | 1 | RWR: 1<br>WC: 16, 20 | Create vocabulary useful for describing robots; practise forming new words using prefixes. | • Can use prefixes to create new words. |
| | 2 | WT: 1<br>WC: 16 | Design a robot, incorporating effective prefix-based words. | • Can apply new vocabulary to good effect. |
| | 3 | WC: 14 | Consider adverbs used to describe movement through physical activity. | • Can understand and use adverbs correctly to describe movement. |
| | 4 | WC: 4, 6, 9 | Practise paragraph skills by writing a description of their robot using a number of headings. | • Can write in paragraphs. |
| | 5 | WT: 7, 8 | Complete handwriting-focused tasks based around writing programmable instructions for their robots. | • Can understand the importance and approaches needed for legible, cursive handwriting. |

# Chapter at a glance

| Week | Lesson | Curriculum objectives | Summary of activities | Outcome |
|---|---|---|---|---|
| 5 | 1 | RC: 14, 16￼ WC: 1 | Recap on the story of The Iron Man, considering language, plot and characterisation. | • Can appreciate and discuss the elements of a story. |
| | 2 | WC: 3, 5 | Plan a story for the robot created in week 4. | • Can combine story elements of character and setting to create a story. |
| | 3 | WC: 4, 19 | Write a robot story, incorporating inverted commas and paragraphs. | • Can organise text into paragraphs and use inverted commas. |
| | 4 | WC: 8, 9 | Proofread, edit and improve their stories. | • Can identify and change punctuation, spelling and grammar, and improve on vocabulary and content. |
| | 5 | WC: 7 | Critically review their own work. | • Can critically reflect on the quality of their own writing. |
| 6 | 1 | RC: 8, 14 WC: 1 | Consider a range of poems and deliver a few lines, discussing how rhythm and rhyme affect poems. | • Can appreciate poetic techniques, and deliver poems using appropriate intonation. |
| | 2 | RC: 6 WT: 1 WC: 1, 16 | Review work on prefixes and plan the basics of a robot poem. | • Can make decisions about poetic style and subject, incorporating appropriate vocabulary. |
| | 3 | WC: 2 RC: 6 | Draft a robot poem using the scientific vocabulary used in the prefix activity. | • Can use and adapt poetic styles for their own work. |
| | 4 | WT: 7, 8 | Revise and then write out copies of their poems for a display or book. | • Can understand the importance and approaches needed for legible, cursive handwriting. |
| | 5 | RC: 6 | Read or recite or perform their robot poems. | • Can orally present a poem using appropriate intonation and expression. |

# Background knowledge

**Heading**: A brief piece of text used to define the focus of a coming passage of text.

**Headword**: Words at the top of dictionary pages showing the range of words on a double-page spread.

**Possessive apostrophe**: Used to show possession, for example *Angela's shoes* and *trees' leaves*.

**Non-fiction**: Any text that deals with factual information.

**Pronoun**: A word used in place of a noun referring to people or things, such as *I*, *you*, *she*, *it* and *this*.

**Simile**: A figure of speech that compares two different things, using *like* or *as...as*.

**Subheading**: A second-level of category under a main heading.

**Syllable**: The natural unit of sound in a word when spoken.

# Week 1 lesson plans

This week introduces children to *The Iron Man*, providing a complete reading of the book over three lessons while focusing on descriptive language, characters and plot, with opportunities for children to look at and emulate the author's use of language, to infer characters' thoughts and attitudes, and to consider how the author has structured the book. Children are challenged to consider the events of the book in depth, preparing statements for what different people might think. In addition, there are related tasks introducing pronouns and developing dictionary skills for checking spellings and meanings of words.

## 1: Where did he come from?

### Introduction
● Dim the lights if possible and, without letting children see any of the illustrations or the cover of the book, start the lesson with a slow-paced, dramatic reading of Chapter 1 of *The Iron Man*.
● Discuss what happened, avoiding speculation about where he came from.

### Whole-class work
● Display photocopiable page 72 'Describing the Iron Man', and ask for volunteers to point out descriptive language. Highlight appropriate words and discuss what effect these have.
● Explain similes to the class, and point out examples in the text, focusing on the use of the words 'like' and 'as...as'. Ask why the author uses these expressions, and what they mean.
● Point out the word 'CRRRAAAASSSSSSH!' and ask: *What effect is the author trying to create?* Briefly mention onomatopoeia, explaining how words sometimes sound like what they mean. Can the children think of any other words they could stretch and/or capitalise to create dramatic effects?
● Next, look for words that describe motion, such as *turned, swayed, tumbled* and *waved*, and look at the sentences they are in to see if there are clues that suggest their meaning. Point out that the author used these words to suggest movement and action and that description is not just about appearance.

### Independent work
● Tell the children to imagine that they were sitting in a boat out at sea and that they saw everything that happened. Explain that they must write a brief letter or diary entry explaining what they saw. They can use the descriptive vocabulary from the passage, or they can use their own words.

### Paired work
● After allowing sufficient time for writing, organise the children in pairs and ask them to share their work with each other.
● Explain that you want them to focus on the descriptive words and phrases they have used, and to work with their partners to make suggestions that might help them to create a stronger picture of the Iron Man and the scene.

### Differentiation
● Support those who find writing difficult by asking them to focus on a description of the Iron Man – either a straight description or a labelled diagram.
● Extend learning by asking children to create original similes for describing the different parts of his body.

### Review
● Gather the class together and ask for volunteers to state some of the descriptive words they have used, and look out for those who have incorporated similes or onomatopoeic words.
● Ask for volunteers who improved their writing with a partner, and discuss the improvements. Assess their understanding of the descriptive phrases used.

### Expected outcomes
● All children will listen to and discuss the language, characters and plot of the book.
● Most children will form questions and offer views on the text, and develop their use of descriptive language, pronouns and dictionaries.
● Some children will offer in-depth comments using rich language.

### Curriculum objectives
● To check that the text makes sense to them, discussing their understanding and explaining the meaning of words in context.
● To assess the effectiveness of their own and others' writing and suggesting improvements.

### Resources
*The Iron Man* by Ted Hughes; photocopiable page 72 'Describing the Iron Man'

### Curriculum objectives
● To choose nouns or pronouns appropriately to avoid repetition.
● To drawing inferences such as inferring characters' feelings, thoughts and motives from their actions, and justifying inferences with evidence.

### Resources
*The Iron Man* by Ted Hughes; interactive activity 'Pronouns' on the CD-ROM; photocopiable page 73 'Why did they do it?'

# 2: Character motives

## Introduction
● Play starter activity 1 'Word pairs' listing family members on the left-hand side (*mother, sisters, twins, grandparents*, and so on). On the right hand side, not in the same order, list possible pronouns (*she, he, they*, and so on).
● Next, open the interactive activity 'Pronouns' on the CD-ROM, and work through it with the class.

## Whole-class work
● Read Chapter 2 to the class, pausing to discuss and clarify as necessary.
● Focus on Hogarth, discussing the different events surrounding him and his actions. What sort of person do the class think he is?
● Write the first phrase from photocopiable page 73 'Why did they do it?' on the board (*Hogarth saw the Iron Man and ran home, he...*) and ask for suggestions, drawing out good vocabulary: *worried, anxious, terrified*, and so on, and stress the pronoun *he*.

## Independent or paired work
● Distributing the photocopiable sheet, explain that you want the children to think about why the different characters acted as they did, and to write the conclusion to each sentence after the pronoun.

## Review
● Gather the class and discuss their ideas. Note those who are able to refer to the text and make inferences.

### Curriculum objectives
● To identify main ideas drawn from more than one paragraph and summarise these.

### Resources
*The Iron Man* by Ted Hughes

# 3: What happened when?

## Introduction
● Write the titles for Chapters 1 and 2 on the board and, talking with the class, recap on the main contents and ideas, making brief notes next to each heading as appropriate.
● Model summarising a chapter in a sentence, such as: *Chapter 2: Everyone is scared, but Hogarth traps the Iron Man in a pit that the farmers have dug.*

## Whole-class work
● Read the final three chapters of the book (this will take slightly longer than previous readings).
● Explain that you will be discussing the themes and meaning of the book in later lessons, but for now you want to concentrate on summarising the book. To help model this for the class, recap the notes made for Chapters 1 and 2, then list the final three chapter headings under these.

## Group work
● Arranging the class in groups of four to six, ask them to discuss and agree on a sentence (or two) that summarises the essence of each of Chapters 3 to 5, with one of the group acting as a scribe.

> ### Differentiation
> ● Arrange children in mixed-ability groups and ensure that groups only write down their sentences once everyone has agreed.

## Review
● Gather the class together and review their summaries. Model and reinforce effective use of language.

## Curriculum objectives
- To participate in discussion about both books that are read to them and those they can read for themselves, taking turns and listening to what others say.
- To ask questions to improve their understanding of a text.

## Resources
A dictionary; A3 paper and felt-tipped pens (one sheet and pen per group of four to six children); *The Iron Man* by Ted Hughes

# 4: Themes

## Introduction
- Write the words *brave* and *kind* on the board and model good dictionary skills to find the precise definitions, then read or write these and discuss. Can children name their opposites (antonyms)? Define these too.

## Group work
- Organise the children into discussion groups and ask them to appoint a scribe; give each group a felt-tipped pen and a sheet of A3 paper, and ask the scribe to divide it into quarters.
- Modelling the process on the board, ask each scribe to write the words *Good or bad?*, *Small or large?*, *Brave?* and *Kind?* – in each quarter, noting the question mark after each.
- Explain that each group must talk together to agree how Hogarth, the Iron Man and the Space-Bat-Angel-Dragon fit into each of those four categories, and choose something from the text to explain their thoughts.

### Differentiation
- Group children with strong verbal reasoning skills and ask them to present balanced arguments as to why these attributes are both true and false for some of the characters.

## Review
- Keeping groups together, facilitate a whole-class discussion. Pose a new question to the whole class: *What will happen when the people of the Earth run out of metal to send to the Iron Man?* Allow the class to discuss freely, noting where ideas are referenced to the book in any way.

## Curriculum objectives
- To use dictionaries to check the meaning of words that they have read.
- To use the first two or three letters of a word to check its spelling in a dictionary.

## Resources
Photocopiable page 72 'Describing the Iron Man'; multiple concise dictionaries, ideally one per child

# 5: Using dictionaries

## Introduction
- Play starter activity 2 'Getting technical', using the words *alphabet*, *dictionary* and *headword*.

## Whole-class work
- Display photocopiable page 72 'Describing the Iron Man' and highlight the word *brink*.
- Modelling good practice, demonstrate how to use the dictionary effectively to locate the word, and then write down the all information given..

## Independent or paired work
- Ask children to work alone or in pairs to locate two or three words from it in their concise dictionary and note their meanings.
- After ten minutes or so, briefly review their work, then remove the photocopiable sheet from view.
- Next, slowly dictate these words (also from the story), and ask the children to write them down: *iron*, *clam*, *torso*, *tractor*, *stove*, *dragon* and *blissful* .
- Children must use their dictionaries to check their spellings and, if they can find the definitions, to note them down.

### Differentiation
- Extend learning by dictating words with more than one meaning or use, such as *bat*, *crane* or *green*, and give children more detailed dictionaries to locate the relevant words.

## Review
- Review children's work, stressing that misspelling words and then not locating them is very much part of the learning, showing the caution needed in using dictionaries effectively.

# Week 2 lesson plans

This week concludes the work on *The Iron Man*. The first lesson is based around a summary of the book, in particular focusing on time and cause words (adverbs, conjunctions and prepositions), with the second lesson introducing these terms and reinforcing the spelling patterns of key words. Next, there is a discrete lesson revising the use of the possessive apostrophe and introducing its use with plural nouns. To conclude, the final two lessons return to the themes of the book and how they are developed through the characters, comparing and contrasting the book with traditional fairy tales.

## 1: Writing a summary

### Introduction
● Use starter activity 5 'Time and cause' words' to introduce the focus of this lesson. It is not necessary to introduce the words *adverb, conjunction* or *preposition* – this will be done in the next lesson.
● Explain that time and cause words help us to understand *when* something happened (or will happen) or *why* something happened (or will happen). They are also essential words for making our writing smoother and easier to read.

### Whole-class work
● Display photocopiable page 74 'Summary of *The Iron Man*'. Read through the Chapter 1 summary with the class and confirm children's understanding as appropriate. Look at the time and cause words that have been highlighted. Model pronunciation and try to decide which of them is a 'time' word, and which is a 'cause' word.
● Next, read through the Chapter 2 summary and check children's understanding again. Then, through discussion, highlight the time and cause words in this paragraph, once again modelling and explaining each in turn.
● Repeat this for the Chapter 3 summary, modelling correct pronunciation and showing how the words help the text to flow more smoothly.

### Independent work or paired work
● Look at the brief lists of events for Chapters 4 and 5 on the photocopiable sheet and confirm that the class agree with these points.
● Ask the class to write their own summaries (either on the photocopiable sheet or on paper) for Chapter 4, including time and cause words wherever they can to help with the flow.
● After a suitable amount of time, focus everyone's attention and take sample contributions, asking the whole class to note when they hear a time and cause word. Use the opportunity to clarify learning where appropriate and model good pronunciation and spelling wherever possible.
● Continue, with children moving on to Chapter 5 only when they are happy with their summary of Chapter 4.

> ### Differentiation
> ● For children who need additional support, distribute photocopiable page 75 'Summary support sheet'.
> ● For children writing their own summaries, it is unlikely that they will finish both chapters in the lesson. This is acceptable – the main thing is to be clear on correctly using the words. If appropriate, children could orally draft any parts they cannot finish in the lesson.

### Review
● Allow children to read from their own writing, the support sheet or to draft sentences orally to allow for equal participation.
● Try to allow plenty of time for the review. Children will need to be able to reflect on their writing and try to improve it.

### Curriculum objectives
● To write from memory simple sentences, dictated by the teacher, that include words and punctuation taught so far.
● To read further exception words, noting the unusual correspondences between spelling and sound, and where these occur in the word.
● To use and understand the grammatical terminology in Appendix 2 accurately and appropriately when discussing their writing and reading.

### Resources
Photocopiable page 'Time and cause words sentences' from the CD-ROM; interactive activity 'Time and cause words' on the CD-ROM

# 2: Practising time and cause words

## Introduction
● Use starter activity 2 'Getting technical' to introduce terms for *adverb*, *conjunction* and/or *preposition*, as desired.

## Whole-class work
● Using photocopiable page 'Time and cause words sentences' from the CD-ROM if you need it, briefly display the sentences you are going to dictate, discussing vocabulary as appropriate, in particular any exception words.
● Adhering to your own 'rules' for dictation, dictate five or six of the sentences to the class, stressing the time and cause word each time. You will need to decide how much to focus on time and cause words (*italic underlined*) and the exception words (bold) in these sentences.

## Independent work
● Ask the children to write short statements about their feelings about each character in the story using time words, such as *at first*, *when*, *before*, *finally*, and so on.

## Review
● Gather the class together and review children's work.
● Scaffold responses for less confident learners and challenge more confident children to identify the word type (*adverb*, *conjunction* or *preposition*). To conclude, open the interactive activity 'Time and cause words' on your CD-ROM. Work through this together with the class, reinforcing spellings of key words as necessary.

### Curriculum objectives
● To indicate possession by using the possessive apostrophe with plural nouns.
● To place the apostrophe accurately in words with regular plurals and in words with irregular plurals.

# 3: Possessive apostrophes

## Introduction
● This is a one-off lesson focusing on the possessive apostrophe.
● Revise the apostrophe for singular possession by having a range of volunteers bring an object they own to the front. Model the process using two sentences, such as *Diane has a pencil. It is Diane's pencil.* Write it and explain as necessary. Explain the first sentence–second sentence approach to this work. (The first sentence must have a subject that 'has' an object.)
● It is suggested that you do not revise apostrophes for contraction at the same time – just look at the apostrophe followed by 's' to show possession.
● Invite other children to suggest initial sentences and ask for volunteers to provide a possessive version.

## Whole-class work
● Teach the correct usage for possession in the plural, looking at both regular and irregular words (such as *cars'* and *children's*).
● Write the following list of words on the board: *children, cars, houses, cats, fingers, women.*
● Challenge someone to come up with a first sentence, not using a possessive apostrophe for it, and for someone else to convert this or make a challenge if the context or structure is incorrect.
● Continue verbally or allow children to write down answers as desired. They might also contribute new plural words that they think will work in sentences containing possessives.

## Review
● Recap on the singular possessive and discuss two or three written examples of the regular and irregular plural possessive. Use traffic light assessment to broadly assess the learning.

# 4: Good and evil

## Introduction
● Whisper the words *good* and *evil* to two volunteers and ask them to mime separate statues for the class. Discuss responses and ask what makes us think such a face or posture is good or evil.

## Whole-class work
● Draw the following 'Good and bad' chart on the board. Taking one colour for the Iron Man, ask where he 'belongs' during Chapter 1 ('OK probably') and mark the graph appropriately. Discussing Chapter 2 and add another mark.

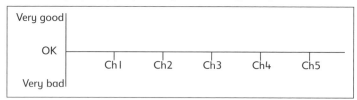

## Paired or group work
● Divide the class into small groups, each drawing the graph as large as possible. Then invite them to plot the behaviour of Hogarth, the Iron Man and the Space-Bat-Angel-Dragon in different colours, adding annotations about character behaviour at key points to explain themselves.

> **Differentiation**
> ● Support children with photocopiable page 74 'Summary of *The Iron Man*'.
> ● Challenge children to refer to the book and plot a continuous line for each character.

## Review
● Ask groups to present their work, taking turns to explain their charts and comments, allowing the class to query and discuss freely.

# 5: Fairy tales

## Introduction
● Briefly narrate, orally, the story of 'Jack and the Beanstalk' to the class.

## Whole-class work
● Ask the class to recall fairy tales they know and, through discussion of contents, build up a list of elements, steering the discussion as necessary. Elements might include: *A fast start with little explanation of character or setting; a good or innocent character; a strange or evil character; royalty; set in unknown lands; magic (good or bad); a problem to be solved; a happy resolution.*
● Write *Jack and the Beanstalk* on the board, and discuss which of the fairy tale ingredients listed appears in the story, and what form it takes. Use this opportunity to model good layout and presentation.

## Independent or paired work
● Ask the children to write *The Iron Man* in the middle of a piece of paper, and to perform a similar exercise for this story.
● With enough time remaining, ask the class to write two or three sentences explaining whether or not they think *fairy tale* is an appropriate description.

## Review
● Gather the class together and ensure equal participation by asking for contributions about the ingredients of the story, ending with volunteers' thoughts about the tag *fairy tale*. Allow discussion as appropriate, challenging contributors to justify their comments.

# Week 3 lesson plans

This week introduces work around the chapter's main theme, robots. The emphasis of the week is researching non-fiction to broaden children's understanding of robot history, technology and use. The first lesson focuses on research skills, moving on to the children finding and organising information that interests them, and finally writing a short piece about these facts, organising their work with headings and paragraphs. To conclude the week's lessons, children must review, edit and improve their work to a high standard. Note that a wide range of books about technology, machines and robotics will make the lessons more effective.

## 1: Research skills

### Introduction

- Start the lesson with the word *Robot* written on the board. Ask what the word means to people. Also ask: *Was the Iron Man a robot?*
- Explain that *etymology* is the study of where words come from. Explain that the word *robot* was invented by a Czech writer around 100 years ago, and that he took the word from *robota*, meaning to force a person to do work.
- Using a dictionary, model how to use the first and second letters to find the word you are looking for and the dictionary definition.

### Whole-class work

- Explain that over the next three lessons they will be researching robots, discovering information that interests them and organising it in a useful way.
- Display and discuss the features and layout of photocopiable page 'Sample contents and index' from the CD-ROM, considering how they could be used for research. Remind children that the index can help them to locate information. Note, this sample is not for reference, it has been written to help teachers demonstrate how to use non-fiction books for effective research.
- Using an appropriate robots reference book (or a good non-fiction book), work with the class to look at the contents and index pages, modelling effective research skills and reinforcing new vocabulary wherever possible.

### Independent or paired work

- Explain that to make research effective and useful, it is best to have an idea of what you are looking for.
- Working individually or in pairs, ask the children to make a note of what they already know about robots, and then to note down the sorts of things that they want to find out about when doing their research.
- Ask the children to keep questioning what they are reading (what they now know, what they still want to find out, what they now want to find out).

### Whole-class work

- Gather the class together again and discuss their initial thoughts and ideas on robot research.
- Move on to discussing how to read for information. Using a suitable book, model how you might reference a specific area of information and then scan for key facts.

> **Differentiation**
> - Support learners with photocopiable page 'Sample contents and index' from the CD-ROM for them to highlight aspects that interest them, encourage them to say why.
> - Challenge children to consider more complicated areas, such as 'robots and health'.

### Review

- Look again at the structure of reference and non-fiction books, reinforcing the skills involved. Ask the class to consider whether the things they want to find out about are likely to be in the books you have to hand.

---

### Expected outcomes
- All children will locate material that interests them, representing it in their own words.
- Most children will organise the information they are interested in effectively.
- Some children will develop a well-organised non-fiction piece, written to a high standard, with continuity.

### Curriculum objectives
- To read books that are structured in different ways and reading for a range of purposes.

### Resources
Photocopiable page 'Sample contents and index' from the CD-ROM; good reference book (ideally about robots and robotics) that has contents and index pages; access to the internet (optional)

**Curriculum objectives**
● To read books that are structured in different ways and read for a range of purposes.
● To retrieve and record information from non-fiction.

**Resources**
Photocopiable page 'Sample contents and index' from the CD-ROM; wide range of books about robots and robotics; access to the internet (optional)

# 2: Researching robots

## Introduction
● Display photocopiable page 'Sample contents and index' from the CD-ROM, and look together at the order of the contents. Is this logical? Could it be better organised?
● Look at the sample index page and consider what is different about it. Why would you look here rather than the contents?

## Independent or paired work
● Ensuring that children have access to a good selection of books, explain that you want the children to familiarise themselves with the robotics books available and, using their lists of what interests them from yesterday, to start researching robots, noting down information as they go.
● (You may need to organise this as a carousel activity if the number of books available is limited.)

> **Differentiation**
> ● Support learners by choosing appropriate texts for them to work with.
> ● Extend more confident children by allowing access to the internet, ensuring that you have established clear e-rules for use and focus.

## Review
● Gather the class and discuss whether their research has been useful and/or successful. Where issues have occurred, is this because their original ideas of what to find are inappropriate, or do they not have the books they need? Finish the session by allowing everyone time to consider how they can each move their research forward.

**Curriculum objectives**
● To discuss and record ideas.
● To ask questions to improve their understanding of a text.
● In non-narrative material, to use simple organisational devices.

**Resources**
Photocopiable page 'Sample contents and index' from the CD-ROM; wide range of books about robots and robotics; access to the internet (optional); completed work (from week 3, lessons 1–2); A3 paper, pens and pencils

# 3: Organising information

## Introduction
● Display photocopiable page 'Sample contents and index' from the CD-ROM and have a quick oral quiz, asking questions such as: *Where would you find out about the work robots do?* or *On what page will you find information about x?*, and so on.
● Discuss what the difference is between each of the mock pages. Focus on how the middle 'chapter' page is organised. What other headings and subheadings might this or other chapters contain?

## Group work
● Explain that they are going to cooperate as a group to share their research work from the previous lessons and effectively organise their information.
● If necessary, model the use of A3 paper and pens to collate information, allowing children to cut and stick facts on rather than rewrite if desired.

> **Differentiation**
> ● Support learners by grouping them appropriately, and allowing ongoing access to suitable books.
> ● Extend learners by challenging them to add further questions to their categories, listing what they are yet to find out.

## Review
● Have groups present their work to the class, with some members reading out headings and others stating the contents under these to allow equal participation.
● Use this as an opportunity to reinforce the use of headings and paragraphs for ordering information.

## Curriculum objectives

- To organise paragraphs around a theme.
- In non-narrative material, to use simple organisational devices.

## Resources

Photocopiable page 'Sample contents and index' from the CD-ROM; completed work (from week 3, lessons 1–3); structured writing frames (optional)

# 4: Writing non-fiction

## Introduction

- Start the lesson with starter activity 2 'Getting technical', focusing on *paragraph*, *heading*, *subheading* and *bullet point*. Display photocopiable page 'Sample contents and index' from the CD-ROM and point out each feature.
- Recap on the benefits of organising texts and how this helps make writing easier, as well as reading.

## Independent work

- Explain that today everyone will be writing their own non-fiction texts about the information on robots that is of interest to them, which they have collected over previous lessons.
- Write the following text on the board: *The main things that interest me about robots are as follows:*
- Explain that this will be the opening line of everybody's work, under which they will put headings for each category that interests them, followed by one or two small paragraphs containing the information for each category.

### Differentiation

- Provide structured writing frames for those who need additional support.
- Extend the task by challenging children to explain why each area interests them.

## Review

- Gather the class together and ask children to work with partners to review each other's work, focusing on the headings and ascertaining whether the content of text under each heading is relevant (spelling, grammar and punctuation will come tomorrow).
- Decide whether the children will need more time to draft their work before they review and improve it.

## Curriculum objectives

- To assess the effectiveness of their own and others' writing and suggest improvements.
- To propose changes to grammar and vocabulary to improve consistency.
- To proofread for spelling and punctuation errors.

## Resources

Completed non-fiction robot work (from week 3, lesson 4)

# 5: Reviewing and improving texts

## Introduction

- Explain that today everyone will be reviewing, improving and finishing their non-fiction texts, reminding the class that the purpose of the texts is to provide a range of information for themselves, that they find interesting and useful for the coming weeks' work on their own robots.
- Through guided discussion, generate a brief checklist for reviewing work: information organised under headings, good punctuation, pronouns for efficient writing, identifying and checking possible spelling errors, and so on.

## Paired work

- Organise the class so that everyone can work with a partner to review each other's work, using the checklist on the whiteboard.

## Independent work

- With the peer reviews done, allow plenty of time for children to edit their texts, asking them to focus on checking for appropriate use of pronouns and apostrophes, and whether the information under each heading is appropriate.

## Review

- Ask volunteers to read their finished pieces to the class, reminding children that they can continue to gather information for their future robot work.
- Use the review to assess effective structuring of their non-fiction texts.

# Week 4 lesson plans

This week's work develops children's vocabulary and language skills by considering and using prefixes and adverbs. They will use new vocabulary and grammar to create language that effectively describes a range of real and imagined robots. The first two lessons focus on introducing and consolidating the language and its associated grammar, leading to individual designs of robots with well-structured written descriptions incorporating paragraphs. The week concludes with a focused lesson on handwriting, writing programmable instructions for a robot that only responds to legible, joined script.

## 1: Robot words

### Introduction
● Preparing suitable lists on the board in advance of the lesson, do starter activity 1 'Word pairs', but using prefixes on the left-hand side (such as 'dis-', 'mis-', 're-', 'un-') and a larger number of root words on the right (such as *pay, take, appear, even, understanding, like, wrap, new*).
● Challenge the class to work alone or in pairs to make as many real words as they can using the prefixes and root words available, then work through these together.
● Recap on what a *prefix* is and discuss how they can be used to create new words when added to root words.

### Whole-class work
● Discuss robot characters that the class might have come across in films and books, such as *R2-D2, Wall-E, Buzz Lightyear*, and so on. Talk also about any real-life robots they know of, including electronic toys. Discuss their qualities – what they do, and how they do it.
● Open the media resource 'Robots' on the CD-ROM on the board and go through the images of different robots, pausing to discuss their possible functions, referring to research from the previous week and gathering ideas for what qualities and abilities each might have.
● Explain that you are going to be looking at a range of prefixes that may provide good vocabulary for describing robots, either real or invented.

### Independent or paired work
● Distribute photocopiable page 76 'Powerful prefixes' and look at the words together, challenging children to identify root words in the examples given.
● Challenge children to create words that might be useful for one of the robots already discussed, or for describing a new robot. Stress that it is acceptable to create new words as well as identifying existing words. The main thing is that the words they choose need to 'fit' with the type of robot they are thinking of.

**Differentiation**
● Provide word cards with prefixes and suitable root words on to allow some children to play with matching these together and consider outcomes.
● Learning can be extended by providing larger dictionaries and asking children to research the range of words available for each of the prefixes given.

### Review
● Gather the class together and share work. It is important to reinforce the terms *prefix* and *root word*, and that while some of the words created may not be found in dictionaries, their prefix and root must be.
● Focus on effective words and consider their sound as well as meaning – which words help create an image of how the robot actually looks or behaves?
● Create a quick display showing the vocabulary covered for reference in coming lessons.
● Request that the children give their opinion of the poem in five words, then three, then one word.

# 2: New robots

## Introduction

● Open the media resource 'Robots' on the CD-ROM on the board and go through the images of different robots, pausing to discuss their possible functions, referring to research from the previous week.
● Consider effective descriptions for each image, recapping prefixes introduced in lesson 1, considering how these might also make other words.

## Independent work

● Distribute photocopiable page 77 'Robot design template' and ask the children to consider the key features and attributes for a robot of their own, completing the template and then describing their creation. Can they use powerful prefixes to describe their robot's features?
● Point out that the logical starting point is to decide on the main function of their robot, as this will affect its size, shape and complexity.

### Differentiation
● Support learning by providing appropriate word banks for children to reference.
● The work can be extended by asking children to highlight any prefix-led words and writing definitions of each on the reverse of their design sheet.

## Review

● Gather the class together and initially ask children to share their work with a partner, carrying out peer reviews and discussing work together.
● Ask for volunteers to share their work, requesting words, phrases or complete descriptions, focusing on different elements of the design sheet.
● To conclude, recap and reinforce the use of prefixes using words from children's texts as model examples if possible.

**Curriculum objectives**
● To use further prefixes and suffixes and understand how to add them (Appendix 1).
● To learn the grammar for Year 3 in Appendix 2.

**Resources**
Media resource 'Robots' on the CD-ROM; completed prefixes work (from week 4, lesson 1); photocopiable page 77 'Robot design template'; wide range of books about robots and robotics

# 3: Robot movements

## Introduction

● Use starter activity 6 'Adverbs', with words for everyday movements.

## Whole-class work

● Ideally in a large space, ask the children to walk around, moving according to the adverbs you call: quickly, lazily, jerkily, and so on.
● Next, ask everyone to think of an adverb and to create a mime doing something in the style of that word (such as typing a letter angrily).
● Pair children and to refine their mimes together, offering feedback.
● Ask for volunteers to demonstrate their mimes to the class, then reinforce the purpose of adverbs by having them re-enact their mime without the adverb modifying it.

## Independent, group or paired work

● With the children back at their desks, and adverb banks displayed if desired, ask them to write about five sentences explaining how the robot they designed would move to do certain tasks (you can list these tasks or let the children identify tasks relevant to their robot).

### Differentiation
● Provide adverb cue cards to support children.
● Challenge children to create metaphors or similes to describe their robots' movements.

## Review

● Discuss the children's work, noting and making a temporary display of strong adverbs. Check whether children can use them correctly – both in context and grammatically.

**Curriculum objectives**
● To use conjunctions, adverbs and prepositions to express time and cause.

**Resources**
Completed robot design work (from week 4, lesson 2); space to move around (optional); bank of adverb cue cards (optional, not provided)

**Curriculum objectives**
● In non-narrative material, to use simple organisational devices.
● To organise paragraphs around a theme.
● To proofread for spelling and punctuation errors.

**Resources**
Completed prefixes and adverbs work (from week 4, lessons 2–3); photocopiable page 'Sample contents and index' from the CD-ROM; structured writing frame (optional)

# 4: My robot

## Introduction

● Display photocopiable page 'Sample contents and index' from the CD-ROM and focus on the middle page, demonstrating the organisational features it contains.
● Recap the meanings of *chapter*, *heading*, *subheading* and *bullet point*. Discuss what sort of information would be in each category of this page.

## Independent work

● Explain that you want the children to imagine that they are going to try and get their robot manufactured, and the first stage is to write a presentational piece about it, encouraging them to use the vocabulary they developed in lessons 2 and 3.
● Discuss the key features of such a text – they will need to be factually accurate while using engaging vocabulary, as well as structuring the information appropriately, perhaps with an introduction, then using headings, such as *Functions*, *Key features*, and so on.

> **Differentiation**
> ● Provide a structured writing frame for those who need support, and allow them to compose orally if needed.
> ● To extend thinking, challenge children to incorporate one bulleted list and one numbered list in their piece.

## Review

● Gather the class together and share effective uses of prefixes, adverbs and good organisation of texts. Ideally the work from this lesson should be extended to allow for a presentation-quality draft of their writing accompanied by a high-quality picture – either done on the computer or by hand.

**Curriculum objectives**
● To increase the legibility, consistency and quality of their handwriting.
● To use the diagonal and horizontal strokes that are needed to join letters and understand which letters, when adjacent to one another, are best left unjoined.

**Resources**
Handwriting paper and pens, as per school policy

# 5: Written instructions

## Introduction

● Before the lesson starts, write a selection of commands on the board in the handwriting style of your school policy, such as *move forward*, *pick up the ball*, *sit down*, and so on.
● In discussion with the class, go over these in a different colour, explaining different strokes and joins as appropriate.

## Independent work

● Explain that a robot has been created that takes instructions by scanning human writing with its camera-lens eyes, but the writing has to be very precise and consistent.
● As such, the children's mission is to create a set of instructions that the robot will be able to follow.
● Point out that to start, the children can simply rewrite the instructions on the whiteboard, but after this they must then create their own.

## Review

● Look at samples of work, ideally enlarging them on the board (if you can use acetates to show how the work should be, so much the better).
● Ask the children to decide which instructions the robot would understand, and why.
● If possible, allow children time to revisit and improve or repeat aspects of their instructions.

# Week 5 lesson plans

This week moves on to focus on the story-writing genre, while allowing children to use language from previous weeks' lessons. The first lesson revisits *The Iron Man*, looking at both language and structure, moving on to children planning their own stories in lesson 2 with structured support. The third lesson reminds the class about the use of paragraphs and direct speech, and then (ideally) will provide an opportunity for extended writing for one or more sessions, allowing the children to craft a satisfying robot story around their plan. Lessons 4 and 5 help children to review their work in depth, editing and improving it, and then finally offering critical reviews of their stories.

## 1: Revisiting *The Iron Man*

### Introduction
● Display photocopiable page 72 'Describing the Iron Man' and read it to the class.
● Recap on the way the author has used vocabulary to create the scene and discuss this, reflecting on the different aspects of vocabulary and grammar that have been encountered since first reading the story in weeks 1 and 2.

### Whole-class work
● Explain that the focus of this week's work is to look at how stories are structured and created, also reviewing them for strengths and weaknesses.
● Tell the class that some people have commented that *The Iron Man* is really two separate stories – the first three chapters deal with the arrival and eventual capture of the Iron Man, with the solution of scrap metal being found to create a happy ending, and the second half deals with the arrival of the Space-Bat-Angel-Dragon, and its contest with the Iron Man (use photocopiable page 74 'Summary of *The Iron Man*' if needed.)
● Display photocopiable page 78 'Story planner' and work through it with the class, completing it for the first three chapters of *The Iron Man*. In particular, discuss how the plot of *The Iron Man* revolves around the mismatch between creatures and location, and elicit that when the robot and the dragon are in the right place they are no longer threats to humans.
● Display photocopiable page 75 'Summary support sheet' and recap the essence of Chapters 4 and 5, using the opportunity to reinforce the time and cause words used.

### Group or paired work
● Ask the children to create a second story plan for Chapters 4 and 5, including effective vocabulary.

> **Differentiation**
> ● Support learning by providing chapter headings and key contents on strips of paper for children to arrange in the correct order and then identify and highlight interesting vocabulary.
> ● Extend learning through children developing extensive vocabulary lists for each chapter and highlighting words according to their type, such as prefixes, and so on.

### Review
● Bring the class back together and review their work – do they think that Chapters 4 and 5 constitute a separate story?
● Explain that Ted Hughes created the story for his own children. Do the children think he made it up as he went along, or did he have it planned? Can children offer reasons for their thoughts?
● Discuss whether the story would have been better ending after Chapter 3, or as two separate stories, or just the way it is. To finish, take a vote.

---

### Expected outcomes
● All children will plan and write their own stories, incorporating paragraphs and direct speech.
● Most children will use paragraphs and direct speech correctly, reviewing and editing their work to improve it.
● Some children will show a good grasp of paragraphs, direct speech, sentence structure and vocabulary.

### Curriculum objectives
● To participate in discussion about both books that are read to them and those they can read for themselves, taking turns and listening to what others say.
● To identify how language, structure, and presentation contribute to meaning.
● To discuss writing similar to that which they are planning to write in order to understand and learn from its structure, grammar and vocabulary.

### Resources
Photocopiable page 72 'Describing the Iron Man'; photocopiable page 74 'Summary of *The Iron Man*'; photocopiable page 75 'Summary support sheet'; photocopiable page 78 'Story planner'

**Curriculum objectives**
● In narratives, to create settings, characters and plot.
● To compose and rehearse sentences orally (including dialogue), progressively building a varied and rich vocabulary and an increasing range of sentence structures (see Appendix 2).

**Resources**
Photocopiable page 78 'Story planner'

# 2: Planning robot stories

## Introduction
● Do starter activity 2 'Getting technical', focusing on the meaning of the following terms in relation to stories: *plot, character, setting, dilemma, resolution*.

## Whole-class work
● Explain that over the next few lessons children will be planning, writing, editing and reviewing a story involving the robot that they created last week.
● Work together to consider and discuss key aspects and options. *Will it take place in space, or somewhere more unexpected?* (Such as a school.) *What is the main focus, or dilemma, of the plot? Will they stick to the fairy tale genre?* (You may wish to guide them here.)

## Independent work
● Distributing photocopiable page 78 'Story planner', explain that they can base it on the story of *The Iron Man* if desired. (You may want to guide some children.)
● Point out the vocabulary boxes in the story planner – they should recall or research effective vocabulary that will help them to portray the different aspects of their story effectively.
● Encourage children to work in pencil, and to modify their work as they think through their plot.

## Review
● Gather the children together and review their work, noting carefully who needs further support to create a plan that will work. In particular, focus on the vocabulary they have added to their plans.

**Curriculum objectives**
● To use and punctuate direct speech.
● To organise paragraphs around a theme.

**Resources**
Completed story planning work (from week 5, lesson 2); structured writing frames (optional)

# 3: Robot stories

## Introduction
● Draw the Iron Man's head on one side of the whiteboard, and Hogarth's head on the other. Draw a giant speech bubble coming out of each one's mouth. Ask for contributions for exchanges between the two, starting off with aspects from the story, but moving on to anything, including the humorous.
● Write utterances in the speech bubbles, then ask the children to talk you through how to write this as direct speech, modelling and explaining correct use of punctuation as you go.

## Independent work
● With their plans from the previous lesson to hand, ask the children to start drafting their stories, with their robots as central characters, reminding them that paragraphs are necessary for new speakers, as in the introduction, but also for changes of subject.

> **Differentiation**
> ● Support children by verifying their plans with them and adjusting if necessary, then provide structured writing frames or allow them to compose orally initially.

## Review
● Ideally you should allow an extended lesson, or two or three sessions, for children to complete their writing. Whatever way you structure the session(s), be sure to bring the children together from time to time and let them share progress – both to give them a breather and to allow you to assess progress and guide as appropriate, focusing on aspects specific to each piece of work.

## Curriculum objectives
• To proofread for spelling and punctuation errors.
• To propose changes to grammar and vocabulary to improve consistency.

## Resources
Photocopiable page 'Correcting text' from the CD-ROM; completed story plans and drafts (from week 5, lessons 2–3)

# 4: Proofreading for improvements

## Introduction
• Display photocopiable page 'Correcting text' from the CD-ROM and work through it with the class, sentence by sentence, to identify spelling, grammar and punctuation errors. Allow children to correct errors verbally then challenge others to explain their thinking.
• Ideally, have a policy for how different types of errors are noted so that spelling errors can be easily distinguished from punctuation issues, and so on.
• Explain that in this lesson they will be performing a similar task for their robot stories.

## Independent work or paired work
• Organising the class as desired, ask the children to proofread their own and or others' work to check for spelling, punctuation and grammar.
• Stress that this lesson is about correcting the accuracy of their texts: 'proofreading'. This is not the same thing as reviewing and rewriting, for which the primary reason is to improve the quality of what the text is *communicating*.

### Differentiation
• To avoid overwhelming some children, tackle this exercise in chunks, focusing only on spellings, or punctuation.
• To consolidate children's technical vocabulary challenge them to note technical explanations for their errors.

## Review
• Gather the class and ask the children to volunteer examples of things they have corrected in their text, stating their original work and the changes. Challenge others to identify the *type* of error. Use this as an opportunity to note children who are having particular problems, or indeed successes.

## Curriculum objectives
• To assess the effectiveness of their own and others' writing and suggest improvements.

## Resources
Completed story plans, drafts and edits (from week 5, lessons 2–4)

# 5: Critical reviews

## Introduction
• Work through starter activity 4 'Hard-to-spell words' for the words: *imagine*, *peculiar* and *strange* (or other words if preferred).

## Independent or paired work
• Remind the class of your previous discussions on whether *The Iron Man* would have been better if it had finished after Chapter 3, then tell them that in this lesson they are going to be reviewing their own stories in a similar fashion. In other words, they are not looking for corrections to grammar, punctuation or spelling, but for strengths and weaknesses in their content and its structure.
• Organise children to review their work alone or in pairs, allowing them to read aloud any variations of their stories.

### Differentiation
• For children with weaker language skills it can be effective to allow them to review work in small chunks orally. If they find offering alternatives difficult, partner them appropriately for a part of the lesson with someone who can offer alternative ideas to them.
• Challenge those children who are able to modify their story effectively to comment (orally, or in writing) about what effect their changes have made and why these improve their story.

## Review
• When finished, ask for volunteers to offer critiques of their own work, discussing how improvements might be made where children are dissatisfied.

### Expected outcomes
● All children will discuss poems about robots and create their own poem for performance.
● Most children will consider different styles, vocabulary and structures for their poem.
● Some children will create well-written poems incorporating relevant vocabulary in the style of their choice.

### Curriculum objectives
● To recognise some different forms of poetry.
● To identify how language, structure, and presentation contribute to meaning.
● To discuss writing similar to that which they are planning to write in order to understand and learn from its structure, grammar and vocabulary.

### Resources
Photocopiable page 'Robot poetry samples' from the CD-ROM; good selection of children's poetry books

# Week 6 lesson plans

The final week of this chapter moves on to poetry, taking a more light-hearted approach to robot texts, with the aim of children creating their own robot poems. Lessons are focused on examining existing poems and discussing different styles and elements, concluding with children having the opportunity to create and perform their own poems.

It is worth noting that this is a difficult unit of work in as much as creating poems to a tight structure, especially with rhyme, is an exacting task. Remember that the important learning for your class is appreciating different forms of poetry, ongoing encounters with new and challenging vocabulary, and the understanding of how to read with expression and intonation.

## 1: Robot poetry

### Introduction
● Play a quick rhyming game. Randomly call out a robot word encountered over the previous lessons and ask the children to find a word that rhymes.

### Whole-class work
● Using photocopiable page 'Robot poetry samples' from the CD-ROM or published ones if preferred (they do not have to have a robot theme), deliver a selection of readings to the class, using intonation and expression to full effect.
● Ideally displaying the poems for everyone to see, discuss their make-up and consider their strengths and weaknesses: *What advantages and disadvantages do they have over writing laid out in sentences?*
● Introduce the terms *voice*, *structure* and *form* as ways to understand a poem.
  ● Form: the type of poem – free verse, rhyming, and so on.
  ● Structure: how it is arranged.
  ● Voice: 'who' is telling the poem, or if it is in the third person.
● Consider how these elements are addressed in the poems you have read with the class.

### Group work
● Arranging the class in groups of four to six, give each group a small selection of poetry books and ask them to compare and contrast the style of each: *Do they rhyme? If so, how? Do they tell a story? Are they funny? What are their strengths and weaknesses?*
● Ask groups to decide on their favourite poem and prepare to read or recite it to the class, and also be prepared to explain it, and their reasons for liking it.
● Give groups enough time to prepare their reading or recital, reminding them that they can take turns with lines or read in chorus.
● After each reading, allow other groups to ask questions as appropriate. Praise and reinforce effective delivery and presentations.

---
### Differentiation
● Support less confident learners by grouping them appropriately and ensuring they are able to present poems and work that is manageable for them.
● Learning can be extended by asking children to categorise poems by form or genre and to analyse rhythms.
---

### Review
● Return to the poems that you originally read to the class and, displaying one or more of them, start to analyse them more thoroughly, initially through numbers – verses, lines per verse, syllables and so on, moving on to reviewing styles and purposes, modelling vocabulary as appropriate.
● Discuss which poems are simpler and which are more effective.

## Curriculum objectives
● To use further prefixes and suffixes and understand how to add them (Appendix 1).
● To discuss writing similar to that which they are planning to write in order to understand and learn from its structure, grammar and vocabulary.
● To prepare poems and playscripts to read aloud and to perform, showing understanding through intonation, tone, volume and action.
● To learn the grammar for Year 3 in Appendix 2.

## Resources
Photocopiable page 79 'Poetry planner'; robot vocabulary lists (optional, not provided); wide selection of children's poetry books

# 2: Planning a poem

## Introduction
● Write the prefixes from week 4's work on prefixes on the board: *auto, hyper, inter, super, trans, ultra.*
● Challenge the class to remember the meaning of each prefix, and ask them to recall vocabulary that uses these prefixes.

## Whole-class work
● Display photocopiable page 79 'Poetry planner' and choose an appropriate poem that the class are familiar with (robotic or otherwise).
● In discussion, complete the first half of the planner together to exemplify how it can help develop a sense of a poem's purpose. Recap the meaning of *structure, voice* and *form* from lesson 1.

## Independent or paired work
● Distributing the photocopiable sheet and, ensuring that a wide range of poetry books are available, ask children to consider what sort of robot-related poem they would like to write.
● Ask the class to use the second half of the lesson to focus on vocabulary.

## Review
● Gather the class together and ask children to share their work in pairs, discussing their reasons for choosing particular forms and themes. Ask them to review vocabulary choices with each other and discuss alternatives. To conclude, share plans as appropriate and reinforce knowledge of poetry styles and strong robot vocabulary.

## Curriculum objectives
● To discuss and record ideas.
● To prepare poems and playscripts to read aloud and to perform, showing understanding through intonation, tone, volume and action.

## Resources
Completed photocopiable page 79 'Poetry planner' (from week 6, lesson 2)

# 3: Drafting robot poems

## Introduction
● Use starter activity 3 'Vocabulary builder', using key vocabulary related to robots from the past weeks' work. In particular, use the opportunity to reinforce week 4's prefix work.

## Independent work
● Ask the children to each draft their own robot poem, using their plans from yesterday to help them. Stress that rhyming is not essential, and that the focus of any poem should be the message or feeling it is trying to convey.
● As work progresses, circulate and discuss work with individuals. Where interesting work is emerging, stop the class briefly and share good words or lines, discussing why particular work seems effective.

### Differentiation
● Allowing children to draft orally can make poetry seem less daunting, for the first few lines at least.
● Thinking can be extended by pushing children to choose a form (such as rhyming couplets) and to stick closely to the rules.

## Review
● Gather the class together and ask children to share their work in pairs, sharing successes and difficulties and discussing strengths and weaknesses, allowing time for children to take comments onboard and adjust their work if desired.
● To conclude, ask for volunteers to share both their work and their process, guiding the children carefully to avoid banal or bland comments – question them to challenge how their draft fulfils their plans and intentions.

**Curriculum objectives**
● To use the diagonal and horizontal strokes that are needed to join letters and understand which letters, when adjacent to one another, are best left unjoined.
● To increase the legibility, consistency and quality of their handwriting.

**Resources**
Dictionaries; handwriting paper and pens as per school policy; completed robot poem drafts (from week 6, lesson 3)

# 4: Polished poems

## Introduction

● Remind the class of the robot instructions they wrote in week 4, lesson 5, and the handwriting techniques practised with them.
● Write the words *We are writing robot poetry* on the board, and go over these words in a different colour to model different strokes and joins.
● Next, ask for volunteers to call out good vocabulary that they have used in their poem drafts. Write appropriate words on the board and work with the class to use a dictionary to check the words, modelling the use of first letter, second letter, and so on.

## Paired and independent work

● Pairing children appropriately, give each pair a dictionary and ask them to work together to review their work, identifying possible spelling mistakes and checking and correcting them.
● Ask the children to write out copies of their poems for a display or book, encouraging them to use their 'best' handwriting.

> **Differentiation**
> ● Support children by writing out parts of their poem for them to model technique, and allow them to copy or trace these parts while writing the rest themselves.

## Review

● When all the poems are completed, recap the desired standards for handwriting, and have a quick 'exhibition', allowing the class to circulate and look at each other's work. Ask the children to mentally note when they see writing that reaches the desired standards.

**Curriculum objectives**
● To prepare poems and playscripts to read aloud and to perform, showing understanding through intonation, tone, volume and action.

**Resources**
Video camera (optional); completed poems (from week 6, lesson 4)

# 5: Robot recitals

## Introduction

● As a reminder, model effective intonation for the class, reading one or two verses from the poem of your choice.

## Paired or group work

● Ask the children to work together to practise their poems with each other. Stress that it is enough to practise only a few lines of recital, as the object is to improve intonation.

## Independent work

● Have children read or recite a part of or their entire poem to the class.
● Depending on how you structure child interaction, this is a good opportunity to allow for peer-to-peer constructive feedback to be given, as in the discussions of other poems earlier in the week.
● You can also take this opportunity to reinforce knowledge and understanding of poetry types through highlighting effective work.

> **Differentiation**
> ● Allowing children to read only a part of their poem will help with equal participation, reminding them it is how they deliver their words that is important.
> ● Demanding a recital will provide a challenge to those who want or need it.

## Review

● To conclude, remind children of the different types of poems they have encountered, and discuss what makes an effective poem – it is not just the poem, but how it is delivered.

## Curriculum objectives
● To choose nouns or pronouns appropriately to avoid repetition.
● To indicate possession by using the possessive apostrophe with plural nouns.
● To place the apostrophe accurately in words with regular plurals and in words with irregular plurals.

## Resources
Interactive activity 'Pronouns' on the CD-ROM; photocopiable page 73 'Why did they do it?'

# Grammar and punctuation: Possessive apostrophes and pronouns

## Revise
● Play starter activity 1 'Word pairs' using the names of people, groups, animals and places on the left-hand side (such as *Jill, the police, Buckingham Palace, elephant*). On the right-hand side, not in the same order, list possible pronouns (*she, he, they, it*).
● Look at photocopiable page 73 'Why did they do it?' previously completed in week 1. Highlight the pronouns and re-read the sentences using the original names rather than the pronouns. Discuss the clumsiness of repetition.
● List further statements indicating possession, such as *All the houses have doors, they are the houses doors*. Discuss where apostrophes should be inserted.

## Assess
● Ask the children to complete the interactive activity 'Pronouns' on the CD-ROM and record their score.
● Provide a text that is written 'clumsily', with no pronouns or apostrophes for possession. Ask children to correct the text.

## Further practice
● Pronouns become more complicated when using them as subjects or objects (*I* and *me*, *he* and *him*, and so on). Although this is the next step, be cautious not to muddle children by introducing too many at once.
● Reiterate the rule that the apostrophe, usually with *s*, means 'of' – it belongs to the person or thing attached to it. Look at texts with the children and, using this rule, ask them to identify possessives, including plurals.

## Curriculum objectives
● To use further prefixes and suffixes and understand how to add them (Appendix 1).
● To write from memory simple sentences, dictated by the teacher, that include words and punctuation taught so far.

## Resources
Photocopiable page 46 'The '-y' suffix'; interactive activity 'Affixes' on the CD-ROM

# Spelling: Adding prefixes and suffixes correctly

## Revise
● Do starter activity 2 'Getting technical' for: *affix, prefix, suffix* and *root word*.
● Recap the work on prefixes and discuss the meanings of each one: *auto, hyper, inter*, and so on. Using the board, or card strips, demonstrate how prefixes and root words come together and form new words.
● Introduce the term *suffix* and work through examples on photocopiable page 46 'The '-y' suffix' from Autumn 1 to illustrate that these often alter the spelling of the root word.
● Dictate sentences containing words with prefixes and suffixes. Once written, ask children to identify these features.

## Assess
● Provide a selection of words that contain prefixes and suffixes. Ask the children to analyse the words and break them down into their parts – prefixes, root words and suffixes.
● Use interactive activity 'Affixes' on the CD-ROM, recording children's scores.
● To check their understanding of morphology *in context*, provide a cloze text, with a bank of root words, prefixes and suffixes at the bottom. They must complete the text using only words formed with the roots and affixes given.

## Further practice
● Introduce a new prefix and suffix each week, showing them on a display alongside a selection of root words. How many words can children make from them, and can they identify other root words that will take these affixes?
● Use starter activity 12 'Word displays'.

**Curriculum objectives**
● To read books that are structured in different ways and reading for a range of purposes.
● To retrieve and record information from non-fiction.

**Resources**
Photocopiable page 'Sample contents and index' from the CD-ROM; wide range of books about robots and robotics; access to the internet (optional)

# Reading: Using contents and indices to research non-fiction

## Revise

● Do starter activity 2 'Getting technical' for the words *contents*, *index*, *headword*, *chapter*, *heading* and *bullet point*.
● Using photocopiable page 'Sample contents and index' from the CD-ROM recap on good practice for using contents and indices.
● Use the opportunity to mention dictionaries and model effective use of one.
● Using a pre-prepared quiz on the board, select an appropriate non-fiction book from those you have been using and work with the class to find a range of information, using all aspects of the book as appropriate, reinforcing key vocabulary and approaches as you go.

## Assess

● Ask the children to complete information-retrieval exercises using a selection of non-fiction books. (For assessing skills it is better to use different books than those used for the topics covered in this chapter.)
● Next, do a review of a non-fiction book. Ask the children to write a review of one of the books they have used. Stress that reviewing non-fiction is different to reviewing fiction. Discuss what elements this review might include, such as:
  ● Structure of book
  ● Ease of use
  ● Quality of information
  ● Layout of information
  ● Use of graphics
  ● Style of writing
● Take the above exercise a step further by asking children to compare two books, rating and comparing each of the qualities listed. This would perhaps be more efficient for children to do orally.

## Further practice

● Try to provide regular practice in reading for information to help develop scanning and skimming skills. Using photocopied texts (beware of copyright issues) and coloured pencils, challenge children to find certain words and facts.
● Ensure that good-quality encyclopaedias are available in the classroom, setting carousel tasks that allow children to use them at least once a week to locate specific information.
● Taking all the usual precautions, develop children's understanding and skills in using the internet for research, stressing in particular that unverified information should not be used.
● Have non-fiction class (or group) reading books, basing their use around specific projects or fact-finding exercises to facilitate varied use.

## Curriculum objectives
● In non-narrative material, to use simple organisational devices.
● To organise paragraphs around a theme.

## Resources
Paper copy of your school's prospectus; access to a range of school websites that have site maps; photocopiable page 'Sample contents and index' from the CD-ROM; range of non-fiction books and leaflets; completed non-fiction writing on robots (from week 3)

# Writing: Organising non-fiction texts

## Revise
● Revisit the children's work on robots and discuss its strengths and weaknesses, recapping on the features they have used and the style of the writing.
● Practise writing lists of instructions, reinforcing the nature of numbered versus standard bullet points.
● Look briefly at your school's prospectus, considering its organisation and structure. Consider its strengths and weaknesses.
● Finally, ask the children to work in groups to create a plan for a new school prospectus. They do not have to write the whole prospectus, but their work should include a contents list and a couple of sample pages. Focus in particular on the logical ordering of information.
● Remind the class of the importance of paragraphs – at the very least they need to consider using subheadings to break up their text. Look at example paragraphs together and discuss what the subject of each one is.
● Using one or more of the prospectus plans, consider how this would translate into a website. Look at the site maps for some school websites and discuss the similarities and differences between these and contents listings. Consider also the differences between a page from a paper prospectus and a webpage with a similar focus.

## Assess
● Ask the children to prepare a guide to something they enjoy as a hobby, such as a sport, art, animals, drama or dance.
● Explain that their work needs to have the following elements: contents, chapters, glossary (optional), and index.
● Encourage them to produce A5 booklets, as these create more pages and make the organisation of the information more prominent. Writing large amounts of information is potentially unfeasible, so suggest they produce a sample chapter with a complete contents listing and a breakdown of the headings for every section of the remaining chapters.
● In assessing the work, look in particular at how children arrange the contents listings – is there a logic to the order of their work? Consider how they have broken down the information in their sample chapters, as well as the quality and continuity of the text therein.
● If desired, you can extend the assessment to a second session, asking the class to provide a site map for a website version of their booklet. They might also list what additional features they would use that interactive web pages can offer.

## Further practice
● Without overwhelming children with too much written work, engage them in analysing and using samples of text from all around them, in particular information leaflets. Ask the children to create their own leaflets for local history and attractions.
● Continue analysing fiction and non-fiction texts for how paragraphs are structured. Challenge the children to write a guide to their family (real or fictitious), creating sections for each member and dividing these into paragraphs appropriately – every family member can have the same structure, or it can be varied according to children's own style, inclinations or abilities. For example, for each person they might cover appearance, interests and personality.

## Describing the Iron Man

■ How many words and phrases can you find that describe the Iron Man? Highlight them and say why you think the author used these words.

The Iron Man came to the top of the cliff.

How far had he walked? Nobody knows. Where had he come from? Nobody knows. How was he made? Nobody knows.

Taller than a house, the Iron Man stood at the top of the cliff, on the very brink, in the darkness.

The wind sang through his iron fingers. His great head, shaped like a dustbin but as big as a bedroom, slowly turned to the right, slowly turned to the left. His iron ears turned, this way, that way. He was hearing the sea. His eyes, like headlamps, glowed white, then red, then infra-red, searching the sea. Never before had the Iron Man seen the sea.

He swayed in the strong wind that pressed against his back. He swayed forward, on the brink of the high cliff.

And his right foot, his enormous iron right foot, lifted – up, out, into space, and the Iron Man stepped forward, off the cliff, into nothingness.

CRRRAAAASSSSSSH!

Down the cliff the Iron Man came toppling, head over heels.

CRASH!

CRASH!

CRASH!

From rock to rock, snag to snag, tumbling slowly. And as he crashed and crashed and crashed

His iron legs fell off.

His irons arms fell off, and the hands broke off the arms.

His great iron ears fell off and his eyes fell out.

His great iron head fell off.

All the separate pieces tumbled, scattered, crashing, bumping, clanging, down on to the rocky beach far below.

A few rocks tumbled with him.

Then

Silence.

# Why did they do it?

- Write how you think each person was feeling or thinking.

**1.** Hogarth saw the Iron Man and ran home. He _____

_____

**2.** Hogarth's mother went pale. She _____

_____

**3.** Hogarth's sister cried. She _____

_____

**4.** Hogarth's father got his gun. He _____

_____

**5.** The first farmer laughed. He _____

_____

**6.** The farmers dug a large hole. They _____

_____

**7.** Hogarth trapped the Iron Man. He _____

_____

**8.** The Iron Man fell into the pit. He _____

_____

I can make inferences from a text about character's thoughts.

How did you do?

## Summary of *The Iron Man*

- Highlight time and cause words in the summaries. The first one has been done for you.
- Write your own summary for Chapters 4 and 5.

| Events | Summary |
|---|---|
| **Chapter 1:** The Iron Man fell down the cliff and smashed on the rocks. A seagull dropped a hand next to an eye. He put himself together. He went into the sea. | The Iron Man was smashed to pieces **when** he fell down the cliff. **Then** a seagull moved his hand next to his eye. **Now** he could put himself together, **but** he could not find one of his ears. After this he vanished **because** he walked into the sea. |
| **Chapter 2:** Hogarth saw the Iron Man. He ran home and told his family. His father told the other farmers. The farmers dug a pit. Hogarth trapped the Iron Man in it. | Hogarth was fishing when he first saw the Iron Man. He ran home and told his family and his father went to tell the other farmers. Next the farmers dug a pit. After a few days Hogarth used a nail and a knife to trap the Iron Man. |
| **Chapter 3:** The Iron Man escaped from the pit. The farmers did not know what to do. Hogarth talked to the Iron Man. Hogarth took the Iron Man to the scrap yard. The Iron Man was happy. | A family were having a picnic but they ran away because the Iron Man escaped from his pit. When the farmers found out they let Hogarth talk to the Iron Man because they trusted him. So Hogarth led him to the scrap yard, and the Iron Man was soon eating scrap metal. |
| **Chapter 4:** The Space-Bat-Angel-Dragon came to Earth. It wanted to eat all the living things. The human armies try to destroy it. Hogarth talked to the Iron Man. The Iron Man decided to fight the dragon. | |
| **Chapter 5:** The Iron Man challenged the dragon. The Iron Man lay down on the fire pit. The dragon flew to the Sun. The dragon was defeated and sang for everyone. | |

I can summarise the main ideas of paragraphs.

How did you do?

## Summary support sheet

- Below are summaries of Chapters 4 and 5 of *The Iron Man*. Use some of these time and cause words to fill the missing gaps.

| |
|---|
| when  so  because  before  after  while  then<br>but  next  soon  during  in  to  of |

### Chapter 4

Everyone was scared _____ the Space-Bat-Angel-Dragon came

to Earth. It wanted to eat all living things, _____ the armies

attacked it _____ they could not hurt it. _____

Hogarth talked to the Iron Man, and he agreed to challenge the dragon.

### Chapter 5

The Iron Man was taken _____ Australia. _____ he

arrived he challenged the dragon. The dragon agreed _____

it thought it would win easily. The Iron Man lay down on a fire pit,

_____ sent the dragon to the sun. _____ two

trips to the sun the dragon was defeated. _____ the dragon

became the Iron Man's slave, and _____ it was flying above

the Earth singing beautiful music for everyone.

I can use time and cause words correctly.

How did you do?

Name: _____     Date: _____

## Powerful prefixes

■ Look at the prefixes below and the words they can make. Can you think of other examples?

| Powerful prefixes | Meanings | Examples |
|---|---|---|
| auto- | by itself | automatic, autofocus, autopilot |
| hyper- | more than normal | hyperactive, hyperdrive, hyperspace |
| inter- | between, or among | intergalactic, interconnect, interplanetary |
| super- | above, or better | supercharge, Superman, supersonic |
| trans- | across, or beyond | transmarine, transmission, transport |
| ultra- | extreme | ultralight, ultrasonic, ultraviolet |

■ Think about some of the words that can describe things, such as size, speed, shape and cleverness.
■ Use strong prefixes to create words that would describe a robot you know, or one you would like to make. You can make real or imaginary words.

| Prefix | Word | New word | Meaning |
|---|---|---|---|
| ultra- | fast | ultrafast | can move extremely fast |
|  |  |  |  |
|  |  |  |  |
|  |  |  |  |
|  |  |  |  |
|  |  |  |  |
|  |  |  |  |

I can use prefixes to create interesting descriptive words.

How did you do?

Name: _____     Date: _____

## Robot design template

- Use this sheet to describe and design your robot. Remember that powerful words will help design a powerful robot.

The robot I am describing is:

Name: _____

Job: _____

Special features:

_____

_____

Size: _____

Speed: _____

Brain power: _____

Draw a diagram of your robot here:

Notes:

_____

_____

_____

_____

_____

I can use new vocabulary to good effect.

How did you do?

Name: _____     Date: _____

## Story planner

- Use this sheet to help you plan your story effectively.

Working title: _____

Genre: _____

| Details | Vocabulary |
|---|---|
| Main characters: | |
| Setting: | |
| Dilemma: | |
| Resolution: | |

**Plot:**

1. _____

2. _____

3. _____

4. _____

5. _____

I can combine elements of plot, character and setting to plan a story.

How did you do?

Name: _____    Date: _____

## Poetry planner

- Use this sheet to help you plan your poem effectively.

Working title: _____

Form: _____

Structure: _____

Voice: _____

Vocabulary: _____

_____

_____

Draft your poem here:

<br><br><br><br><br><br><br><br><br><br><br><br><br><br><br>

I can use and adapt poetic styles for my own work.

How did you do?

# Kings, queens and castles

This chapter adopts a medieval theme, using castles as its starting point, allowing you to introduce links to the history curriculum. Week I focuses on castles themselves, basing work around a real or virtual visit, moving on to look at the lives of those who live in castles. For weeks 3 and 4, after exploring fairy tales set in fictional castles, children have the opportunity to create an adventure story based in their own unique castle. The final fortnight moves on to rulers with problems, such as King Midas, with a debate on the morality and issues surrounding such rulers, and concludes with royalty themed poetry.

## Expected prior learning

- Can understand how a setting can add to a story.
- Know what a verb is.
- Can understand word families and suffixes.
- Can discuss the features of a sentence.
- Can understand the convention of direct speech.
- Can identify themes.
- Can use the story structures: beginning, middle and end.
- Can use preposition, adverbs, time and cause words.
- Can understand basic techniques for performing a poem.

## Overview of progression

- As well as consolidating skills from the previous chapters in working with a range of text types and an ongoing focus on adverbs, conjunctions and prepositions, the chapter introduces the perfect form of verbs, using this to mark relationships of time and cause.
- There is a particular emphasis on proofreading and correcting work using correct terminology for grammar and punctuation, and producing coherent and well-structured texts.

## Creative context

- With its focus on medieval Britain there are many clear links to history.
- This chapter could link to design technology via artefacts, as well as PSHE (considering fairness in social structures and debating character and qualities in rulers).

## Preparation

If possible, arranging a trip to a real castle, or carefully reviewing a virtual tour available online, such as:

- Warwick Castle: www.warwick-castle.com – click on 'Explore Castle', then '3D Panoramas Viewer...'
- Windsor Castle: www.royal.gov.uk – click on 'The Royal Residences', then 'Windsor Castle' and 'Virtual Rooms'.

A range of books about castles and their inhabitants, novels involving fantasy castles, and information about kings and queens of England would also useful.

**You will also need:**
Access to the internet is optional, but could be useful for extending research for some learners; access to a large indoor space with play equipment; dictionaries; a comic; king outfits and props; storyboard templates (optional); character card templates (optional); video camera (optional); a video clip from 'Sleeping Beauty' (optional).

**On the CD-ROM you will find:**
Media resources 'UK castles map', 'Castles'; interactive activities 'Joining clauses', 'Using the perfect form', 'Using dictionaries', 'Correcting work'; photocopiable pages 'The Princess and the Pea', 'Sleeping Beauty', 'King Midas and the Golden Touch', 'The Emperor's New Clothes', 'The King's Breakfast', 'God Save the Queen'

# Chapter at a glance

An overview of the chapter. For curriculum objective codes, please see pages 8–10.

| Week | Lesson | Curriculum objectives | Summary of activities | Outcome |
|---|---|---|---|---|
| 1 | 1 | RC: 15 WC: 2 | Arrange a real or virtual castle visit and research information about castles. | • Can record relevant facts in an ordered manner. |
| | 2 | RC: 3 | Investigate the layout and associated vocabulary of castles. | • Can use dictionaries to check the meaning of words. |
| | 3 | WC: 14 | Develop the use of prepositions for their writing (on, through, around, down, and so on), to describe moving around a castle. | • Can use the terms conjunction, adverbs and prepositions, and identify and use prepositions in sentences. |
| | 4 | WC: 6 | Write a first-person recount about the castle visit (virtual if necessary). | • Can use devices such as headings to organise a text. |
| | 5 | WC: 7, 8, 9 | Edit and improve work, paying particular attention to time and cause words. | • Can add interest to writing by using time and cause words. |
| 2 | 1 | RWR: 1 RC: 15 | Research the range of people who lived and worked in a medieval castle. | • Can find information in non-fiction texts. |
| | 2 | WC: 11 | Develop sentences using conjunctions to join clauses. | • Can write sentences with more than one clause. |
| | 3 | WC: 12 | Introduce the perfect form of verbs through examples where they are used to create time and cause relationships. | • Can recognise the perfect form of verbs. |
| | 4 | WC: 12, 19 | Enact conversations between castle dwellers, structured around use of the perfect form and conjunctions. | • Can create and transcribe short conversations using correct punctuation. |
| | 5 | WC: 11, 12 | Complete a jobs rota in role as workers in a castle. | • Can write in context using the perfect form and conjunctions to create longer sentences. |
| 3 | 1 | RC: 4, 5 | Look at and discuss castles from different stories, and consider the features and language that describe a good fictional castle. | • Can discuss descriptions from a range of books. |
| | 2 | RC: 4 WC: 1 | Read and discuss a short version of 'The Princess and the Pea', then retell it, incorporating more adverbs and descriptive vocabulary. | • Can retell stories with their own language. |
| | 3 | WT: 1 WC: 20 | Discuss examples of the suffix '-ly' and '-ing' and their effect on spellings. | • Can understand and use suffixes to create new words and use them effectively. |
| | 4 | RC: 4 WC: 1 | Analyse the text of 'Sleeping Beauty' to understand its structure and style. | • Can identify different aspects of a story. |
| | 5 | WC: 5 | Rewrite a small scene from 'Sleeping Beauty' with enhanced vocabulary, incorporating prepositions and adverbs. | • Can use prepositions and adverbs to create interest in a story. |
| 4 | 1 | WC: 2, 5 | Plan a castle-based story. | • Can plan a story with a clear beginning, middle and end. |
| | 2 | WC: 5 | Craft a character for their story. | • Can create characters appropriate to story type. |
| | 3 | WC: 3 | Use their plan and character sketch to roughly storyboard and orally compose a castle story. | • Can draft and constructively review stories. |
| | 4 | WC: 11, 13, 14 | Write the first draft of the story focusing on adverbs and prepositions, then conduct peer reviews. | • Can use prepositions and adverbs to create interest in a story. |
| | 5 | WC: 7, 8 | Review and improve their castle stories. | • Can effectively review and improve their work. |
| 5 | 1 | RC: 4 | Listen to and discuss the stories of 'King Midas' and 'The Emperor's New Clothes' (and King Canute if desired). Prepare questions that would be interesting to ask each ruler. | • Can appreciate stories and ask questions about them. |
| | 2 | RC: 10 | Ask questions to adults in role as the kings. | • Can ask appropriate questions and draw conclusions. |
| | 3 | RC: 5, 16 | Compare and contrast the kings they have learned about. | • Can compare stories and recall and comment on events in them. |
| | 4 | RC: 16 | Discuss what is important in life: money, health, love, and so on. What would the group have as their wish if they had one? | • Can participate in discussions and debates. |
| | 5 | WC: 2, 4 | Write royal decrees about the importance of values. | • Can justify a point of view or idea. |

## Chapter at a glance

| Week | Lesson | Curriculum objectives | Summary of activities | Outcome |
|---|---|---|---|---|
| **6** | I | RC: 1, 8 | Read and summarise 'The King's Breakfast'. | • Can summarise the narrative of a poem. |
| | 2 | RC: 6 | Recite sections of 'The King's Breakfast'. | • Can recite poetry to an audience. |
| | 3 | RC: 6 | Plan a royal poem. | • Can plan a poem. |
| | 4 | RC: 6 WC: 8, 9 | Write poems about rulers to the style of their choice. | • Can write a poem in a chosen style. |
| | 5 | WT: 7, 8 WC: 10 | Present and recite royal poems. | • Can present work legibly and neatly. |

## Background knowledge

**Adverb**: In their most common use, adverbs modify verbs to give us more information about how something is done.

**Clause**: A phrase that has as its main word a verb that describes the state of things.

**Conjunction**: Links two words or phrases together.

**Preposition**: The link between a noun or pronoun to another word in the sentence.

**The perfect form**: The perfect form of a verb is generally used to draw attention to the consequence of a situation. It is also used to raise questions about things that have happened.

**Verb**: A word that often describes actions, identifiable by the changes in tense it can take.

**■ SCHOLASTIC**

# Week 1 lesson plans

This week is based around a visit of a castle, allowing children to appreciate and understand its past and features. If a real tour is unfeasible, a virtual tour will suffice. After the initial tour children have opportunities to research and develop their understanding of the features and to imagine moving around a castle, with a focus on prepositions. The week culminates in a recount of their visit, written as a tour, in an appropriately structured text, which they have the opportunity to draft and then improve. Note: it may be easier for you to plan the visit separately to lesson 1, then follow up with the remaining tasks in lesson 1.

## 1: A castle tour

### Introduction
● Introduce the subject of castles. Discuss which ones the children know and what they know about them. Limit the discussion at this stage to real castles – why were they built, and by who.

### Independent or paired work
● Distribute photocopiable page 104 'Castle features collection form' and tell the children to collect as much information as they can on their tour (real or virtual), stressing that if they do not know the function of a particular feature they should make a guess – they can research it further afterwards. Also remind them to write their impression of the feature, such as *The moat looked very deep and cold*.
● Conduct the tour in whatever way you prefer, using the opportunity to reinforce as much subject-related vocabulary as possible.

### Whole-class work
● Follow up the visit with further research about the castle, investigating how they were built, of what materials, by who and when.
● Watch the media resource 'Castles' on the CD-ROM.
● Display the media resource 'UK castles map' on the CD-ROM. Discuss their locations and consider what they tell us about life at the time. Explain that some are on high ground and ask why this might be. Discuss why they are so big and strong.

### Independent or paired work
● Return to reviewing the facts about the castle you have toured.
● Write on the board: *I did not like the moat because it looked cold and deep.*
● Explain the reasoning behind this sentence – it is very much a personal feeling rather than the function of the moat. Point out the use of the conjunction *because*, which makes the sentence longer.
● Ask the children to list five things they would like about living in the castle and five things they would not, writing a brief explanation of each point as per the example.

> **Differentiation**
> ● Children's thinking can be extended here by challenging them to write a further sentence for each or their like and dislike points. The sentence should consider what it must have been like to actually live in the castle, and what they would think of the feature. Using the example from above: *I did not like the moat because it looked cold and deep, but it probably made the people who lived there feel safer.*

### Review
● Discuss children's impressions of the castle and their likes and dislikes list – do they disagree on anything? Finish the lesson by reviewing the main features of castles, eliciting any further information that has been researched about them.

---

**Expected outcomes**
● All children will create a range of castle texts and participate in debates, using new vocabulary.
● Most children will incorporate prepositions, conjunctions and the perfect form into their writing.
● Some children will effectively use grammar and punctuation to create more complex sentences.

**Curriculum objectives**
● To discuss and record ideas.
● To retrieve and record information from non-fiction.

**Resources**
Real or virtual castle tour; wide selection of books about castles; photocopiable page 104 'Castle features collection form'; media resource 'Castles' on the CD-ROM; media resource 'UK castles map' on the CD-ROM

## Curriculum objectives
● To use dictionaries to check the meaning of words that they have read.

## Resources
Photocopiable page 105 'Castle layout' (ideally enlarged to A3), photocopiable page 106 'Castle vocabulary'

# 2: Castle facts

## Introduction
● Start the lesson by adapting starter activity 2 'Getting technical', to cover three to five words for castle features, such as *moat*, *barbican*, and so on.

## Whole-class work
● Explain that everyone is going to use their knowledge to create a labelled diagram of a castle. (Photocopiable pages 105 'Castle layout' and 106 'Castle vocabulary' are provided for this, although you may wish to focus on the castle you have toured.)
● Focusing on the word *moat*, work with the class to model good dictionary use to find its definition, and show how they can add these notes to their diagrams. In discussion, add any further knowledge they have of moats to extend the notes.

## Group work
● Distributing resources as desired, including dictionaries, ask the children to work together to create a detailed information diagram about castle features.

### Differentiation
● Provide written definitions of the features on separate strips of paper to the definitions themselves, allowing children to cut these out and stick them on the diagram to ensure equal participation.
● For more confident children, provide larger dictionaries and ask them to note the etymology, or historic origin, of the words wherever possible.

## Review
● Ask groups to circulate and look at each others' work, noting additional information that would support their work.

## Curriculum objectives
● To use conjunctions, adverbs and prepositions to express time and cause.

## Resources
Completed castle diagrams or photocopiable pages 105 'Castle layout' and 106 'Castle vocabulary' (from week 1, lesson 2); access to a large indoor space with play equipment (optional)

# 3: Using prepositions

## Introduction
● Use starter activity 8 'Prepositions' to focus on spatial prepositions *down*, *on*, *through*, *around*, and so on.
● Explain how these words help us understand objects in relation to each other, and how we move in relation to the things around us.

## Paired work
● Explain that everyone will be taking turns to invent routes through a castle, with partners drawing the route as they go. Model an example by initiating one or two sentences and drawing very rough plans on the board, such as *To start, go across the drawbridge and under the portcullis.*
● Once their route or tour is complete they should show their plan to the describer, and then swap roles.

### Differentiation
● To support children give them a set of vocabulary cards for castle features, preposition cards (numbered one to six), and dice. Invite them to roll the die to select the appropriate preposition, and a castle area that will fit in a sentence with the preposition. Once they have created six sentences ask them to arrange these in a logical order.

## Review
● Discuss children's routes and reinforce prepositions for different castle features. If time allows, or as an extra activity, go to a large indoor space and, using equipment, create an imaginary castle to navigate, dictating routes to reinforce preposition meanings.

**Curriculum objectives**
● In non-narrative material, to use simple organisational devices.

**Resources**
Completed photocopiable page 104 'Castle features collection form' (from week 1, lesson 1); wide selection of books about castles; internet access (optional)

# 4: Recount of a visit

## Introduction
● Recap on the previous castle tour, talking through the class's information sheets and checking knowledge of different castle features.
● Discuss also how to plan the structure of a recount, considering possible headings and subheadings for the aspects of the castle that the children want to use to structure their report (history, function, features, and so on).

## Paired work
● Encourage children to discuss the events with a partner to help with checking their notes and creating a plan for their recount, creating an appropriate structure around what interests them the most about the castle.

## Independent work
● Ask children to draft a recount of their castle visit. Make books and, if desired, internet access available for checking facts and vocabulary.

> **Differentiation**
> ● Support less confident writers with a writing scaffold to structure their recount, including sentence openings if necessary.
> ● To extend the task, ask more confident writers to provide a glossary for the features they encountered.

## Review
● Gather the class together and ask the children to share their plans and initial drafts with a partner. Ask them to feed back to each other on structure as well as content. Have they used headings and subheadings effectively? Share appropriate examples and discuss approaches to organising texts.

**Curriculum objectives**
● To assess the effectiveness of their own and others' writing and suggest improvements.
● To propose changes to grammar and vocabulary to improve consistency.
● To proofread for spelling and punctuation errors.

**Resources**
Completed drafts of castle visit recount; wide selection of books about castles

# 5: Improving writing

## Introduction
● Before the lesson starts, write a brief paragraph on the board about something you did at the weekend, or something about the school. Include in it one or two errors of punctuation and grammar.
● Challenge the class to identify the errors, explaining and correcting them, as well as reaching consensus on one constructive comment that would lead to improvement of the text, again explaining why.

## Paired work
● Ask children to review each others' drafts in their original pairings, covering content, grammar, punctuation and spellings, using agreed notation.
● In particular, allow time for the children to discuss improvements of content with each other, considering carefully whether changes are meaningful or not.

## Independent work
● Allow a final session for children to take changes on board and improve their texts. Provide extra time if you want them to develop it for presentation.

> **Differentiation**
> ● Reviewing peers' work can be difficult for some children. Support children by setting limits, such as finding a number of spelling mistakes and making an overall comment.

## Review
● Gather the class together and share work as appropriate. Ask the children to consider whether their work contains much information about castles, and if they have been successful in clarifying the information to their readers.

# Week 2 lesson plans

Staying with castles, though moving on to look at the people who lived and worked in them, this week's work has a substantial focus on grammar, introducing conjunctions as a way of joining phrases or clauses, and then using them in conjunction with the perfect form of verbs. For example: *He has cleaned the moat because it was dirty.*

## 1: Castle dwellers

### Introduction
● Use the internet to find a photograph of a medieval queen or king and display it on the board along with some factual information, including which castle they lived in.
● In discussion, elicit what sort of person they appear to be and what their life might have been like.
● Work with the class to sketch out a simple 'character card' for this ruler, with key information on it. Use a dictionary to model finding the meaning of *queen* or *king*, and add this to the details.

### Group or paired work
● Explain to the class that their work for today is to research the lives and work of the types of people who lived in castles.
● Giving each group a range of books and photocopiable page 107 'Castle dwellers', ask them to create a set of 'character cards' providing essential facts about the different roles and jobs of people who lived in castles. The group should produce a different character card for every group member.
● If necessary, prompt thinking with different cues, such as:
  ● *Would they have had contact with the queen and king?*
  ● *Would they have worked inside or outside the castle?*
  ● *Where would they sleep?*
  ● *Did they need special equipment?*
  ● *Was their work dangerous?*
  ● *Would you like their job?*
● Stress that, in addition, you would like them to use their dictionaries to find precise meanings for each job type.
● To conclude, ask children to write a sentence or two at the bottom of their card saying what they think life was like for their character.
● Once all groups have concluded their work, so that each child has a character card that is different from the rest of their group, form totally new groups. Ask the children to compare their character cards and consider similarities and differences with the work their group did.

> **Differentiation**
> ● Support the task by providing templates for the children to work on.
> ● Provide extension by supplying larger dictionaries and asking children to find the origins of the job titles.

### Review
● Bringing the class together, in discussion note the different characters they have discovered and try to position them according to their importance in the hierarchy of castle life. Use this as an opportunity to recap on dictionary skills, and draw attention to the meanings and origins of some of the job titles.
● To conclude, use the internet to show children lists of the names that medieval people may have had (there are many websites for this) and ask them to consider what name they would give to their characters.

**Curriculum objectives**
● To extend the range of sentences with more than one clause by using a wider range of conjunctions.

**Resources**
Photocopiable page 105 'Castle layout'; photocopiable page 106 'Castle vocabulary'; interactive activity 'Joining clauses' on the CD-ROM

# 2: Using conjunctions

## Introduction
● Start the lesson with starter activity 7 'Conjunction challenge'.

## Paired work
● Write a range of conjunctions on the board, such as: *after, and, because, but, for, if, or, since, so, until, when.*
● Explain that the children have the task of thinking about instructions for keeping a castle in good working order, and that these will be written on notices in the appropriate places around the castle.
● Distribute or display photocopiable pages 105 'Castle layout' and 106 'Castle vocabulary' if necessary, and explain that you would like them to create a list of tasks that would be needed around the castle.
● Explain also that each 'task notice' must contain a conjunction.
● Model some examples, such as *Repair the roof if it is leaking,* or *Clean the dungeon after the prisoners leave,* or *Scrub the fireplaces until they are clean.*

> **Differentiation**
> ● Create a range of task-related commands on cue cards to help prompt those who need support.

## Review
● Gather the class together and share ideas for what sort of jobs might be needed in different parts of the castle. Discuss the conjunctions they have used, reinforce effective sentences and address any errors.
● To conclude, open interactive activity 'Joining clauses' on the CD-ROM and work through it with the class to consolidate understanding.

**Curriculum objectives**
● To use the present perfect form of verbs in contrast to the past tense.

**Resources**
Photocopiable page 108 'Perfect sentences'; interactive activity 'Using the perfect form' on the CD-ROM

# 3: The perfect form of verbs

## Introduction
● Preparing sentences on the board beforehand, use starter activity 9 'The perfect form' to introduce the perfect form of verbs, and discuss how it is used to create time and cause relationships.

## Independent or paired work
● Distribute photocopiable page 108 'Perfect sentences' and ask children to complete the sentences choosing appropriate verbs and conjunctions.
● To finish, ask small groups to share and check their work together.

> **Differentiation**
> ● Support learning by completing the photocopiable sheet yourself and photocopying it, then cut to separate the sentences, and cut again to separate the phrases and clauses of each sentence. Ask the children to match these together, checking for sense. You can take this a step further by separating the conjunctions also.
> ● Extend the learning by providing a list of verbs and conjunctions (such as *go, because*) and asking children to create a sentence using the perfect form for each.

## Review
● Gather the class together and open the interactive activity 'Using the perfect form' on the CD-ROM, stressing the use of the verb *to have* and how it works with conjunctions to clarify and develop the meaning of a sentence. For example: *I have eaten the cake because I was hungry.*

**Curriculum objectives**
● To use and punctuate direct speech.
● To use the present perfect form of verbs in contrast to the past tense.

**Resources**
Photocopiable page 107 'Castle dwellers'; photocopiable page 106 'Castle vocabulary'

# 4: Castle conversations

## Introduction
● Adapt starter activity 2 'Getting technical' to focus on the different people and jobs in a medieval castle.

## Whole-class work
● Recap the perfect form with the class, using it in questions. For example: Q. *Have you done your homework?* A. *Yes, I have. / No, I haven't.* Discuss the order of the words and the use of *haven't* at your discretion.
● Move this a stage further by recapping on conjunctions as a way of joining clauses: Q. *Have you done your homework?* A. *Yes, I have done my homework but it was very hard.*
● Then move on to the castle theme: Q. *Have you raised the drawbridge?* A. *Yes, I have raised the drawbridge as it was getting dark.*

## Independent or paired work
● Ask children to choose two castle dwellers from photocopiable page 107 'Castle dwellers', and then create a conversation of two or three questions between a knight and one of their choices, and another between the lady of the castle with their other choice. Stress that conversations should include question and answer dialogue, as explained.
● Explain that the conversations can be long or short, but must have a logical purpose. Let children refer to photocopiable page 106 'Castle vocabulary'.
● Once they are happy with each conversation they should write it down as direct speech.

## Review
● Have volunteers enact their conversations and ask the class to check on their use of the perfect form and conjunctions.

**Curriculum objectives**
● To use the present perfect form of verbs in contrast to the past tense.
● To extend the range of sentences with more than one clause by using a wider range of conjunctions.

**Resources**
Photocopiable page 106 'Castle vocabulary'; photocopiable page 107 'Castle dwellers'; completed castle conversations (from week 2, lesson 4)

# 5: Completing the daily rota

## Introduction
● Using starter activity 9 'The perfect form', write three things you have done at work today, such as: *I have marked all the maths books because there is a lesson this afternoon.* Use these sentences to reinforce understanding of both the perfect form and conjunctions.

## Independent work
● Explain that the children will be taking on the role of a worker in a castle. Unfortunately, the queen who rules their castle is rather strict and at the end of every day the workers must complete the work rota. This entails writing a brief introduction and a list of all the jobs they have done and why they did them. The queen rewards the best worker by inviting them to the feast.
● Let children refer to photocopiable pages 106 'Castle vocabulary' and 107 'Castle dwellers' if required. Either assigning roles or allowing children to choose, invite them to write their 'rota entry' for the day.

---
**Differentiation**
● Challenge children to use a different conjunction for every sentence on their job list.
---

## Review
● Taking on the role of the queen, ask children to read their rotas to you. Reinforce good use of the perfect form and conjunctions. Who will sit at the feast today?

# Week 3 lesson plans

This week moves the emphasis on to fiction, considering castles from literature and creating vivid descriptions of them. Children have the opportunity to read and listen to fairy tales, and understand how they are constructed (plot, characters, and so on), and then to write evocative descriptions of a scene from 'Sleeping Beauty'. There is also specific grammar work focusing on the suffixes '-ly' and '-ing' and their effect on words and meaning.

## 1: Fictional castles

### Introduction

● Display photocopiable page 106 'Castle vocabulary' and distribute some dictionaries if desired.
● Ask for volunteers to give a definition, either their own or from a dictionary, and challenge the rest of the class to indicate the word they are thinking of.
● Use this as an opportunity to reinforce the correct spellings and meanings of the words.

### Whole-class work

● Talk about the corridors, narrow twisting staircases and dungeons at any castles you have visited (online or in reality), looking at photographs if possible. What words can the children use to best describe what they have seen and experienced?
● Explain that you are now moving on to imaginary castles, giving lots of scope for imagination and invention.
● Discuss why castles might make for good settings in stories – what are the qualities they have that make them interesting?
● Talk about stories or films that are set in castles. Discuss the features of castles: *impressive halls and secret corridors and dungeons.*
● Reading from novels that you have bookmarked in advance, share extracts set in castles with the children and, in discussion, consider what these books have in common with each other, and in what ways they are different.
● Discuss what separates fictional castles from real ones.

### Independent work

● Challenge the children to write a paragraph or two describing the sort of castle they would really like to visit or live in. *What sort of features would it have? What sort of atmosphere? What condition would it be in?*
● After children have been working a while, ask them to write down three or four key words or phrases that describe their castle.
● Finally, ask the class to each draw two columns under their work, putting the headings *Pros* and *Cons* at the top of each one. Ask them to list four or five pros and cons of them living in their ideal castle, discussing their ideas with their classmates to support their thinking.

> **Differentiation**
> ● Use the photocopiable sheet to offer support where it is needed. If time permits, the children could also produce labelled sketches of their castle.

### Review

● Gather the class together and share their work, drawing attention to novel and interesting ideas.
● Remind them of the fictional castles they heard about and discussed at the start of the lesson: *Which of these appeal most, and why?*

---

**Expected outcomes**
● All children will use effective language to describe being in a fictional castle.
● Most children will create effective descriptions of imaginary castles and appreciate how a traditional fairy story is structured.
● Some children will employ increasingly complex vocabulary and grammar in their descriptions.

**Curriculum objectives**
● To increase their familiarity with a wide range of books, including fairy stories, myths and legends, and retelling some of these orally.
● To identify themes and conventions in a wide range of books.

**Resources**
Dictionaries; photocopiable page 106 'Castle vocabulary'; photos from castle visits or online castle tours; good selection of fiction involving castles (bookmark descriptive passages in advance)

## Curriculum objectives
• To increase their familiarity with a wide range of books, including fairy stories, myths and legends, and retell some of these orally.
• To discuss writing similar to that which they are planning to write in order to understand and learn from its structure, grammar and vocabulary.

## Resources
Photocopiable page 'The Princess and the Pea' from the CD-ROM

# 2: Understanding fairy tales

## Introduction
• Revise adverbs, playing a drama game where volunteers mime actions using a variety of adverbs and the other children must guess the word, using it in a full sentence.
• Challenge the children to suggest adverbs for how someone might move in different parts of a castle, with volunteers to mime this.

## Whole-class work
• Display and read photocopiable page 'The Princess and the Pea' from the CD-ROM to the class, and discuss what it is about it that links it to the fairy-tale genre (*simple plot, royalty, castle setting, problem to be resolved*).
• Noting that the story is very brief, talk with the class to consider where descriptions could have been used to good effect, and elicit suggestions for amendments to the text.

## Group or paired work
• Ask the children to prepare their own retelling of 'The Princess and the Pea', but incorporating descriptions of parts of the castle into it.

---
### Differentiation
• Challenge children to also describe how the characters move through the castle.
• Support those who need it by giving them copies of the original story to work from.
---

## Review
• Gather the class together and group children to retell each other parts of their stories. Share successes with the whole class.

## Curriculum objectives
• To use further prefixes and suffixes and understand how to add them (Appendix 1).
• To use and understand the grammatical terminology in Appendix 2 accurately and appropriately when discussing their writing and reading.

## Resources
Photocopiable page 'Sleeping Beauty' from the CD-ROM; photocopiable page 109 'Using suffixes'

# 3: Using suffixes

## Introduction
• Begin the lesson with starter activity 2 'Getting technical', focusing on the words *adverb*, *suffix* and *root word*.

## Whole-class work
• Display photocopiable page 'Sleeping Beauty' from the CD-ROM and, without reading it, ask the children to locate words ending in '-ly' and '-ing'.
• In discussion, elicit which are words that have been modified by adding suffixes – write the root words down and look at the different spellings.
• Display photocopiable page 109 'Using suffixes' and work through the explanations with the class for the '-ing' and '-ly' suffixes. Explain the grammar involved and develop further examples if desired. In particular, ensure that children appreciate the present and past continuous is distinguished from the present tense.

## Independent work
• Ask children to complete photocopiable page 109 'Using suffixes'.

---
### Differentiation
• While the children are working, write a selection of adjectives and verbs on the board, and challenge early finishers to combine different verbs and adjectives to make complete sentences using the present or past continuous and an adverb.
---

## Review
• Gather the class and check work, reinforcing why these suffixes are used.
• When looking at children's sentences note variations where both are correct, as well as correcting spelling errors where rules have not been recognised.

## Curriculum objectives
● To increase their familiarity with a wide range of books, including fairy stories, myths and legends, and retell some of these orally.
● To discuss writing similar to that which they are planning to write in order to understand and learn from its structure, grammar and vocabulary.

## Resources
Photocopiable page 'Sleeping Beauty' from the CD-ROM, or any other castle-based fairy tale that you want to focus on; photocopiable page 110 'Castle story planner'

# 4: 'Sleeping Beauty'

## Introduction
● Displaying photocopiable page 'Sleeping Beauty' from the CD-ROM, ideally showing both pages at once, ask the class to identify any words that have the '-ing' suffix added, being sure to distinguish these from words that simply end in 'ing', such as *King*.
● Reinforce children's understanding of these words by discussing what sort of words they are and what they convey.

## Whole-class work
● Read 'Sleeping Beauty' (or the fairy tale of your choice) to the class, and briefly discuss its links to the fairy-tale genre.
● Look at the text with the class and discuss features of the text, highlighting any descriptive language.

## Independent or paired work
● Display or distribute photocopiable pages 'Sleeping Beauty' from the CD-ROM and page 110 'Castle story planner' and ask children to *work backwards*. Explain that you want them to use the planner to identify the different *ingredients* of 'Sleeping Beauty' and note them on the sheet.
● Ask the children to note down any words, phrases or expressions that provide description in the story. If time, ask them to identify alternatives.

## Review
● Ask individuals or pairs to share their work with each other and discuss. In particular, look at descriptive words and phrases they have gathered, sharing these with the class and discussing alternative ways of wording these.

## Curriculum objectives
● In narratives, to create settings, characters and plot.

## Resources
Photocopiable page 'Sleeping beauty' from the CD-ROM; video clip from 'Sleeping Beauty' cartoon, film or ballet (optional, not provided)

# 5: Describing a scene in detail

## Introduction
● Play starter activity 8 'Prepositions' with the class, focusing on prepositions for moving through a building. Challenge children to describe moving from the school entrance to their classroom in an interesting (or even forbidden) way.

## Whole-class work
● Re-read the section of 'Sleeping Beauty' when she walks through the castle to find the spinning wheel and pricks her finger.
● If possible and desired, show children a video clip of the same scene, discuss the interpretation and elicit descriptive language.

## Independent work
● Ask the children to rewrite the scene just read or watched, using their knowledge of prepositions, adverbs and castles to make their scene as atmospheric as possible.
● Stress that the exercise is about capturing atmosphere, not presentation, and that they should feel free to alter and change their texts freely.

> **Differentiation**
> ● Provide a 'skeleton' of the passage (key points in the sequence of events) and allow children to write words they wish to incorporate around these points.
> ● Challenge others to use similes to enhance their creation of atmosphere.

## Review
● Arrange children into small groups and invite them to review each other's work. To conclude, gather the class and share successes, reinforcing good use of prepositions, adverbs and strong descriptions.

# Week 4 lesson plans

This week gives children the opportunity to bring all their newfound knowledge and skills together in creating their very own adventure story set within a castle. They can choose whether to base it on an existing castle or whether to make it pure fantasy, as well as consider the style of story they wish to create.

## 1: Story planning

### Introduction
● Write in large letters and different colours a selection of story genres on the board, such as: *Adventure, Mystery, Scary, Funny, Exciting, Historical, Fairy tale.*
● Explain the word *genre*, and ask for suggestions for different stories or films the children may know that fit into one or more of the categories listed. For example, the *Shrek* films fit within several of the categories listed above.

### Whole-class work
● Briefly talk through and look at your previous work on castles and stories set in them, reminding the children that they now have a good understanding of life in castles and that they know lots of relevant vocabulary.
● Display photocopiable page 110 'Castle story planner' and, taking contributions from everyone, create a class plan, modelling good vocabulary and thinking processes, freely changing ideas and adding notes as you see fit. Stress that a plan is a fluid thing and can easily end up looking very different from how it started, or indeed from what was originally intended.
● Explain the term *authenticity* and that, whatever the genre chosen, certain details must be carefully noted to ensure the story is authentic to a medieval castle.

### Independent or paired work
● Distribute photocopiable page 110 'Castle story planner' and explain to the class that their task for this lesson is to develop ideas for a story set in a castle, written in the style of their choice. The main thing is to include lots of what they know about castles and their inhabitants to create an authentic story.

---

**Differentiation**
● The planning process can be supported by supplying banks of cue cards containing pictures and names for castles, people and objects. Encourage children to stick these onto their plans and make additional notes.
● The task can be made more challenging by setting children a target of listing and including at least four locations in a castle that must be part of the story, three different types of person (*knight, king, servant,* and so on) and a central object that is the key to the story.

---

### Review
● Gather the class and ask children to share their plans with each other, encouraging them to offer suggestions and modify their plans as much as they see fit.

## Curriculum objectives
● In narratives, to create settings, characters and plot.

## Resources
Completed photocopiable page 110 'Castle story planner'

# 2: Crafting characters

## Introduction
● Find an image of a well-known character from a film or story that the children will be familiar with (it does not have to be castle-related) and display it on the board.
● In discussion, create a bank of words around the image that describe the character. These should describe physical features, personality and attitudes.

## Whole-class work
● Model the use of effective adjectives and, if desired, recap and use some similes to provide more striking descriptions.
● Introduce the idea of a catchphrase. Do the children know of any characters that have one?
● Discuss special attributes (*powers*, *skills*, *artefacts*) that key characters from stories might have.

## Independent work
● Explain to the class that they will be developing more detailed character profiles for their stories, bringing one or more of their characters to life, and ask them to draw one or more of their characters (face or full-body) in an appropriate outfit, and to write descriptive words and labels around them.

### Differentiation
● You can support this task by providing vocabulary banks for different features and attributes for children to use to aid their illustrations.
● Extend the task by challenging children to create similes to describe facial features.

## Review
● Share and comment on work. Do children want their character to have a catchphrase or special powers?

## Curriculum objectives
● To compose and rehearse sentences orally (including dialogue), progressively building a varied and rich vocabulary and an increasing range of sentence structures (see Appendix 2).

## Resources
Completed photocopiable page 110 'Castle story planner'; completed character work (from week 4, lesson 2); comic for demonstrating storyboards and speech bubbles; storyboard templates (optional, not provided)

# 3: Composing orally

## Introduction
● Display a comic and recap that speech bubbles hold spoken words. Contrast this with captions that explain scenes and plot. Talk around the scenes on the comic and ask the children to make oral contributions to flesh out the story.

## Independent work
● Using their completed photocopiable page 110 'Castle story planner' ask the children to create between two and four large storyboard panels showing the main problem of their story and its resolution. Remind them that sketches on the storyboard should be very rough so as not to waste time.

## Paired work
● Once children have worked for a while ask them to share their work with a partner, using their work to help compose their story orally, then tweak their work after mutual feedback.

### Differentiation
● Support children by providing figures, glue sticks and speech bubbles and encourage them to use sheets of A4 paper per storyboard scene to help structure their work.
● Challenge children to annotate each scene to show additional details. Remind them also of the perfect form for characters' dialogues.

## Review
● Gather the class and have volunteers present their scenes. Discuss effective work and offer comment and guidance as appropriate.

**Curriculum objectives**
● To use conjunctions, adverbs and prepositions to express time and cause.
● To choose nouns or pronouns appropriately to avoid repetition.
● To extend the range of sentences with more than one clause by using a wider range of conjunctions.

**Resources**
Completed scene descriptions (from week 3, lesson 5), or photocopiable page 'Sleeping Beauty' from the CD-ROM

# 4: First drafts

## Introduction
● Re-read one or two of the children's versions of the scene from 'Sleeping Beauty' and discuss effective writing, pointing out prepositions, pronouns and adverbs, as appropriate.
● Alternatively, re-read the actual scene from photocopiable page 'Sleeping Beauty' from the CD-ROM and discuss its strengths and weaknesses.

## Independent work
● Allow five minutes for children to review their previous planning and character work, and remind them of the oral drafting they did in lesson 3.
● Now ask the children to write the first draft of their own castle story, challenging them to use their knowledge of time and cause words, prepositions and adverbs and pronouns to write a richly descriptive story.

> **Differentiation**
> ● Scribe for children who write slowly, and allow access to vocabulary banks to support learning.
> ● To provide extension, ask children to focus on richer descriptions of appearance and scenes and to consider their use of conjunctions for extending sentences.

## Review
● Initially, bring the class together and have them read scenes from their stories to each other for constructive feedback.
● Next, ask children to work through their drafts identifying one or more time and cause words, adverbs and/or pronouns. Provide more time for children to conclude their drafts.

**Curriculum objectives**
● To assess the effectiveness of their own and others' writing and suggest improvements.
● To propose changes to grammar and vocabulary to improve consistency and accuracy.

**Resources**
Completed initial drafts (from week 4, lesson 4); draft text to demonstrate editing (optional, not provided)

# 5: Improving stories

## Introduction
● Explain that in this lesson children will review and finalise their stories.
● Either display one of the children's drafts or use some writing that you have prepared.
● Spend time looking at the work and reviewing its different elements, focusing in particular on how the quality of the writing can be improved, annotating freely and clearly.

## Independent or paired work
● Ask the children to review and alter their own drafts accordingly, sharing work with each other and providing constructive advice.
● Encourage children to think of a limited number of changes that will genuinely enhance their work, and to focus on these before considering grammar and punctuation.

> **Differentiation**
> ● For children who find improving work hard, providing checklists can make life easier for them, such as identifying three spelling mistakes, suggesting one change that makes their story more exciting, and so on.
> ● Extend the work by insisting on effective paragraphing, drawing on the lessons on plot and speech bubbles.

## Review
● To conclude, have a final session for the children to read their stories aloud, or at very least their favourite parts, to their peers. If you want to 'publish' the stories you may need more time for children to write out to presentation standards.

# Week 5 lesson plans

This week changes the tone, with a focus on mythical 'silly' kings, through retelling the stories of 'King Midas and the Golden Touch', and 'The Emperor's New Clothes' by Hans Christian Andersen. The stories are read, considered and compared, with opportunities for the children to think about the kings' behaviour and prepare questions to ask of them, leading to preparation for and participation in a debate on what makes a good ruler. The story of King Canute is also added for variety, though the teacher will need to tell this, and it can be omitted if a more focused approach is preferred. The essence of the week is very much on discussion and debate, using comparative language to consider the stories in depth.

## 1: Silly kings

### Introduction

● Talk about the difference between open and closed questions, explaining that a closed question has a definite answer, such as *right* or *wrong*, whereas an open question leads to further consideration and discussion. Provide examples of each and ask the children to identify them.
● Ask: *What is a king?* Discuss this, encouraging children to think broadly as well as literally.
● Explain the term *emperor* (someone who rules over a state or empire) and explain the similarity to the word *king*.
● Briefly tell the children the tale of King Canute (or Cnut) – the real-life king, of whom it is rumoured that he believed he could command the sea to stop if he wished. He was taken to the beach and it all went wrong – the moral being one of the vanity of rulers' beliefs in their own powers.
● As a class, create some interesting questions to ask King Canute.

### Whole-class work

● Talk about the characters of kings in stories that children may know, then introduce the background of the two stories ('King Midas' is from Ancient Greece; 'The Emperor's New Clothes' is by Hans Christian Andersen, who said that the story was originally Spanish).
● Provide a retelling, or reading, of each story to the class, adding as much drama and atmosphere as possible.
● After each story, pause and ask questions to ensure children understand the meaning, and elicit the themes and moral in each one.

### Group work

● Arranging the children in appropriate groups, ask them to imagine that they could have the opportunity to meet these kings, and challenge them to come up with a list of interesting questions that they would like to ask of, and about, the kings in each story.
● Explain that these do not need to be questions that can be directly answered, in other words they can be 'open questions'.

---

**Differentiation**
● Support learners by grouping them appropriately, and ensure that at least one question per group member is generated.
● The questioning process can be effectively extended by guiding children to think more broadly about the family, such as: *What would Midas's family have thought? How would the people of the country feel about having such a silly king?*

---

### Review

● Gather the class and recap on the stories and the morals of the tales.
● Discuss the groups' work, noting questions and asking for volunteers to suggest answers.

**Curriculum objectives**
● To ask questions to improve their understanding of a text.

**Resources**
Different 'outfits' or motifs for each king (not provided); extra adults who are happy to be hot seated in role; large space to work in (optional)

# 2: Meet the kings

## Introduction
● Recap on the concept of open and closed questions and offer examples.
● Briefly recap the tales presented in yesterday's lesson: 'King Midas', The Emperor's New Clothes' and 'King Canute'. Remind children of the questions they prepared.

## Group work
● Prepare for this session by having yourself and/or other adults in role as the kings. Ideally the lesson should take place in a hall, with the kings seated in different parts so that groups can circulate.
● Ideally, do not have groups of more than six, with separate tasks arranged for those who are not questioning a king.
● Explain that today the children are going to have the opportunity to meet the kings from the stories and ask questions about them, particularly in relation to the events of the stories.
● Before meeting the kings they should discuss and agree on a selection of questions, but do stress that impromptu questions are valid, and will be answered if worthwhile.
● Also ask groups to consider if they want to ask the same questions of each king (to allow for easier comparison), or different ones.

> **Differentiation**
> ● Ask groups to plan and assign questions to their members beforehand to ensure equal participation.

## Review
● Gather the groups together and consider what the children have heard that has improved their understanding of the stories.

**Curriculum objectives**
● To participate in discussion about both books that are read to them and those they can read for themselves, taking turns and listening to what others say.
● To identify themes and conventions in a wide range of books.

**Resources**
Questions and notes meetings with kings (from week 5, lesson 2)

# 3: Comparing kings

## Introduction
● Write the name of three things you can compare, such as football teams, meals or, if appropriate, bring three children to the front of the class. Compare the three things you have chosen by looking at like-for-like qualities and modelling comparative language (*taller than*, *as…as*), as well as comparative and superlative adjectives (*faster*, *fastest*).

## Independent work
● Recap how the tales of kings and emperors from this week are moral tales.
● Split the class into three sections: King Midas, the Emperor and King Canute. Ask the children to work independently to list good and bad points about their assigned ruler. What can they use from the stories to help them? Did they learn anything from talking to the kings to help with their thinking?

## Group work
● Create groups of around six, with two children for each ruler, and ask them to compare and discuss their thoughts about their rulers. Ask: *What can you find in common? What is different?*
● Challenge them to work as a group to create five or so sentences comparing particular aspects of two (or three if desired) of the kings studied.

## Review
● Gather the class and allow groups to present some of their sentences, opening up discussion with others as appropriate.
● Model good language and prompt thinking with references to the stories.

**Curriculum objectives**
• To participate in discussion about both books that are read to them and those they can read for themselves, taking turns and listening to what others say.

# 4: What makes a good ruler?

## Introduction

• This is a class-based debate. Write the following words large on the board (or on card) so that they can be moved around: *Happiness, Health, Safety, Money, Love, Shelter, Food.*

• Ask for volunteers to come to the whiteboard and, without speaking, arrange any one word into order of importance, with the most important first and the least important last.

• After a while, decide whether consensus has been reached or which words are contentious, and discuss children's reasons for their choices as well as collating views on the overall order.

• Discuss which order King Midas would give to these words, before and after his experience.

## Group work

• Explain that, in the time of castles, the kings and queens of England had great powers and control over the country. They had the power to raise taxes, make people join the army, take away their jobs, and also to provide safety and food for them. Some rulers were mainly concerned with themselves, others were concerned for their country.

• Arranging the class into groups, ask them to debate: *What makes a good ruler?* Follow your usual rules for discussion. Conclude with a group statement: *We think the things that make a good ruler are...*

## Review

• To conclude, gather the groups together and have them read out their statements, allowing others to query and challenge them. Can the class reach consensus?

**Curriculum objectives**
• To discuss and record ideas.
• To organise paragraphs around a theme.

**Resources**
Completed statements on good rulers (from week 5, lesson 4)

# 5: If I were on the throne

## Introduction

• With some pomp and ceremony, unroll a piece of paper and 'issue' a royal decree to the class, such as: *On this day, his majesty King Canute, has decreed that the sea will obey him, and henceforth will not come higher than he so wishes. This means all children will be able to paddle in safety.*

• Explain that decrees are statements that will affect how society will function.

## Independent or paired work

• Remind the class of the words they ordered in importance for lesson 4 (*Happiness, Health, Safety, Money, Love, Shelter, Food*). Explain that they will be using these words today.

• Next, ask the children to write at the top of a piece of paper: *If I were Queen/King.* Modelling the first decree, explain that you want them to write a royal decree for each of these seven words they have discussed, reminding them to write *how* they will make it happen and *what* their decree will achieve.

> **Differentiation**
> • To extend the learning ask children to write decrees for all seven words in the style of a fictitious ruler (evil, funny, mad, or so on) of their choice, adding wacky reasons to support their decrees.

## Review

• Gather the class and share their decrees, discussing which are a good use of power, and which are not.

# Week 6 lesson plans

The final week of this chapter moves on to poetry. Initially, children listen to 'The King's Breakfast', enjoying its comic elements and considering ways of breaking it down to help memorise it. Children then enjoy performing aspects of the poem, guided to consider intonation and expression to good effect. Lesson 3 moves on to looking at a version of 'God Save the Queen' as a national anthem and tribute, contrasting this with the style and intent of 'The King's Breakfast', then allowing children time to consider the sort of poem they want to create. They end the week drafting their own royal poems and reciting them.

## 1: 'The King's Breakfast'

### Introduction
● Read photocopiable page 'The King's Breakfast' from the CD-ROM to the class, using dramatic techniques and voices to bring the poem to life and convey the story it tells. (Before you start you may wish to explain that an *Alderney* is a breed of cow and that *porringer* is porridge.)

### Whole-class work
● Display the poem and in discussion consider the four characters in it and their roles and relationships.
● Look in detail at the first verse. Consider how many lines it has, which words rhyme, and how such short lines can still be so effective.
● Next, look at the overall poem. Consider how many verses it has, which words rhyme, and if the structure is maintained throughout. Focus on all the words that rhyme with *bread*, considering both spellings and their positions in the poem.
● Use the opportunity to look again at inverted commas, which are less common in poetry than in ordinary narratives.

### Paired work
● Display the poem or distribute copies as desired.
● Distributing photocopiable page 111 'Summarising a poem' to pairs of children, explain that you want them to work together to summarise the structure of the poem, by tracking all the conversations that took place through it. Using the photocopiable sheet forces children to review the poem in detail, thinking about each exchange and tracing its flow.
● As instructed on the photocopiable sheet, when they have summarised the plot ask them to write about one or more of the characters and summarise their thoughts on them.

> **Differentiation**
> ● For children who find working with the poem summary sheet too difficult, you might give them multiple drawn figures of the characters, as well as numbered verses on a separate sheet of paper. Children can then work together using A3 paper and glue sticks to look at each verse and stick characters next to their relevant parts.

### Review
● Gather the class together and review their summary work. Gradually elicit that the whole poem would lose its point if the cow had just said *yes* from the start. Focusing on the king, ask the class to decide on what sort of person he is, using quotes from the poem to substantiate their views. How do the children think the other characters in the poem perceive the king?
● To conclude, discuss the purpose of the poem. Explain that the author (AA Milne) also wrote *Winnie the Pooh*, and was well known for his whimsical poetry.

## Curriculum objectives
● To prepare poems and playscripts to read aloud and to perform, showing understanding through intonation, tone, volume and action.

## Resources
Photocopiable page 'The King's Breakfast' from the CD-ROM; completed photocopiable page 111 'Summarising a poem' (from week 6, lesson 1); video camera (optional)

# 2: Reciting verses

## Introduction
● Open the lesson with a class rendition of 'Sing a Song of Sixpence', both to loosen children's voices and inhibitions, as well as reminding them of the royal theme of this week's literacy work.

## Group work
● Explain that in this session they will be considering recitals (orally presenting poetry from memory). Distributing all or parts of 'The King's Breakfast' to each group (or displaying the poem on the board), explain that you want each group to plan a recital of all or part of the poem.
● If desired, you can turn the exercise into a whole-class rendition, with each group being assigned a verse and each group assigning specific lines to its members. Alternatively, a choral approach may be preferred.

### Differentiation
● Using the completed summary sheets from lesson 1 can act as effective memory aids while learning the poem.

## Review
● Ensuring that the actual poem is not on view (or at least only for the eyes of anyone checking), ask the groups to recite their verse(s) in turn. Ask chosen children (or do this yourself) to note where errors occurred, and then allow children to receive feedback or indeed watch themselves though video playback. Discuss the skills and difficulties involved in effective recital, and any techniques used to help.

## Curriculum objectives
● To prepare poems and playscripts to read aloud and to perform, showing understanding through intonation, tone, volume and action.

## Resources
Photocopiable page 'The King's Breakfast' from the CD-ROM; photocopiable page 'God Save the Queen' from the CD-ROM; photocopiable page 79 'Poetry planner'

# 3: Poem research

## Introduction
● Open photocopiable page 'God Save the Queen' from the CD-ROM and explain that although this is a song it retains a poetic form. Look at the lyrics and explain words that the children do not know.
● Briefly discuss the format. Are there any rhymes or repeated lines? How long is each verse? And so on.
● Ask why this is used as a country's national anthem, and compare it with 'The King's Breakfast'. Do children prefer a serious or light-hearted approach to royal poetry?

## Independent work
● Explain that the children are going to be creating their own poems for the ruler of their choice. It can be a real king or queen from past or present, one from a story, or a fictitious one of their own creation.
● They can choose the style of their choice – rhyming is optional; they can tell a story or praise (or indeed politely ridicule) their chosen ruler.
● Photocopiable page 79 'Poetry planner' can be used to support planning.

### Differentiation
● The task can be extended by explaining the role of a 'poet laureate', and asking the children to prepare a poem for a particular occasion, such as a royal wedding.

## Review
● Allow time for the children to explain their plans to each other and adjust them according to comments.

## Curriculum objectives
● To prepare poems and playscripts to read aloud and to perform, showing understanding through intonation, tone, volume and action.
● To proofread for spelling and punctuation errors.
● To propose changes to grammar and vocabulary to improve consistency.

## Resources
Completed poetry planning work (from week 6, lesson 3); dictionaries

# 4: Drafting a royal poem

## Introduction
● Work though starter activity 3 'Vocabulary builder', introducing vocabulary relevant to royalty, such as *regal*, *enthroned*, *glorious* and *reign*.
● Discuss the use of appropriate vocabulary to give a ruler a certain air, whether powerful, silly, or otherwise.

## Independent work
● Ask the children to draft their poems, then work with partners to review work from the point of view of spelling, punctuation and meaning. Do their poems have a central message or story?
● When checking work, ask the children to consider the consistency of the verses – does their poem follow any pattern or rules?

> **Differentiation**
> ● Many children find writing structured poetry difficult. For those that do, work with groups to model how initial drafts can be altered to become more coherent. Showing how choosing different words can help and ensuring that grammar is consistent can quickly give a poem more shape. Also, look at lines that can be repeated – a common feature of poems that can help create rhythm and structure.

## Review
● Allow time to review children's drafts together, asking others to decide on the style and aim of each poem they read or hear.
● If possible, children should adjust and finalise their drafts.

## Curriculum objectives
● To use the diagonal and horizontal strokes that are needed to join letters and understand which letters, when adjacent to one another, are best left unjoined.
● To increase the legibility, consistency and quality of their handwriting.
● To read aloud their own writing, to a group or the whole class, using appropriate intonation and controlling the tone and volume so that the meaning is clear.

## Resources
Props such as a throw for a throne and a royal crest of arms; completed poetry drafts (from week 6, lesson 4); handwriting equipment; video camera (optional)

# 5: Presenting and reciting royal poems

## Introduction
● Use the props to present an air of seriousness for the recitals or, if desired, go the whole way and have a medieval themed day.
● Develop the theme and aims of the lesson, presenting your own royal poem (or one of those already studied) to the class, using all your acting skills to add flourishes, drama and humour as appropriate.

## Independent work
● Explain that everyone must produce a high-quality handwritten copy of their poem for presentation to their chosen king or queen, using handwriting equipment and methods as per your school handwriting policy.

## Group work
● With the poems written for presentation, gather the children into groups and ask them to plan a performance of recitals, deciding on the best order to read their poems (they can read independently or share the readings of each other's work in a group).
● When ready, have each group present its different poems in whichever way they prefer.

> **Differentiation**
> ● Allow children who find public reciting difficult to work in pairs appropriately, or read only sections of their work.
> ● For confident writers, introduce italic pens and ask them to try and create a script with some flourish. They might also 'illuminate' their poem with colour illustrations.

## Review
● While listening to readings, challenge children to note particular words and phrases that they hear (and do likewise yourself). Discuss aspects of poems that seem particularly successful, and why.

## Curriculum objectives

- To use the present perfect form of verbs in contrast to the past tense.
- To extend the range of sentences with more than one clause by using a wider range of conjunctions.

## Resources

Photocopiable page 108 'Perfect sentences'; interactive activity 'Using the perfect form' on the CD-ROM; interactive activity 'Joining clauses' on the CD-ROM

# Grammar and punctuation: Using conjunctions and the perfect form

## Revise

- Recap on the meaning of the perfect form and the situations it is used in.
- Display photocopiable page 108 'Perfect sentences' and talk again about the use of the verb *to have* and the need for prepositions to extend the explanation or meaning of the first part of the sentence.

## Assess

- Ask the class to imagine that they are servants in a bygone era (medieval is fine), and that they are undergoing training. Explain that you are going to ask them some questions. (It is OK to write these on the board too.) The purpose of the questions is to see how well they understand their jobs.
- Work through a sample question together, such as: *Have you polished my sword?* And model a response: *Yes, I have polished the sword because it was rather dirty.* Focus on the use of *have* and *because.*
- Repeat five to ten questions regarding servant duties and ask the class to write answers to each one (oral responses are fine if you have time to rotate children).

## Further practice

- Work through interactive activities 'Using the perfect form' and 'Joining clauses' on the CD-ROM.
- Challenge the children to ask each other *Have you...?* type questions and to answer them fully.

## Curriculum objectives

- To use dictionaries to check the meaning of words that they have read.
- To apply their growing knowledge of root words, prefixes and suffixes (etymology and morphology) as listed in Appendix 1, both to read aloud and to understand the meaning of new words they meet.
- To use the first two or three letters of a word to check its spelling in a dictionary.

## Resources

Set of class dictionaries; online dictionary; photocopiable page 106 'Castle vocabulary'; interactive activity 'Using dictionaries' on the CD-ROM

# Spelling: Using dictionaries to find the meaning of words

## Revise

- Recap the use of alphabetical order for first and second letters when locating dictionary entries, reminding children of the use of headwords.
- Play 'call my bluff' type games for difficult topic-related vocabulary.
- Introduce the children to online dictionaries and how to access them quickly using search engines. (Typically, to find the meaning of a word just type it into a search engine with the word *dictionary* after it.)
- Look again at photocopiable page 106 'Castle vocabulary'. Remind the children of the words they had researched and then research some more.
- Look at word origins in a suitable dictionary.

## Assess

- Using the format of starter activity 4 'Hard-to-spell words', present children with a listing of five to ten words that may be new to them (perhaps getting progressively more complex). Ask them to find each of the words in a dictionary and complete the information for each word.
- Example words: *man, manacle, dictionary, envoy, costume, locomotion, tranquil, harbour, preen.*

## Further practice

- Rotate the class through the interactive activity 'Using dictionaries' on the CD-ROM.
- Set a 'word of the day' for a fortnight with children tasked, perhaps during registration, to find the word in their dictionary and confirm its meaning.
- Develop good classroom routines for dictionary access and use.

## Curriculum objectives

● To identify themes and conventions in a wide range of books.
● To increase their familiarity with a wide range of books, including fairy stories, myths and legends, and retell some of these orally.
● To participate in discussion about both books that are read to them and those they can read for themselves, taking turns and listening to what others say.

## Resources

Photocopiable page 'The Princess and the Pea' from the CD-ROM; photocopiable page 'Sleeping Beauty' from the CD-ROM; range of fairy tales and myths, old and modern; photocopiable page 110 'Castle story planner'

# Reading: Appreciating the features of fairy tales

## Revise

● Allow the children to re-read photocopiable pages 'The Princess and the Pea' and 'Sleeping Beauty' from the CD-ROM, and provide a small range of comprehension questions to check their understanding of the key features of fairy tales (royalty, castle setting, simple plot, magic, and a problem to be resolved).
● Look at other fairy tales and use photocopiable page 110 'Castle story planner' to 'deconstruct' them, breaking them down into their parts.
● Research and explain the difference between fairy tales, myths, fables and legends.
● Talk about folklore and how this helped create fairy tales and other stories. Provide information about how the stories originated, telling children about the Brothers Grimm and Hans Christian Andersen.

## Assess

● Provide a selection of fairy tales for the class, such as 'Rapunzel', 'Beauty and the Beast', and 'Hansel and Gretel' (the last one is deliberately listed as it is quite different from the others). Ask the children to read them through and identify the conventions of a fairy tale in each one. How many does each story have? Are there any missing?
● Ask the children to retell the stories for a younger person, and note what they retain and what they remove from the story – do they keep the essential ingredients?
● Although the focus here is reading, children's own stories connected to this genre will help you assess if they appreciate its style and conventions.

## Further practice

● Look at modern versions of fairy tales, such as Babette Cole's marvellous 'Prince Cinders' and Lauren Child's wonderful retelling of 'The Princess and the Pea'. After enjoying the books, talk about how they retain the themes and conventions of fairy tales.
● Compare and contrast different versions of tales, such as Phillip Pullman's retelling contrasted with the Brothers Grimm's originals.
● Provide groups with randomly chosen piles of fiction books, asking them to sort the books according to their own criteria into generic sets. When the books are sorted, ask: *How did you decide which books went together? How much help were the titles? Were some already known to you? Did you read the blurbs and use the cover illustrations? Did you read any of the text? Which type of book did you find most of? Were any books particularly difficult to define?*
● Look at modern texts that may belong to the genre, such as *The Iron Man*. Debate whether it is reasonable to call these books 'fairy tales'.

## Curriculum objectives
● To assess the effectiveness of their own and others' writing and suggest improvements.
● To discuss writing similar to that which they are planning to write in order to understand and learn from its structure, grammar and vocabulary.

## Resources
Interactive activity 'Correcting work' on the CD-ROM

# Writing: Improving writing – drafting and amending original fairy tales

## Revise
● The first and foremost technique for checking work is simply whether it looks right or wrong. This is hard for children to check in their own work, as they tend to skim as they already know what is there. Asking them to read out loud can be much more effective – if they have to pause, encourage them to think why.
● Use 'review partners', as reading someone else's work can make errors much easier to spot.
● The need for children to self-correct is an obvious one, but it is not simply a case of spotting errors and changing them. Children need to be guided carefully in the techniques and approaches to correcting and altering work.
● With so much variation in errors it is important not to overwhelm or confuse children. Try to separate this work into specific areas, concentrating on particular aspects at different times. Use the following checklist to guide their work: *vocabulary*, *meaning*, *style*, *spelling*, *punctuation* and *grammar*.
● As children become familiar with the notations introduced, have them review longer texts with different types of errors in, but do not make it mandatory to find every error.

## Assess
● Ensuring that you have thoroughly covered the fairy-tale genre in previous lessons, ask the children to plan and write their own fairy tale based on an existing plot or creating one of their own, part of which they should relate to a partner.
● Provide children with a fairy tale checklist or writing template, as preferred, explaining that it is an extended piece of writing that should encompass the key elements of fairy tales, and allow planning time as per your usual approaches, with sufficient writing time to create good stories.
● Once the children have completed their stories, allow them ample time to re-read and correct their work. Guide the children to use the checklist above and any conventions of notation that you have taught.
● Depending on their preference they might make several passes through their draft, focusing on a different element (such as spelling) each time they go through it. Others may prefer to read carefully, spotting all types of error and amendment as they go.
● Comparing drafts and finished pieces will show the level of self-improvement and should guide you as to next steps for developing these skills.
● The finished work will also help you to assess how well the children have assimilated the structure, grammar and vocabulary of the fairy-tale genre.

## Further practice
● Run regular short sessions, maybe to introduce lessons, looking at a sentence or two with errors in, and using agreed conventions for indicating errors and then correcting them.
● Return to older work. It is interesting once in a while for children to look at their work from several months ago. Seeing words afresh helps to focus on them, and their growing skills should make error identification easier and improvements in style more obvious.

Name: _____ Date: _____

## Castle features collection form

- Use this sheet to help you make notes when touring a castle.

Castle name: _____

Location: _____

Built by: _____

Built in: _____

| Feature | Function | My impression |
|---------|----------|---------------|
| Moat | To protect the castle from attackers. | It looked very deep and cold. |
|  |  |  |
|  |  |  |
|  |  |  |
|  |  |  |
|  |  |  |
|  |  |  |

- Make further notes on the other side.

I can identify features and describe them.

How did you do?

**PHOTOCOPIABLE**

## Castle layout

■ Label this diagram of a castle. Check any new terms using
a dictionary.

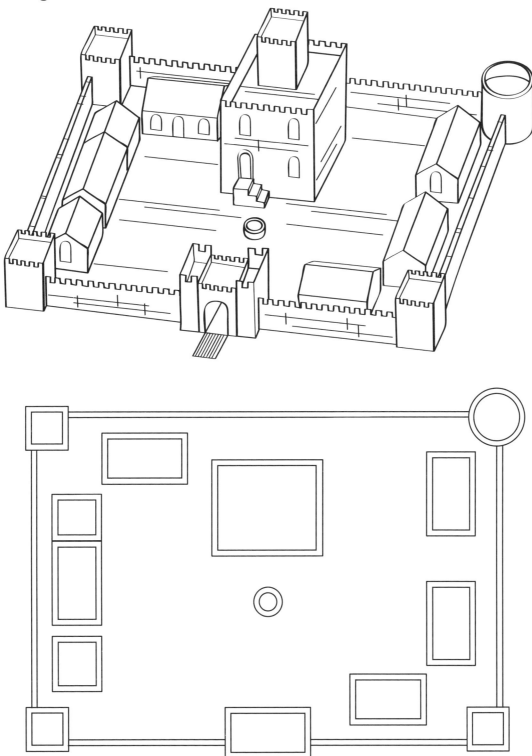

I can label a diagram and use a dictionary to check new terms.

How did you do?

**PHOTOCOPIABLE**

## Castle vocabulary

**A**

armour

armoury

arrow loops

**B**

bailey

barn

bastion

battering ram

battlements

**C**

castle

catapult

chain mail

chateau

crenellations

crest

crossbow

curtain wall

**D**

donjon

drawbridge

dungeon

**F**

fortress

**G**

garderobe

gatehouse

great hall

**H**

heraldry

**K**

keep

kitchens

**M**

mangonel

manor

medieval

moat

**O**

onager

**P**

palace

peel tower

portcullis

**R**

round tower

**S**

shield

siege

solar

spiral staircase

square tower

stables

**T**

tower

trebuchet

turret

**W**

walkway

walls

watchtower

well

Name: _____ Date: _____

## Castle dwellers

■ Look at the different people who lived and worked in a castle. Which ones do you want to find out about?

| chaplain | lady-in-waiting | cook | blacksmith | steward |

| knight | lady | groom | constable | lord |

## Perfect sentences

- Can you make perfect sentences? Try filling in the gaps below.
For example:

*I _____ been to the doctor _____ I wasn't feeling well.*

Becomes:

*I have been to the doctor as I wasn't feeling well.*

**1.** They _____ gone to Spain _____ they need a holiday.

**2.** She _____ gone to the cafe _____ they fix her car.

**3.** We _____ called the police _____ we can hear noises.

**4.** It _____ been six months _____ it happened.

**5.** Ann _____ eaten all the sandwiches _____ she is hungry.

- The next sentences are harder. Try to complete the following.
For example:

*Jo has walked to school because she has no money.*

**6.** He _____ dog _____ lazy.

**7.** We _____ shops _____ empty.

**8.** I _____ computer _____ broken.

**9.** They _____ pizza _____ late.

- Can you write one more sentence like those above?

**10.** _____

I can use the perfect form in sentences.

How did you do?

## Using suffixes

- A suffix is added to the end of a word to change its meaning. It can also change what sort of word it is. Look at the below two suffixes.

---

**-ing**

- **-ing** can be added to the end of verbs to make the continuous form.
- Instead of **I run**, we can say **I am running** when we talk about something that is happening now.
- We can also say **I was running** if we are talking about the past.
- Beware, short words (such as **run**) double the last letter when you add **-ing**.

---

**-ly**

- **-ly** can be added to the end of some adjectives to make adverbs.
- Adverbs modify verbs.
- Instead of **she is a quick runner** we can write **she runs quickly**.
- If an adjective ends in **y** we have to change the spelling: **lazy** becomes **lazily**.

---

- Can you use '-ing' and '-ly' to alter the bold words and improve these statements? The first one has been done for you.

**1.** He **run slow**.      **He is running slowly**.

**2.** You **behave stupid**. _____

**3.** I **eat** my lunch **messy**. _____

**4.** The dog **walk lazy**. _____

**5.** Last night I **sleep deep** when a noise woke me up. _____

_____

I can use the '-ing' and '-ly' suffixes correctly.

How did you do?

## Castle story planner

**Genre:** _____

**Setting:** Describe your castle here. Mention any features that will be in the story.

```



```

**Characters:** You need two or three main characters. Describe them here.

Hero:

Other characters:

**Objects:** What objects will be in your story?

```



```

**Plot:** What is the main problem your characters face, and how is it resolved?

Problem:

Resolution:

I can plan a story.

How did you do?

## Summarising a poem

■ Use this sheet to help you to summarise 'The King's Breakfast'. To start, write the trail of conversations that took place.

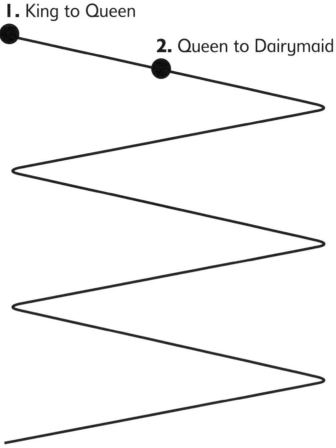

**1.** King to Queen

**2.** Queen to Dairymaid

■ Choose one or more of the characters and write your opinion of them here.

■ I can summarise a poem.

How did you do?

# Aliens

This chapter takes its focus from the word 'alien', and its different meanings – from fantasy creatures from space to feeling 'alien' to places and people. Initial lessons are based on the picture book *Beegu* – a lovely story about an alien lost on Earth. The picture book format allows for greater class discussion and interpretation, and provides stimuli for summarising stories and inferring character and emotions.

Stemming from this are separate chapters covering clear instruction writing (for aliens of course), moving to more thoughtful chapters on being and feeling alien. Children study an excerpt from *King of the Cloud Forests* by Michael Morpurgo, then writing diaries, followed by creating a play for younger children on the theme of 'being alien'. The chapter then concludes on a more light-hearted note, with humorous alien poetry.

## Expected prior learning

- Can remember homophones encountered in Year 2.
- Know the difference between a sentence and a clause.
- Familiar with some coordinating and subordinating conjunctions.
- Can use headings to order information.
- Can create settings.
- Understand the conventions of a playscript.
- Understand a variety of poetry types.

## Overview of progression

- This chapter has ample opportunities for discussion, oral composition and planning, helping children to compose dialogues, instructions, diary entries, plays and poems, with the latter two being performed.
- Grammatical input covers determiners, noun phrases and homophones, clauses and the perfect form for increasingly complex sentences.
- Several lessons throughout the chapter focus specifically on a range of suffixes and word endings.

## Creative context

- There are good potential links to science (Space), art and design (creating fantasy creatures and locations), and PSHE (thinking about emotions and empathy). Also, the work on playscripts encourages awareness of a younger audience and suggests a range of formats (acting, mime, puppets and stop-frame animation).

## Preparation

You will need to familiarise yourself with several books with alien themes, as well as the extract and poem on the CD-ROM. Titles referenced within lessons include *Beegu* by Alexis Deacon, *The Way Back Home* by Oliver Jeffers, or *Cloudland* by John Burningham; *King of the Cloud Forests* by Michael Morpurgo (optional, but preferable); some well-illustrated fun alien books, such as *The Aliens Are Coming* and *We're Off to Look for Aliens* by Colin McNaughton, and *Aliens Love Underpants* by Claire Freedman and Ben Cort. One or more copies of *Aliens Stole My Underpants* by Brian Moses.

**You will also need:**
Dictionaries; a list of everyday tasks; a short non-fiction text; globe; internet access (optional); coloured pencils; video camera (optional); performance space; a selection of alien poetry.

**On the CD-ROM you will find:**
Media resources 'Aliens', 'Making a cake', 'Emotions'; interactive activities '/shun/ words', 'Joining clauses', 'Sequencing instructions', 'Homophones'; photocopiable pages 'Beegu's Tale', '*King of the Cloud Forests* extract', 'Roald Dahl biography', '*The Twits* playscript', 'Aliens Stole My Underpants'

# Chapter at a glance

An overview of the chapter. For curriculum objective codes, please see pages 8–10.

| Week | Lesson | Curriculum objectives | Summary of activities | Outcome |
|------|--------|----------------------|----------------------|---------|
| 1 | 1 | WC: 16, 20 | Introduce and discuss aliens, using determiners correctly. | • Can understand rules for indefinite or definite articles, and use determiners correctly. |
| | 2 | WC: 5 | Describe aliens using multiple adjectives. | • Can understand ordering adjectives and can use similes. |
| | 3 | WT: 2, 5, 6 | Select and write homophones for spelling and meaning. | • Can accurately spell a range of homophones. |
| | 4 | WC: 5 | Invent aliens and create fact files for them. | • Can develop a simple character profile. |
| | 5 | WC: 3, 11 | Work together to create dialogues between aliens. | • Can create dialogues with rich vocabulary. |
| 2 | 1 | RC: 14 WC: 2 | Collaborate to create sets of instructions using pictures. | • Can read and interpret instructions. |
| | 2 | WC: 2, 6 | Write simple instruction lists from pictures. | • Can write instructions in lists using appropriate language. |
| | 3 | WT: 3, 6 | Spell words with the ending /shun/. Gather words and discuss how they are spelled. | • Can begin to spell words ending in /shun/ correctly. |
| | 4 | WC: 2, 6 | Develop advice for different everyday situations using freeze-frame techniques. | • Can collaborate to create logical instructions. |
| | 5 | WC: 4, 6 | Write *The Intergalactic Space Traveller's Guide* – useful advice for different everyday situations. | • Can write information in paragraphs, incorporating new vocabulary. |
| 3 | 1 | RC: 1, 10 WC: 6 | Read, discuss and summarise the picture book *Beegu*. | • Can summarise a picture book. |
| | 2 | WC: 3 | Consider explanations for adult characters' actions. | • Can infer characters' feelings, thoughts and motives from their actions. |
| | 3 | WT: 1, 6 WC: 16, 20 | Introduce the rules for adding suffixes starting with a vowel. | • Can use rules to spell words correctly. |
| | 4 | WC: 11, 20 | Introduce and practise simple, compound and complex sentences using main and subordinate clauses. | • Can identify sentences and clauses, and combine two clauses using a range of connectives. |
| | 5 | RC: 11 WC: 11 | Write a page from Beegu's diary after she returns home, using clauses. | • Can use clauses to support more complex writing. |
| 4 | 1 | RC: 1, 7, 11 | Look at a synopsis of *King of the Cloud Forests* by Michael Morpurgo. | • Can infer aspects of plot and character from a book synopsis. |
| | 2 | WC: 1, 10 | Listen to and discuss an extract from *King of the Cloud Forests*. | • Can identify and discuss the main ideas in a text. |
| | 3 | WC: 3. 19 | Create an imaginary dialogue between the main character of *King of the Cloud Forests* and another character. | • Can correctly punctuate direct speech. |
| | 4 | RC: 13 WC: 4 | Plan a diary entry about arriving somewhere strange and 'alien'. | • Can effectively structure a text and prepare appropriate vocabulary. |
| | 5 | WC: 4, 12, 14 | Write a diary entry about 'feeling alien'. | • Can create a sense of atmosphere when writing about a new place. |
| 5 | 1 | WC: 6 RC: 6 | Plan a short play on the theme of 'feeling alien'. | • Can identify the main elements of a story. |
| | 2 | WT: 3, 6 | Develop an understanding of the ' ation' suffix. | • Can use '-ation' to convert verbs to nouns, adhering to appropriate spelling rules. |
| | 3 | WC: 3 | Improvise and practise their play in pairs. | • Can develop a playscript through improvisation. |
| | 4 | RC: 6 | Write plays as playscripts, adhering to the usual conventions. | • Can correctly punctuate a playscript. |
| | 5 | WC: 10 | Perform their alien plays. | • Can perform a short play to peers. |

## Chapter at a glance

| Week | Lesson | Curriculum objectives | Summary of activities | Outcome |
|------|--------|----------------------|----------------------|---------|
| 6 | 1 | RC: 1, 8 | Consider alien-themed poetry and try to rewrite a well-known poem. | • Can understand and can talk about different aspects of poetry. |
| | 2 | WT: 3, 6 | Spell words with the ending '-ous'. Gather words and discuss the spelling rules that affect them. | • Can begin to spell words ending in '-ous' correctly. |
| | 3 | WC: 1, 2 | Plan a short narrative poem about an alien invasion. | • Can incorporate aspects of other people's poetry in their work. |
| | 4 | RC: 6 WC: 2 | Develop poems about an alien invasion. | • Can write a poem in a narrative style. |
| | 5 | RC: 6 | Present alien poems. | • Can perform poems using intonation and movement. |

## Background knowledge

**Article**: A type of determiner (see below). The articles are *a* and *an* (indefinite) and *the* (definite).

**Clause**: A special type of phrase whose main word is a verb that describes the situation.

**Determiner**: A word that modifies a noun and comes before other modifiers, such as adjectives. It can be an article (see above), demonstrative (such as *that*), possessive (such as *your*), quantifier (such as *any*) or numeral (such as *seven*).

**Intonation**: The variation in voice tone and pronunciation.

**Noun phrase**: A group of words with a noun as the main word.

**Sentence type**: This can be simple, compound or complex. A simple sentence has one clause, a compound sentence has two or more equal clauses, and a complex sentence has a main clause and a subordinate clause.

**Subordinate clause**: This provides information about another word or clause.

# Week 1 lesson plans

## Expected outcomes
● All children will use adjectives to describe aliens and create an imaginary dialogue. They will also learn about homophones.
● Most children will develop effective extended noun phrases.
● Some children will use complex adjectives, similes and homophones to add humour and interest.

## Curriculum objectives
● To use and understand the grammatical terminology in Appendix 2 accurately and appropriately when discussing their writing and reading.
● To learn the grammar for Year 3 in Appendix 2.

## Resources
Good full-colour alien book, such as *The Aliens Are Coming* and *We're Off to Look for Aliens* by Colin McNaughton, or *Aliens Love Underpants* by Claire Freedman and Ben Corts

This week opens the chapter by focusing on considering and describing aliens, using a picture book to allow the class to appreciate that aliens may have 'inner' lives beyond their outward appearances.

Lessons 1 and 2 revise using determiners correctly with extended noun phrases by describing features and explaining their use. The third lesson focuses on understanding and spelling homophones, with the remaining sessions allowing children to create their own alien characters, who then go on to meet and get to know each other, developing their characters all the while.

## 1: Introducing aliens

### Introduction
● Start the lesson with a rousing reading from your chosen alien book – if this is rhyming poetry with big colour illustrations so much the better.
● Explain that this chapter of work is all to do with aliens, of the humorous rather than the serious kind.

### Whole-class work
● Discuss what the children think an alien is, and explain the dictionary definitions to them:
    ● **Noun:** *a foreigner, especially someone staying in a country they were not born in.*
    ● **Noun:** *a mythical being from another planet.*
    ● **Adjective:** *belonging to another country; feeling unfamiliar or strange.*
● Explain also that the word *alien* was first used hundreds of years ago, and comes from the Latin *alius*, meaning 'other'.
● Introduce determiners and, if appropriate, clarify that *a*, *the* and *an* are types of determiner called *articles*.
● Explain that the difference between *a* and *the* is *indefinite* (any example of a noun: *a horse*), or *definite* (a particular object: *the horse*), and exemplify this with some examples.
● Explain also that if nouns start with a vowel sound we must use *an*, not *a*, hence *an alien*. Write a range of topic-related vocabulary on the board and in discussion consider which words take *a* or *an*. Sample vocabulary might include: *alien, emergency, planet, spaceship*.
● Remind the class that words that have *a*, *an* or *the* before them are nouns, but that they can be extended by putting adjectives in front of them. So, *a bus* can become *a red bus*. Now, reminding the class that you would say *an alien*, ask what they would say if it were red, and gradually elicit that the article changes depending on whether the first letter of the next word is a vowel or a consonant sound.

### Group work
● Discuss the aliens that children may know from other books or films (*Ben 10, Star Wars, Wall-E, ET*, and so on).
● Organising the children in groups, ask them to discuss both the aliens they know of, and what they themselves imagine aliens to be like, or perhaps what they *would like* them to be like. Prompt discussion by asking: *Might they be like us? Might they be friendly or aggressive? Why would they want to visit Earth? Why would we want to visit them?*
● To extend children, pose the question *Do aliens really exist?* Ask them to research this, think it through, and then debate.

### Review
● Facilitate a class discussion on aliens, gathering ideas and knowledge from all groups. To conclude, remind children of the determiners *a* and *an*, and the rules that they use.

**Curriculum objectives**
● In narratives, to create settings, characters and plot.

**Resources**
Media resource 'Aliens' on the CD-ROM

# 2: Describing aliens

## Introduction
● Have a small collection of objects on show, and challenge children to describe each one using as many words as possible, such as *A long, red pencil* or *A small, square, white rubber*, and so on. Elicit that the describing words are adjectives, and explain that these are positioned according to rules: size, shape, colour, material (there are more categories, but this is enough for now).

## Independent work or paired work
● Open the media resource 'Aliens' on the CD-ROM and work through them, pausing to elicit extended descriptions of different features. Pause on the final screen, which shows all the aliens.
● Remind the children of the scene where Little Red Riding Hood mistakes the wolf for her grandmother (*What big, sharp teeth you have...*).
● Working individually or in pairs, ask the children to choose an alien from the media resource and imagine meeting it. Their challenge is to create one or two statements per alien, using at least two adjectives per statement, and add what explanation the alien would give for having these features.

> **Differentiation**
> ● Allow pairs to create their sentences orally before transcribing them.
> ● To stretch children's learning ask them to substitute similes for every adjective.

## Review
● Gather the class and have them read or recite their best sentences. Can everyone guess which alien they are talking about?

**Curriculum objectives**
● To spell further homophones.
● To use dictionaries to check the meaning of words that they have read.
● To write from memory simple sentences, dictated by the teacher, that include words and punctuation taught so far.

**Resources**
Interactive activity 'Homophones' on the CD-ROM; photocopiable page 136 'Homophones'; dictionaries

# 3: Homophones

## Introduction
● Begin with interactive activity 'Homophones' on the CD-ROM, or starter activity 1 'Word pairs', putting a list of five or six homophones on one side of the board, and a jumbled list of their partners on the other. Choose from: *accept/except, affect/effect, ball/bawl, berry/bury, brake/break, fair/fare, grate/great, groan/grown, here/hear, heel/heal/he'll, knot/not, mail/male, main/mane, meat/meet, medal/meddle, missed/mist, peace/piece, plain/plane, rain/rein/reign, scene/seen, weather/whether, whose/who's*. Work through the activity and discuss the differences between pairs, reinforcing the meaning of the words.

## Paired work
● Suggesting that it must be hard for aliens to understand that two words which sound the same mean something different, distribute photocopiable page 136 'Homophones' and ask the children to write the correct meaning for each one, using dictionaries if they need to.

## Independent work
● Read out sentences containing a range of homophones and challenge the children to write them correctly. Then ask children to make two or three sentences with strange meanings by using the wrong homophones.

> **Differentiation**
> ● Support children with the homophone list visible when you are dictating sentences.

## Review
● Quickly confirm the meaning of homophones and compare one or two.
● Ask children to read their sentences and discuss their choice of words.

**Curriculum objectives**
● In narratives, to create settings, characters and plot.

**Resources**
Media resource 'Aliens' on the CD-ROM; photocopiable page 137 'Alien fact file'

# 4: Create an alien

## Introduction
● Begin with starter activity 3 'Vocabulary builder', using the words *spaceship, tentacle, antennae, interplanetary* and *slime*.

## Whole-class work
● Look again at the media resource 'Aliens' on the CD-ROM, and recap on the work from lessons 1 and 2 and explain that they are to create their own alien, which they must consider from a practical perspective. In other words, they must offer reasons for *why* it has the features and attributes they have chosen to give it (such as an eye on a stalk for looking over high walls).
● Display photocopiable page 137 'Alien fact file', and in discussion complete it for a member of the class or perhaps yourself (after all, we would be aliens elsewhere...). Use this as an opportunity to model good language and ideas.

## Independent work
● Distribute the photocopiable sheet and ask the children to complete it.

> **Differentiation**
> ● To support learning prompt children to visualise the alien arriving at their school and imagine how it would react and behave.
> ● Challenge children to take their creation further and write some background to their alien's life on the reverse of the fact file.

## Review
● Don't share children's work at this stage (this happens in lesson 5), only review. In particular, does their physical description use expanded noun phrases, and do they explain what its features are used for?

**Curriculum objectives**
● To compose and rehearse sentences orally (including dialogue), progressively building a varied and rich vocabulary and an increasing range of sentence structures (see Appendix 2).
● To extend the range of sentences with more than one clause by using a wider range of conjunctions.

**Resources**
Completed photocopiable page 137 'Alien fact file' (from week 1, lesson 4)

# 5: Alien chatter

## Introduction
● Begin the lesson with starter activity 7 'Conjunction challenge' using sentences about an alien of your own creation. Try using cues from photocopiable page 137 'Alien fact file', for example *My alien eats sausage...*
● Try to elicit extended sentences using a small range of conjunctions.

## Paired work
● Ensuring that everyone has their alien templates from yesterday, explain that the children are going to imagine that their aliens have both travelled to Earth separately, and by amazing coincidence they have met each other.
● Their task is to work together to develop a dialogue between the two aliens, using and misusing English as they see fit to create something humorous.
● Prompts to encourage conversation might include:
  ● get to know each other
  ● find out information about things that humans do
  ● plan a way to get home
  ● go in search of food.

> **Differentiation**
> ● Support children by allowing them act out the dialogue.
> ● Challenge children to relate the dialogue in the third person.

## Review
● Gather the class together and ask for volunteers to enact their dialogues, asking the viewers to consider how well these reflect the apparent personalities of their aliens.

# Week 2 lesson plans

Instructions are the focus of this week; specifically with reference to helping aliens to understand what to do on Earth should they ever come here. Initially children have to read instructions and convert them to pictures, considering carefully how the language is used. Next they must create their own set of instructions for an everyday task. The middle of the week has a discreet lesson focusing on the spelling of /shun/ words, followed by considering more complex instructions and guidance for everyday situations, which children first address through mime and gesture, finishing with written pieces for *The Intergalactic Traveller's Guide*.

## I: Non-verbal instructions

### Introduction
● Watch the video 'Making a cake' on the CD-ROM. Play it through a second time pausing after each step to discuss what is happening at each point.
● Talk about the language you would use in creating instructions for making a cake, particularly the use of imperative commands *do this, do that*, and so on.

### Whole-class work
● Display photocopiable page 138 'How to make toast' and read through the instructions in each box. Point out the numbered stages and the features of the language, such as imperative verbs.
● In discussion, consider what would be the best thing to draw in the first box, and model the level of detail you wish children to work at.

### Paired work
● Explaining the time allowed (around 15 minutes), distribute the photocopiable sheet to pairs of children, ask them to discuss and then illustrate the captions effectively and efficiently.
● Once time is up, ask pairs to share their work with others, and then briefly discuss the process and their outcomes. Ask: *Would your sketches be useful?*

### Independent work
● For the second half of the lesson, explain that children will be working alone to provide drawn instructions for an everyday task, which must include no words whatsoever.
● Discuss possible tasks that the children might illustrate (in a maximum of eight sketches), filtering out any that are too difficult, and noting good ideas.
● Possible tasks for illustration include:
  ● writing and sending a letter
  ● doing the washing up
  ● ordering a pizza to be delivered
  ● getting washed and cleaning teeth before bed.

> **Differentiation**
> ● For children who struggle with the concept of this work you may find it preferable to provide a set of illustrations to one of the tasks mentioned and have them organise it in the correct order.

### Review
● Once their illustrations are complete, ask children to look at each other's work and, before giving feedback, provide a sentence for what each illustration represents, such as *4. Put the pillows in the pillow cases.*
● Allow time for children to tweak their illustrations to try and make them less ambiguous, then gather the class together and discuss the task, asking: *What was the hardest part? Why can things be misinterpreted? What would you do to improve your pictures further?*

# 2: Written instructions

## Introduction

● Work through interactive activity 'Sequencing instructions' on the CD-ROM with the class.
● Next, watch the video 'Making a cake' on the CD-ROM. Play it through a second time, pausing after each step to note the instruction for that point. Model written instructions, including numbered steps, for the whole task, reinforcing the use of imperative commands, such as *do this*, *do that*, and so on.

## Independent work

● Review the children's work from lesson 1, particularly the list of instructions for making toast and the children's other drawn instructions.
● Displaying photocopiable page 138 'How to make toast', draw the class's attention to finer aspects of the language, such as words *begin* and *next*, as well as adding safety warnings and a conclusion.
● Challenge the children to write a list of numbered steps for their chosen task from lesson 1. They can use their drawings to help them if desired.

> **Differentiation**
> ● Support learning by writing the instructions as captions on the work from week 1.
> ● To extend children's learning, ask them to write instructions for preparing and cooking a simple meal, using sub-categories for different types of task.

## Review

● Working in pairs, ask the children to review each other's instructions, providing constructive feedback and pointing out errors and inconsistencies. In particular, ask them to check for the use of imperative verbs.

# 3: /shun/ words

## Introduction

● Write /shun/, '-tion', '-ssion', '-sion' and '-cian' on the board. Reinforce the difference between the spelling patterns and the pronunciation.
● Open the interactive activity '/shun/ words' on the CD-ROM on the board and work through it with the class.

## Independent or paired work

● Distribute photocopiable page 139 '/shun/ words' and ask children to look carefully at the root words and how they change to make a /shun/ word. They should write what they notice, looking for rules and patterns. Encourage them to note these rules if possible.
● When ready, discuss the work done so far and consider the rules and variations they have seen.
● Dictate five or six sentences containing /shun/ words and ask the children to try and write them down correctly.

> **Differentiation**
> ● To avoid overwhelming some children, focus only on the most common spelling pattern ('-tion') and provide a range of words for them to learn.

## Review

● Gather the class and reinforce the rules for /shun/ words:
  ● '-tion' is the most common spelling for root words ending in 't' or 'te'
  ● '-ssion' is used if the root word ends in 'ss' or 'mit'
  ● '-sion' is used if the root word ends in 'd' or 'se'
  ● '-cian' is used if the root word ends in 'c' or 'cs'.

**Curriculum objectives**
● To discuss and record ideas.
● In non-narrative material, to use simple organisational devices.

**Resources**
List of everyday tasks, such as going to the shops (not provided)

# 4: The alien's guide to everyday situations

## Introduction

● With the class watching in silence, mime some everyday actions, such as eating a banana. For each action, ask the class to identify the steps involved in the procedure.
● Discuss what makes body language effective (strong poses, clear gestures, facial expressions).

## Group work

● Organise the children into groups and provide a list of specific events: *how to shop at the supermarket*, *how to behave in school*, and so on.
● Explain that you want groups to plan and create a series of tableaux (freeze-frames) with no spoken words to convey the actions and etiquette of the situation to a non-English speaking alien. *What should they do? What shouldn't they do?* They can use sign language if desired.
● Point out that they can imagine this task as a human storyboard.
● Review each group's non-verbal instructions, firstly as a mime and then with each child explaining their role in the sequence.
● To conclude, ask the groups to write a heading for each section of their instructions.

## Review

● Gather the class and review their scene titles, explaining that these are effectively the themes of paragraphs for longer, written pieces.

**Curriculum objectives**
● In non-narrative material, to use simple organisational devices.
● To organise paragraphs around a theme.

**Resources**
Short non-fiction text (not provided); completed headings (from week 2, lesson 4); completed photocopiable page 139 '/shun/ words' (from week 2, lesson 3)

# 5: *The Intergalactic Space Traveller's Guide*

## Introduction

● Display a short non-fiction text on the board, ensuring that there are three or four paragraphs available. Read the piece together then talk with the class to elicit the theme of each paragraph. Write these themes above or next to each paragraph.

## Group work

● Arranging the children in the same groups as in lesson 4, ask them to review or rewrite their lists of headings.

## Independent work

● Explain that an intergalactic publisher would like you all to produce a guide for them about these everyday situations. They will translate the English into many alien languages.
● As such, children must write a few small paragraphs explaining what to do and how to behave in everyday situations.
● There are two main requirements: firstly, children must organise the text clearly and logically; secondly, they must use /shun/ words, as intergalactic translators love these words and will pay extra every time they see one used (and spelled) correctly! Let them refer to their completed photocopiable page 139 '/shun/ words' if they desire.

## Review

● Ask for volunteers to share their work and focus on how they have structured their text. Do they use paragraphs effectively, and does their language help to clarify the situations they describe?

# Week 3 lesson plans

This week moves on to work based around empathising with a lost alien: Beegu. Although a picture book, *Beegu* is full of lovely ideas that provide many starting points for discussion and literacy development. After discussing and summarising the story, children move on to inferring characters' thoughts and feelings. Then, after discrete work on spelling and clauses, children write a diary entry for Beegu.

## 1: *Beegu*

### Introduction

● Start the lesson by looking at the front and back cover of *Beegu*. Ask the class to use appropriate adjectives to describe Beegu and her features.
● Ask what the images on the front suggest about the setting, and why Beegu is looking at the leaf.
● Looking at the back cover, focus on the change in posture and expression in Beegu and what this might mean. What about the speech bubble?
● Talk about alien work from previous lessons. Ask: *Does this book feel the same or different?*
● Briefly discuss the style of illustration. Ask: *How have the pictures been made, and does this add to the impact of the text?*

### Whole-class work

● Share the whole book with the class, carefully considering the text and images to infer what Beegu is feeling at different points of the story. Infer why the adults in the story are reacting to Beegu in the way that they do, and how this appears to differ from the children Beegu meets.
● Encourage the children to ask questions about the text to help them uncover their thoughts.
● Beegu's speech bubble in the first three illustrations is the same as the one on the back cover of the book. Discuss what it might mean.

### Independent work

● Distribute photocopiable page 'Beegu's tale' from the CD-ROM, which contains the final speech bubble showing Beegu explaining her adventure to her parents. Look at this with the class and discuss the images in it.
● Tell the children that you want them to write a summary of Beegu from memory, but using the pictures in the speech bubble to help them, as best they can.
● Explain they can write in whatever way they wish, but they may find that creating a numbered list of the events will be easiest.

> **Differentiation**
> ● Support learners by numbering the events in the speech bubble and provide a numbered list that corresponds to this.
> ● Challenge children, in addition to the summary, to write Beegu's feelings for each event listed.

### Review

● Initially, ask children to share their work with each other and discuss their ideas, offering constructive feedback as per your usual procedures.
● Next re-read the story, asking the class to check their summaries as you read. Use this as an opportunity to reinforce the various emotions involved, both for Beegu and the human characters.
● To conclude, discuss the final pages of the book, where Beegu describes the older people as *unfriendly*, but the smaller ones as *hopeful*. Ask: *What does she mean by 'hopeful'?*

---

**Expected outcomes**
● All children will summarise *Beegu*, develop their understanding of suffixes and clauses and write an empathetic letter.
● Most children will write a letter using clauses to good effect.
● Some children will use new spellings and clauses to construct extended sentences.

**Curriculum objectives**
● To listen to and discuss a wide range of fiction, poetry, plays, non-fiction and reference books or textbooks.
● To ask questions to improve their understanding of a text.
● In non-narrative material, to use simple organisational devices.

**Resources**
*Beegu* by Alexis Deacon; photocopiable page 'Beegu's tale' from the CD-ROM

---

**Curriculum objectives**
● To compose and rehearse sentences orally (including dialogue), progressively building a varied and rich vocabulary and an increasing range of sentence structures (see Appendix 2).

**Resources**
Media resource 'Emotions' on the CD-ROM

# 2: Other characters

## Introduction

● Open the images 'Emotions' on the CD-ROM and discuss the different images. Eliciting or providing vocabulary, build up a bank of words for the emotions that the faces are suggesting.
● Ask for volunteers to create sentences explaining each word, such as *I think he/she is sad because...*, and also to suggest when they themselves feel that way, such as *I was happy when...*

## Paired work

● Look through *Beegu* again, focusing on the man at the stray dogs' home, and the teacher in the school. Consider their statements, expressions and actions.
● Ask the children to work in pairs to discuss each adult and their actions, and to put together two short statements explaining why they think each adult behaved as they did.
● Explain that each statement should have four parts to it:
  ● what job the adult had
  ● how they reacted to Beegu
  ● why the adult did this
  ● their opinion about the adult's actions and the consequences.
● The statements should be composed orally, but if time permits, encourage pairs to write down their thoughts.

## Review

● Gather the class together and briefly discuss the adults' actions. Ask: *Did anyone feel that the adults actually helped Beegu? What would you have done if you had discovered her?*

**Curriculum objectives**
● To use further prefixes and suffixes and understand how to add them (Appendix 1).
● To write from memory simple sentences, dictated by the teacher, that include words and punctuation taught so far.
● To learn the grammar for Year 3 in Appendix 2.
● To use and understand the grammatical terminology in Appendix 2 accurately and appropriately when discussing their writing and reading.

# 3: Adding suffixes with vowels

## Introduction

● Begin with starter activity 2 'Getting technical' for the terms *consonant*, *vowel*, *suffix* and *word family*.

## Whole-class work

● Write a range of root words on the whiteboard that take suffixes with vowels to form new words, such as *begin*, *cry*, *forget*, *open*, *prefer*, *sleep* and *suppose*. Also write up the suffixes '-ing', '-ed' and '-er'. Ask the children to create word families using the words and suffixes provided.
● After a while, ask for words, and compile lists on the board.
● Ask if anyone notices any unusual changes in spelling, and offer an initial explanation as to why this occurs. (If the last syllable of a word is stressed and ends with one consonant letter that has just one vowel letter before it, the final consonant letter is doubled when an ending that begins with a vowel letter is added.)
● Remind the class that although the rule is complicated, the words considered today can be learned with your usual classroom approaches to spelling.

## Independent work

● Dictate a small range of sentences including forms of the words used with the relevant suffixes, such as *Beegu was lost at the beginning*.

## Review

● Ask children to check each other's work and note incorrect spellings of the focus words. Remind the children of the rules involved, modelling the correct technical language.

## Curriculum objectives
● To extend the range of sentences with more than one clause by using a wider range of conjunctions.
● To use and understand the grammatical terminology in Appendix 2 accurately and appropriately when discussing their writing and reading.

## Resources
Interactive activity 'Joining clauses' on the CD-ROM; photocopiable page 141 'Clauses'

# 4: Clauses

## Introduction
● Open interactive activity 'Joining clauses' on the CD-ROM on the board and work through it with the class, recapping on the difference between a sentence and a clause.
● Take time to explain the terms *simple*, *compound* and *complex*, using examples to clarify this (there are some on photocopiable page 141 'Clauses').
● Also explain the terms *main clause* and *subordinate clause*.

## Independent work
● Distribute the photocopiable sheet and ask children to complete it.

## Whole-class work
● Review the children's work on clauses, working in order through their work on simple, compound and complex sentences. Use this opportunity to remind the class about conjunctions and their role in joining clauses.

### Differentiation
● To support learning, write different clauses and conjunctions on separate pieces of card and ask children to arrange them to make complete sentences. Then try to consider sentence and clause types.

## Review
● To conclude, write a range of conjunctions on the board, such as *and*, *because*, *but*, *for*, *never*, *or*, *so*, *that*, *until* and *when*. Then return children's attention to *Beegu*. Prompt them to complete sentences using clauses by providing openings, such as *Beegu was sad...* and *Beegu was lost...* Challenge children to create compound or complex sentences using different conjunctions.

## Curriculum objectives
● To draw inferences such as inferring characters' feelings, thoughts and motives from their actions, and justifying inferences with evidence.
● To extend the range of sentences with more than one clause by using a wider range of conjunctions.

## Resources
Completed photocopiable page 'Beegu's tale' from the CD-ROM

# 5: Beegu's diary

## Introduction
● Remind children of the work done on clauses from the previous lesson, and how they can be used to make longer and more interesting sentences.
● Recap the closing activity from lesson 4, creating compound or complex sentences using conjunctions based on initial prompts such as *Beegu was lost...*

## Independent work
● Ensuring that children have to hand their work on photocopiable page 'Beegu's tale' from the CD-ROM, recap on the story as desired.
● Model a typical diary entry based on the opening page: *I was lost because my spaceship crashed.*
● Ask the children to imagine that they are Beegu. Now that they are home safe and sound, they want to write a diary entry explaining how they were feeling at different points of the story.
● Explain that children can write the diary entry as a list of sentences, or as flowing prose.

### Differentiation
● Challenge the children to use at least six different conjunctions in their diary entry, and ask them to underline any subordinate clauses once they have finished.

## Review
● Challenge the children to find two examples in their writing where two sentences can be combined using a connective indicating time or cause.
● Consider if children can improve their vocabulary to create greater empathy.

# Week 4 lesson plans

Lessons for this week stem from the Michael Morpurgo novel, *King of the Cloud Forests*. This is used to explore the feeling of being alien for a human, which children explore further via imagined dialogues and diaries. These lessons are used to look at a text in detail and to consider how the senses are used in evocative descriptions, recap on inverted commas and further develop children's use of the perfect form and conjunctions. It is not essential to read the book to the class, but if there is scope to do this it would be beneficial. The opening lesson provides a synopsis of the book and an excerpt.

## 1: The *King of the Cloud Forests*

### Introduction
● Begin with starter activity 2 'Getting technical', adapted for the terms *yeti*, *cloud forest*, *Himalayas*, *Tibet*, and *Buddhist*.
● Display photocopiable page 140 '*King of the Cloud Forests* synopsis' and read through it together. Discuss the main points of each paragraph, and work with the class to reduce the synopsis to a sentence or two (orally or written).
● If you want to, read extracts from the book, though not beyond Chapter 5.
● Use a globe or map to investigate the setting of the story – where the main character has travelled from and to.
● Use reference books or the internet to provide images and information to allow you to discuss the Himalayas and Tibet. Look also at China and India and consider distances relative to the UK.

### Whole-class work
● Distribute photocopiable page '*King of the Cloud Forests* extract' from the CD-ROM, and explain that the task is to highlight any language that evokes sensation or describes characters or setting.
● After a while discuss the children's findings and clarify any meanings.
● Focus on Ashley's senses, and elicit sentences that stem from each of them.
● Ask the class to imagine they were Ashley and imagine how he must have felt. Ask: *What do you think the yetis are doing? Who is Leelee?*
● Remind the children that 'alien' also has a meaning as an adjective: *belonging to another country; feeling unfamiliar or strange*. Discuss what might make Ashley 'feel alien' in the yeti's cave.
● Prompting if necessary, discuss the factors that might make any of us feel alien: language, customs, appearances and unfamiliarity. If any of the class has had this experience, talk about it and how they felt. Discuss what might make such feelings go away. Remember to be sensitive to children's experiences.

### Paired work
● Ask the pairs to draw the scene from the extract, referencing the highlighted words in their text such as *smell of smoke* and *flickering glow*, labelling where they have created an illustration of the text.

> **Differentiation**
> ● Support learning by talking through the meaning of more complex language in the extract and offering simpler alternatives.
> ● Extend the task by asking the children to add further illustration and descriptive words of their own for the setting and characters.

### Review
● Gather the class together and ask the children to share their sketches with each other, taking turns to explain their illustrations. Recap on the descriptive language used and consider how the senses can be used to help convey descriptions and feelings.

## 2: Describing with the senses

### Introduction
● Writing a suitable passage on the board, begin with starter activity 10 'Being descriptive'. Discuss the use of vocabulary that considers the senses in helping to create images in our minds.

### Whole-class work
● Re-read photocopiable page 'King of the Cloud Forests extract' from the CD-ROM and discuss the vocabulary that was considered in lesson 1, reminding the class of the use of the senses in evoking feelings and sensations in texts.
● Writing the five words sight, smell, touch, hearing and taste on the board, brainstorm words that might be used to evoke these senses and note them accordingly. (Remember that nouns and verbs are as valid as adjectives here.)

### Independent work
● Either prompting the class with chosen scenarios or allowing them to choose their own, ask them to describe the experience of encountering a room or place for the first time, evoking as many senses as possible.

> **Differentiation**
> ● To support children, ask them to simply list five sentences describing the place through each of their senses.
> ● To challenge more confident learners, forbid the use of direct references to senses or their attributes (such as listen/sounded and smell/smelt).

### Review
● Have volunteers read their work aloud, using intonation and expression to heighten their descriptions. Ask the listeners to spot references to the senses.

---

## 3: Imaginary conversation

### Introduction
● Using speech bubbles, recap the use of these for recording speech, and then transcribe this as a short conversation using direct speech.

### Paired work
● Using photocopiable page 'King of the Cloud Forests extract' from the CD-ROM to remind children of the theme of King of the Cloud Forests, explain that you want them to imagine that the main character, Ashley, has left the yetis and has been reunited with his Uncle Sung. Remind them also that Sung is a Tibetan Buddhist and had heard of the yetis, though had never seen them.
● Ask the children to orally develop a conversation between the two characters, with Uncle Sung asking questions and Ashley responding. (If the class are not familiar with the rest of the book allow them to invent sensible facts.) In particular, request that descriptive language is used, as well as exploring how Ashley felt.
● After a while, ask pairs to note the essence of their conversation, then work towards recording it as direct speech – either independently or still in pairs.

> **Differentiation**
> ● To support the task provide cue cards for question prompts, aimed at eliciting descriptive language about how Ashley felt.

### Review
● Have volunteers enact their conversations, drawing attention to good descriptions and effective exploration of Ashley's feelings. Transcribe some lines on the board to reinforce the use of punctuation for direct speech.

---

### Curriculum objectives
● To discuss writing similar to that which they are planning to write in order to understand and learn from its structure, grammar and vocabulary.
● To read aloud their own writing, to a group or the whole class, using appropriate intonation and controlling the tone and volume so that the meaning is clear.

### Resources
Photocopiable page 'King of the Cloud Forests extract' from the CD-ROM

---

### Curriculum objectives
● To use and punctuate direct speech.
● To compose and rehearse sentences orally (including dialogue), progressively building a varied and rich vocabulary and an increasing range of sentence structures (see Appendix 2).

### Resources
Photocopiable page 'King of the Cloud Forests extract' from the CD-ROM

---

**Curriculum objectives**
● To identify main ideas drawn from more than one paragraph and summarise these.
● To organise paragraphs around a theme.

**Resources**
Photocopiable page 'Roald Dahl biography' from the CD-ROM (optional); photocopiable page 140 'King of the Cloud Forests synopsis'; direct speech work (from week 4, lesson 3)

# 4: Planning a diary entry

## Introduction

● Display a short text (such as photocopiable page 'Roald Dahl biography' from the CD-ROM) and, in discussion with the class, summarise each paragraph as a single brief sentence. Recap on how paragraphs are used to structure texts.

## Independent work

● Recap on photocopiable page 140 'King of the Cloud Forests synopsis' and the children's imagined dialogue with Uncle Sung, and discuss the experience of Ashley and how this would make him feel alien.
● Ask the children to plan one or more diary entries for Ashley while living with the yetis, listing the themes for each paragraph.
● Explain that they will need to give their entries a good structure, as well as recounting events and experiences.
● If you prefer, ask children to invent one or more diary entries for themselves instead – either with yetis or in a situation where they feel alien.
● Explain that when the children have finished their plan they should start considering vocabulary that will evoke their feelings and emotions, as per previous lessons in this chapter.

### Differentiation
● To support the task, initiate a discussion covering imagined aspects of life with the yetis, listing actions and tasks as appropriate.

## Review
● Review children's plans and ensure that they present a solid structure for their diary entries.

**Curriculum objectives**
● To use conjunctions, adverbs and prepositions to express time and cause.
● To use the present perfect form of verbs in contrast to the past tense.
● To organise paragraphs around a theme.

**Resources**
Photocopiable page 140 'King of the Cloud Forests synopsis'; diary planning (from week 4, lesson 4)

# 5: Writing a diary entry

## Introduction

● Explain that everyone will shortly be writing diary entries for Ashley (or otherwise if desired), and how the perfect form along with time and cause words is very effective for such a text.
● To begin the lesson do starter activity 9 'The perfect form' using a selection of sentences relating to everyday tasks (if desired these can relate to King of the Cloud Forests).

## Independent work

● Remind the class of the work they have done so far on King of the Cloud Forests and about feeling alien, using photocopiable page 140 'King of the Cloud Forests synopsis' if necessary.
● With everyone's diary plans from lesson 4 to hand, explain that the main task for this session is to use the plan to help write a diary entry that conveys a sense of 'feeling alien'. Review the sort of vocabulary that might aid such an entry, as well as using paragraphs to structure writing.

### Differentiation
● To extend the task, ask children to include the writer's inner life – thoughts on themselves, loved-ones and what might come next.

## Review
● Ask the class to rate their own work for paragraph structure, then, organising the children in pairs, ask them to share their diary entries with one another, acting as 'critical friends' to spot good language and vocabulary, sharing contributions that convey a sense of 'feeling alien'.

# Week 5 lesson plans

This week focuses on creating and presenting plays in the theme of 'feeling alien'. In particular, it considers how stories can be told by small casts using props, puppets and simple narration. Teachers are encouraged to source local drama companies who specialise in such children's theatre, or at the least videos of such performances. The main task for the children is to work in pairs to produce a short play for younger children, producing initial plans then fleshing these out through oral improvisation, and then converting this work into a playscript, which is performed at the end of the week. There is also a discrete lesson on the '-ation' suffix.

## 1: Planning a play

### Expected outcomes
● All children will draft and perform plays about 'feeling alien' through collaboration, oral composition and improvisation.
● Most children will use vocabulary and sentences to evoke empathy.
● Some children will use ideas, techniques and vocabulary that evoke empathy and hold an audience's attention.

### Curriculum objectives
● In non-narrative material, to use simple organisational devices.
● To prepare poems and playscripts to read aloud and to perform, showing understanding through intonation, tone, volume and action.

### Resources
Video or actual performance of children's play (optional); selection of children's picture books around the theme of being alien or lost, such as *Beegu* by Alexis Deacon; *The Way Back Home* by Oliver Jeffers, or *Cloudland* by John Burningham; photocopiable page 142 'Play planning template'

### Introduction
● Tell the class that this week they will be creating short plays based on the theme of 'feeling alien' or alone, recapping on previous weeks' work to exemplify this as necessary.
● If possible, show children a live or video performance of a scene or whole play for younger children. Discuss the themes and how the play presents them, focusing in particular on any use of props or puppets.
● Present and discuss the range of ways of representing stories – acting, mime, puppetry or animation.

### Whole-class work
● Introduce the class to the picture books you have collated around the theme of feeling alien or lost, sharing and discussing them as appropriate.
● Brainstorm ideas for how the books might be converted into plays for younger children, discussing, in particular, the use of props to support storytelling, and the use of gestures and speech to convey the main theme of 'feeling alien' or alone.

### Paired work
● Distributing photocopiable page 142 'Play planning template', either at your direction or allowing the children to choose, ask them to work in pairs to plan the sort of play that they want to create.
● Before they start working, run through the template with the class, clarifying each section, in particular looking at the last section and considering how stories can be broken down into scenes.

> **Differentiation**
> ● For children who need support, pairing them appropriately, guide them to create a play for *Beegu*, using their own or prepared work about the structure of this book from previous lessons.
> ● To provide significant challenge to those who relish it, explain that each of their scenes must flow seamlessly into the next, providing one continuous retelling.

### Review
● Ask the children to share their plans with each other and explain their intentions, flagging issues and possible problems.
● Focus in particular on how children have broken the story down into scenes. Will this work? Will transitions between scenes be easy?
● To conclude, review any props or materials that children think they will need, assessing feasibility and ensuring they will be able to collate these.

**Curriculum objectives**
● To spell words that are often misspelled (Appendix 1).
● To write from memory simple sentences, dictated by the teacher, that include words and punctuation taught so far.

# 2: The '-ation' suffix

## Introduction
● Begin with starter activity 2 'Getting technical' for the terms *verb*, *noun* and *suffix*.

## Whole-class work
● Explain that the suffix '-ation' is added to verbs to form nouns. Stress that verbs ending in 'e' drop the 'e' when '-ation' is added, and words ending in 'ate' drop the 'e' and take '-ion'.
● Write on the board a range of verbs that can have '-ation' added to form a noun, mixed with verbs that cannot, such as *admire*, *admit*, *adore*, *inform*, *innovate*, *inspire*, *prepare*, *repeat*, *sense* and *think*.
● Spend time looking at the words that do take '-ation' and those that do not, considering changes to spelling and considering meanings. Can the children think of any other words?

## Independent work
● Dictate a small range of sentences including forms of the words used with the '-ation' suffix, such as *There is a difference between adoration and admiration*.

> **Differentiation**
> ● Support learning by providing root words and suffixes on separate cards for children to combine and break down into syllables to aid pronunciation.

## Review
● Ask children to check each other's work and note incorrect spellings of the focus words. Remind the children of the rules involved, modelling the correct technical language.
● Remind the class that although the rule is complicated, the words considered today can be learned with your usual classroom approaches to spelling.

**Curriculum objectives**
● To compose and rehearse sentences orally (including dialogue), progressively building a varied and rich vocabulary and an increasing range of sentence structures (see Appendix 2).

**Resources**
Photocopiable page 'The Twits playscript' from the CD-ROM (optional); completed photocopiable page 142 'Play planning template' (from week 5, lesson 1); video clips of performances of children's plays (optional)

# 3: Improvised scripts

## Introduction
● Remind the children of their work on planning a small play, and introduce them to the following performance checklist – aspects that they need to consider when preparing a play:
  ● using their body: actions, gestures and facial expressions
  ● using their voice: intonation, tone and volume
  ● directing the whole play: organisation, timing and props.
● Using volunteers, reinforce their understanding of each of the above categories, acting out brief vignettes from a known playscript (such as photocopiable page 'The Twits playscript' from the CD-ROM).

## Paired work
● Tell the children that this is the main session for them to create their play, which they will be doing orally. Stress the need for strong vocabulary to engage their audience.
● Allow them plenty time to develop their plays through discussion and improvisation, referring to, and annotating, their plans as necessary.

## Review
● Provide time and space for pairs to explain and present sections of their plays to each other, asking their peers to check that they are meeting the three categories of the performance checklist.
● Gather the class together and discuss successes, problems and solutions.

## Curriculum objectives

● To prepare poems and playscripts to read aloud and to perform, showing understanding through intonation, tone, volume and action.

## Resources

Relevant plans and notes from lessons earlier this week; photocopiable page 'The Twits playscript' from the CD-ROM

# 4: Writing playscripts

## Introduction

● Display photocopiable page 'The Twits playscript' from the CD-ROM, and use it to remind the class of the features of a playscript: the use of a narrator, capital letters to identify speakers, square brackets to separate directions, and so on.
● Discuss how it helps other people to perform the play, and explain that imagining that someone else has to understand it is an effective way of making sure their script is clearly drafted.
● Consider how the majority of the text is, in effect, non-fiction – it is instructions for how the actors should move and talk.

## Paired work

● Arrange the children with their 'play partners' as in earlier lessons.
● Remind the children to stick with the 'type' of play they have been working on. Then, referring to their plans and oral work, ask them to draft their playscript.

### Differentiation

● Challenge children to make sure their script notes acknowledge the performance checklist from lesson 3.

## Review

● Gather the class and review work so far, asking children to look at each other's scripts to assess whether they make sense and could be used by others.
● Allow children time to modify and improve their scripts as desired.

## Curriculum objectives

● To read aloud their own writing, to a group or the whole class, using appropriate intonation and controlling the tone and volume so that the meaning is clear.

## Resources

Play plans and scripts from previous lessons; large space to perform in (optional); video camera (optional)

# 5: 'Feeling alien' plays

## Introduction

● Start the lesson with voice and body warm-up exercises, allowing the children to move around and explore a range of movements and uses of their voice. Prompt them by stating a noun and an adjective, such as chimp – happy or teacher – stern. Ask them to represent this.
● Recap on effective dramatic techniques for clarity and expression when speaking, and the importance of these for creating interesting characters.

## Whole-class work

● Explain that everyone is going to be presenting their short play based on 'feeling alien'.
● Discuss the key elements for an effective performance.
● Depending on space and adult availability, have two separate performances happening at the same time.

### Differentiation

● An additional challenge for children when watching plays is to 'rate' them based on the performance checklist (body, voice and direction). Suggest that those who can manage it, do this discreetly, and that every rating has to have a sensible statement to justify it.

## Review

● If possible, watch video clips of children's performances and, reminding children of the performance checklist from lesson 3, discuss successes and consider further improvements.
● When watching each clip, ask the class to consider how well it conveys its theme of 'feeling alien'.

**Expected outcomes**
● All children will plan their own poems, drafting, editing and presenting it.
● Most children will create their own poems based on a specific idea.
● Some children will create poems in the form of their choosing, incorporating strong vocabulary to good effect.

**Curriculum objectives**
● To listen to and discuss a wide range of fiction, poetry, plays, non-fiction and reference books or textbooks.
● To recognise some different forms of poetry.

**Resources**
Range of alien poetry; photocopiable page 'Aliens Stole My Underpants' from the CD-ROM

# Week 6 lesson plans

The final week of this chapter brings some lighter relief with humorous alien poetry. Initially children experience a wide range of alien poems, ideally from *Aliens Stole My Underpants*, a collection of alien-based poetry compiled by Brian Moses. The poem of this title is provided in this book, but ideally you should have one or more copies of the book to hand as a range of poetry is needed. Children have the opportunity to listen to and discuss poems, in particular focusing on the elements of a specific poem, which they then try to rewrite. After a discrete lesson focusing on the '-ous' suffix, the children must brainstorm their own narrative poems, then draft, edit and present them.

## 1: Alien poetry

### Introduction

● Introduce the book *Aliens Stole My Underpants* by Brian Moses, and deliver a selection of readings to the class, using intonation and expression to full effect. (Avoid reading the title poem for the moment.)
● After each poem, have a quick question and answer session to elicit each poem's focus or intention, and any humorous or interesting words.

### Whole-class work

● Recap the terms *voice*, *form* and *structure* as techniques for understanding poetry:
  ● **Voice:** who is telling the poem, or if it is in the third person.
  ● **Form:** the form of the poem – free verse, rhyming, narrative and so on.
  ● **Structure:** how it will be arranged.
● Reviewing some of the poems that have been read, consider how these elements are addressed in the poems you have read with the class.
● Display photocopiable page 'Aliens Stole My Underpants' from the CD-ROM and elicit that it is more or less a narrative poem with some strange speculations. Explain how these enhance the humour and structure of the poem.

### Paired work

● Arranging the class in pairs, distribute copies of the poem and ask them to make notes around it, highlighting the focus of each verse, underlining rhyming words, and suggesting improvements.
● In particular, ask the children to focus on voice, form and structure.
● After a while, discuss findings, then ask the children to each decide on their favourite verse and prepare to read or recite it to the class. They should also be prepared to explain their reasons for liking it.
● Ask for volunteers to recite a verse they like from the poem, using the opportunity to reinforce the key aspects of delivery – the effective use of intonation and tone. After each recital, allow other groups to ask questions as appropriate. Praise and reinforce effective delivery.
● Next, with children remaining in their pairs, ask them to rewrite one or more verses of the poem from the aliens' point of view, stressing that they can reuse vocabulary and style as much as they wish.

> **Differentiation**
> ● To challenge children's thinking, insist that their rewriting of the poem utilises the same structure and rhyming words as the original.

### Review

● Gather the class and share any rewritten verses as desired. Do these follow the style of the original?
● Return to the poems that you originally read to the class, and start to analyse them more thoroughly. Ask: *Which are narrative poems? What structures do they have? In which voice are they written?*

**Curriculum objectives**
● To spell words that are often misspelled (Appendix 1).
● To write from memory simple sentences, dictated by the teacher, that include words and punctuation taught so far.

**Resources**
Photocopiable page 143 'The '-ous' suffix'

# 2: The '-ous' suffix

## Introduction
● Remind children of the meaning of 'root word' and 'suffix'. Then, writing the word *poison* on the board, demonstrate how adding the suffix '-ous' can create a new word.
● Elicit that *poison* is a noun (or verb) and that *poisonous* is an adjective.

## Independent or paired work
● Explain that various rules are used for making longer words. Stress that no one is expected to learn all of this at once.
● Distribute photocopiable page 143 'The '-ous' suffix' and read the words together.
● Ask children to complete the task on the photocopiable sheet, identifying root words and highlighting which rule each word is governed by.

## Whole-class work
● When the children have completed the main task, ask them to work individually, and dictate a small range of sentences for them to write, each one incorporating one or more words ending in '-ous'.

> **Differentiation**
> ● For support, create cue cards with a range of root words which take '-ous' to form new meanings, as well as distracters, asking children to identify and create new words.
> ● Early finishers should try and think of more words ending in '-ous' and categorise them according to the rules.

## Review
● Gather the class together and review words and rules encountered. Note children who have had some success in spotting the rules.

**Curriculum objectives**
● To discuss writing similar to that which they are planning to write in order to understand and learn from its structure, grammar and vocabulary.
● To discuss and record ideas.

**Resources**
Photocopiable page 'Aliens Stole My Underpants' from the CD-ROM

# 3: Planning poems

## Introduction
● Begin the lesson with starter activity 3 'Vocabulary builder' for a range of words ending in '-ous', either some of those used in lesson 2 or new ones.

## Whole-class work
● Display photocopiable page 'Aliens Stole My Underpants' from the CD-ROM and recap on the key elements discussed in lesson 1.
● Remind children of the voice, form and structure used, and consider whether any verses are not essential to the overall success of the poem.

## Independent or paired work
● Explain that the focus of this session is planning an alien poem (not writing one). The preferred theme is 'alien invasion' in a narrative style, but this is not obligatory.
● Ask the children to brainstorm ideas for the overall 'story' of their poem; the way in which they intend to break it down into verses; and to begin listing any vocabulary and phrases they want to use. Reassure them that taking ideas from other poems is absolutely fine.

## Review
● Gather the class together and ask children to share their work in pairs, discussing their reasons for choosing particular plots and vocabulary. Ask them to review vocabulary choices with each other and discuss alternatives.
● To conclude, share plans as appropriate and reinforce knowledge of poetry styles and strong vocabulary choices.

**Curriculum objectives**
● To discuss and record ideas.
● To prepare poems and playscripts to read aloud and to perform, showing understanding through intonation, tone, volume and action.

**Resources**
Alien poem plans (from week 6, lesson 3)

# 4: Alien poems

## Introduction
● Begin with starter activity 4 'Hard-to-spell words' for a range of words ending in '-ous' – either some of those used in lessons 2 and 3 or new ones.

## Independent work
● Recap on work from the previous days and weeks with the class – remind them of the alien descriptions they have written, the books they have looked at and the plays that they created. In particular, focus on the vocabulary and themes encountered.
● Ask the children to each draft their own alien-invasion poem, using their plans from lesson 3 to help them. Encourage them to use each other for constructive feedback, freely sharing vocabulary and ideas.
● As work progresses, circulate and discuss work with individuals. Where interesting work is emerging stop the class briefly and share good words or lines, discussing why particular work seems effective.

> **Differentiation**
> ● Allow children to avoid rhyme and a tight structure if preferred – the main purpose is to get a good, descriptive narrative across.
> ● Challenge children to use some of their newly learned words ending in '-ous'.

## Review
● Gather the class together and ask children to share their work in pairs, sharing successes and difficulties and discussing strengths and weaknesses. Allow time for children to adjust their work if desired.

**Curriculum objectives**
● To prepare poems and playscripts to read aloud and to perform, showing understanding through intonation, tone, volume and action.

**Resources**
Video camera (optional); completed poems

# 5: Alien poetry day

## Introduction
● As a reminder, model effective intonation for the class, reading the poem of your choice.

## Paired or group work
● Ask the children to work together to practise their poems with each other. Stress that it is enough to practise only a few lines of recital, just to improve intonation.

## Individual work
● Have children read or recite a part of or their entire poem to the class.
● Depending on how you structure child-interaction, this is a good opportunity to allow for constructive feedback to be given peer-to-peer, as with the discussions of poems earlier in the week.
● You can also take this opportunity to reinforce knowledge and understanding of poetry types through highlighting effective work.

> **Differentiation**
> ● Allowing children to read only a part of their poem will help with equal participation, reminding them it is how they deliver their words rather than the quantity that is important.
> ● Demanding a recital rather than a reading will provide a challenge.

## Review
● To conclude, remind children of the different types of poems they have encountered, and discuss what makes an effective poem – it is not just the poem, but how it is delivered.

**Curriculum objectives**
● To learn the grammar for Year 3 in Appendix 2.

**Resources**
Selection of suitable digital texts; children's written work

# Grammar and punctuation: Determiners

## Revise

● Use starter activity 2 'Getting technical' to recap for children what a determiner is (something that changes a noun) and define the difference between definite article (*the*) and indefinite articles (*a*, *an*).
● Look at texts with the class and highlight the articles, considering how meaning changes or is lost by changing definite to indefinite, and vice versa.
● Provide cloze sentences for children to add the appropriate article to.
● Look at texts with the class and highlight the determiners, reinforcing the concept that not only do they modify nouns, but they also precede any other modifiers, such as adjectives. For example:
  ● *It is a very old dog.*
  ● *It is an old dog.*
  ● *It is the old dog I saw yesterday.*

## Assess

● When marking writing, check that indefinite and definite articles are used appropriately, and that *an* is used correctly when followed by a vowel letter. Also, check that *a*, *an* and *the* make sense in context.

## Further practice

● Move children on to considering a larger range of determiners. They can be:
  ● articles (*a*, *an*, *the*)
  ● demonstratives (*this*, *that*, *those*)
  ● possessives (*his*, *hers*, *yours*)
  ● quantifiers (*any*, *every*, *some*)
  ● numerals (*seventy-three*, *five*).
● Use starter activity 13 'A or an?'.

**Curriculum objectives**
● To spell further homophones.

**Resources**
Children's work from week 1; photocopiable page 136 'Homophones'; interactive activity 'Homophones' on the CD-ROM

# Spelling: Spelling homophones

## Revise

● Recap on the meaning of 'homophone' via examples, ensuring that children clearly see the differences in spelling and meaning.
● Try to provide texts that use the homophones correctly in context to help consolidate spelling and meaning.
● Revisit children's work from the chapter, checking the meanings and recapping dictionary usage.
● Provide a selection of sentences, some with incorrect homophones in them. Ask children to check and correct them accordingly.

## Assess

● Using photocopiable page 136 'Homophones' for reference, dictate a range of sentences with homophones in each one, ensuring that partner words are also covered in other sentences.
● Rotate children through the interactive activity 'Homophones' on the CD-ROM, noting scores and errors.

## Further practice

● Where children have problems distinguishing between homophones, it may not be beneficial to push them to memorise them correctly. More importantly, note specific and repeated difficulties and consider the significance to their literacy development.
● To take work further, introduce a range of further homophones and near homophones, such as those on page 116.
● Continue to provide sentences with the new homophones in context to clarify meanings, and ask children to verify these using dictionaries.

## Curriculum objectives
● To recognise some different forms of poetry.
● To prepare poems and playscripts to read aloud and to perform, showing understanding through intonation, tone, volume and action.
● To read aloud their own writing, to a group or the whole class, using appropriate intonation and controlling the tone and volume so that the meaning is clear.

## Resources
Good selection of poetry books; 'This Listeners' by Walter de la Mare; selection of audio or video recordings of poetry recitals; children's own poems

# Reading: Recognising, preparing and performing poems

## Revise
● Throughout any revision of poetry, be sure to use a range of forms, clarifying these as you go.
● Review the key elements of poetry delivery with the class: intonation, tone, volume and action. Model each to help consolidate children's understanding of them. Ideally you should do this regularly using a range of poetry styles.
● When you read to the class, use these key elements for the children to rate your performance. With practice, the children will become adept at assessing you on each criterion.
● To practise poetry readings, take children to an open space and ask them to read to each other across a larger distance, again focusing on volume, tone and intonation.
● Try to have regular poetry readings in class, maybe setting a rota for a poem a day.
● In preparation for the assessment, read the children 'The Listeners' by Walter de la Mare. It is quite tricky, but is an ideal model for an evocative narrative poem.

## Assess
● Try to assess the preparation and delivery of poems separately. While children usually enjoy writing poetry it is often easier to deliver a published poem.
● Your assessment will depend on whether you want to assess children's ability to mimic a poetic style and/or their creative use of language. The key to successful poetry is effective expression, and you may find that children work more easily with less restrictive structures.
● Retaining the 'feeling alien' theme from this chapter, display a photograph of a gloomy, old interior and ask the children to imagine being in the location when something happens to them. Set the class the task of conveying the experience through a poem, and reassure them that rhyming is not important.
● Once the class have had time to plan, draft, edit and finalise their poems, prepare for readings by considering the four qualities that they will be assessed by (intonation, tone, volume and action – you should assess their use of form separately).
● Ideally children's readings or recitals should be videoed so that they can watch and rate themselves and each other, prompting them to identify the different poetic forms used by their peers.

## Further practice
● Writing poetry is hard. Ensure that tasks are focused and well modelled in advance to give children a feel for possible structures. Reading lots of published poetry is the best way to develop an ear for it, while regularly considering form and style.
● Expressive readings can be difficult for less confident children, so try to give them space to practise with only their friends watching, videoing their recitals whenever possible.
● To continue developing confidence, try inviting parents in to listen or have readings in assembly.
● Reading to younger children can also be very beneficial for improving confidence and clarity of speech.
● Look at poems that use alliteration and onomatopoeia to good effect, building up vocabulary banks on display in class.

# Writing: Extended sentences

**Curriculum objectives**
● To compose and rehearse sentences orally (including dialogue), progressively building a varied and rich vocabulary and an increasing range of sentence structures (see Appendix 2).
● To extend the range of sentences with more than one clause by using a wider range of conjunctions.

**Resources**
Photocopiable page 141 'Clauses'; interactive activity 'Joining clauses' on the CD-ROM; completed work on Beegu's diary (from week 3, lesson 5)

## Revise

● Using one or more of the suggestions below will help reinforce the meaning and use of clauses and conjunctions:
  ● Use starter activity 2 'Getting technical' to reinforce the meanings of 'conjunction' and 'clause'.
  ● Use starter activity 7 'Conjunction challenge' to recap on their use.
  ● Use interactive activity 'Joining clauses' for further reinforcement.
  ● Displaying photocopiable page 141 'Clauses', discuss the three different sentence types: simple, compound and complex, and the way each of them uses clauses, in particular the use of subordinate clauses.
  ● Revisit and re-read children's diary entries for Beegu, and highlight correct use of conjunctions and clauses.
● Focusing on vocabulary development, remember that children need to be exposed as much as possible to a wide range of words used in meaningful contexts. Bear in mind that children will probably have 'passive' vocabularies far greater than their 'active' ones. This is fine, but allowing both to keep growing through exposure to and use of rich vocabulary is essential.
  ● Play audio stories whenever possible (and build up a collection in your library).
  ● Use digital voice recorders to allow children plenty of opportunities to compose orally – they usually know many more words than they reveal through writing.
  ● Debate and discuss regularly, ensuring you model good language use all the time.

## Assess

● To assess recognition of conjunctions and clauses provide worksheets with appropriately constructed sentences (as on photocopiable page 141 'Clauses') and ask the children to identify the relevant terms.
● To assess whether children can reproduce this knowledge in a different context, explain that they have been given the task of writing a set of rules for a new school (realistic or fantastic). They must write a list of six to ten rules with a justification in each, using a different conjunction every time.
For example:
  ● *Do not play football on the grass when it is raining.*
  ● *Please walk in the corridors because it is safer.*
● Finally, to assess the development of children's use of vocabulary and sentence construction, set a more open task, asking them to imagine they have been on a perilous journey where they made a brave rescue, discovered a precious treasure, and had a close shave with something nasty. Ask them to write a letter or diary entry explaining how everything happened.

## Further practice

● Look at texts with the class and pick out conjunctions (note that spotting clauses may be harder due to more complex constructions).
● Have a 'conjunction of the day' for a fortnight, and have a display board that children can add sentences to using that conjunction.
● Provide prewritten plays and poems that have strong vocabulary to support practice in using it.
● Provide good, vocabulary-rich model texts to inspire and motivate children.

## Homophones

■ Explain the meaning of each of these words.

| Homophone | Meaning |
|---|---|
| ball | |
| bawl | |
| fair | |
| fare | |
| here | |
| hear | |
| grate | |
| great | |
| groan | |
| grown | |
| medal | |
| meddle | |
| plain | |
| plane | |

I can explain the meanings of homophones.

How did you do?

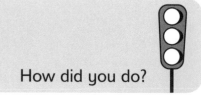

**PHOTOCOPIABLE**     **■SCHOLASTIC** www.scholastic.co.uk

Name: _____  Date: _____

## Alien fact file

■ Use this sheet to create your own alien. Remember to consider the reasons for its features and what benefits these might bring.

Name: _____

Home planet: _____

Distance from Earth: _____

Transport: _____

Favourite food: _____

Favourite drink: _____

Intelligence: _____

Special features: _____

Special skills: _____

Sketch your alien here

Loves: _____ because _____

_____

Hates: _____ because _____

_____

Do say: _____ because _____

_____

Don't say: _____ because _____

_____

Physical description: _____

_____

_____

I can create my own alien.

How did you do?

## How to make toast

■ Instructions are great, but what if an alien cannot read them?
Draw pictures to explain these instructions.

| | |
|---|---|
| **1.** To begin, collect all the things you need: bread, toaster, knife, butter. | **2.** Next, put the slice of bread in the toaster. |
| **3.** Carefully turn the dial on the toaster to the right temperature. | **4.** Pull the lever down on the toaster. |
| **5.** Wait for the toast to pop up. | **6.** Use a knife to butter the toast. |
| **7.** Cut the toast into two or four pieces with the knife. | **8.** Your toast is ready to eat! |

I can present clear instructions in pictures.

How did you do?

## /shun/ words

■ Look at the /shun/ words below. Write down what you notice about their spellings and how the root words change.

| Root word | Adding /shun/ | What do you notice? |
|---|---|---|
| invent | invention | |
| inject | injection | |
| act | action | |
| hesitate | hesitation | |
| complete | completion | |
| express | expression | |
| discuss | discussion | |
| confess | confession | |
| permit | permission | |
| admit | admission | |
| expand | expansion | |
| extend | extension | |
| comprehend | comprehension | |
| tense | tension | |
| music | musician | |
| electric | electrician | |
| magic | magician | |
| politics | politician | |
| mathematics | mathematician | |

I can understand different rules for making /shun/ words.

How did you do?

## King of the Cloud Forests synopsis

Ashley Anderson lives in China with his father, a Christian missionary. But when the advancing Japanese soldiers threaten their peace, Ashley is forced to flee with his beloved Uncle Sung, a Tibetan Buddhist.

The journey they plan is immense and full of danger. It will take them over the Himalayan Mountains to Tibet, Nepal, and then India. It seems impossible, but it is their only chance. The journey sounds even more dangerous when Uncle Sung tells Ashley about the strange creatures called yetis who are rumoured to live in the mountains.

High in the Himalayas, blizzards strike, and Ashley and Uncle Sung must shelter in a hut without food, where wolves are scratching at the door. Desperately hungry, Uncle Sung tells Ashley to stay in the hut while he goes in search of food.

Ashley senses he is not alone: strange shapes in the snow and hairy faces at the window terrify him. Dying of hunger, he finds himself rescued by the yetis and taken to live with them in a remote cloud forest.

Ashley is cared for by the yetis, but soon realises that they think he is someone very special – a king: "Leelee", as they call him. An old tin containing a pipe, a knife and a photograph tells Ashley that someone else has been here before him, but who can it be, and what do the yetis want from him?

## Clauses

■ Look at the three sentence types below.

| Type | Explanation | Example |
|------|-------------|---------|
| Simple | One clause | Raj ate a pizza. |
| Compound | Two equal clauses | Raj ate a pizza and Jen had some pasta. |
| Complex | Main clause and a subordinate clause | Raj didn't have pudding because he was full. |

■ Complete these simple sentences.

1. Zara went _____.

2. The game was _____.

3. London _____.

■ Using one of these conjunctions, complete the compound sentences below – you can only use each conjunction once.

| or | and | but |
|----|-----|-----|

4. You can catch a train to London _____.

5. The dog slept on the sofa _____.

6. His home-made cola is delicious _____.

■ Using one of these conjunctions, complete the complex sentences below – you can only use each conjunction once.

| when | if | that | because |
|------|-----|------|---------|

7. She put up her umbrella _____.

8. The water was really hot _____.

9. They will never win the cup _____.

10. It was the first time _____.

I can add clauses to make compound and complex sentences.

How did you do?

Name: _____  Date: _____

## Play planning template

■ Use this sheet to plan a play for younger children.

**Play title:** _____.

**Story it is based on:** *Beegu / The Way Back Home / Cloudland*

Other: _____

**Style of play:** acting / mime  with a narrator / finger puppets / stop-frame animation

**Roles (who does what):**

1. _____

2. _____

**Props needed:**

_____

_____.

**Scene-by-scene summary of the story:**

| 1. | 2. | 3. |
|---|---|---|
| 4. | 5. | 6. |

Continue your plan on the other side if you need to.

I can plan a play.

How did you do?

**PHOTOCOPIABLE**   ■SCHOLASTIC
www.scholastic.co.uk

## The '-ous' suffix

- Look at the '-ous' words below.
1. Can you spot the root word for any of them? Underline each one you find.
2. Highlight each of the five rules at the bottom of the page a different colour. Then highlight each word you can find that belongs to that rule the same colour.

mountainous   famous   curious   obvious

dangerous   outrageous

courageous

courteous   poisonous

tremendous   vigorous

jealous   humorous

serious

hideous

glamorous   enormous   various   spontaneous

---

**Rules**
- Sometimes the root word is obvious and the usual rules apply for adding suffixes beginning with vowel letters, such as dropping **'e'**, and **'y'** becomes **'i'**.
- Sometimes there is no obvious root word.
- **'-our'** is changed to **'-or'** before **'-ous'** is added.
- A final **'e'** must be kept if the **/j/** sound of **'g'** is to be kept.
- If there is an **/ee/** sound before the **'-ous'** ending, it is usually spelled as **'i'** (but a few words have **'e'**).

---

I can identify the rules for adding the '-ous' suffix.

How did you do?

# Chocolate

The ideal topic for children (and maybe teachers), 'chocolate' mixes non-fiction with fantasy through researching the history and production of chocolate, and moving on to the ever-popular *Charlie and the Chocolate Factory*. After delivering presentations on chocolate in week 1, children investigate the central characters of Dahl's classic in week 2. Week 3 moves on to consider Dahl's use of vocabulary to evoke the deliciousness of chocolate and sweets, preparing the class for weeks 4 and 5, where they will be creating their very own fantasy chocolate products, listing ingredients and then scripting and performing adverts for them. The chapter concludes with confectionery-focused poetry, including readings, recitals and looking at a real-life chocolate poet. (Note that in week 5 children will study chocolate product wrappers, so ask them to start collecting these from week 1.)

## Expected prior learning

- Can use headings to locate information.
- Recognise the themes found in the work of Roald Dahl.
- Can use inference skills.
- Can break down words into syllables to aid spelling.
- Can use inverted commas to record direct speech.
- Familiar with /shin/ spellings.
- Familiar with *Charlie and the Chocolate Factory*.
- Aware of advertising.
- Can appreciate the basic features of poetry.

## Overview of progression

- The chapter combines an emphasis on two quite different skills: researching and presenting information, and effective speaking and reading. Embedded in all the tasks surrounding these skills is an ongoing emphasis on exploring and understanding texts' contents and meanings. As such, the work on grammar and spelling is relatively light, although several tasks (and the end of chapter assessment) require high-quality written pieces.

## Creative context

- This chapter brings together history and geography in understanding the origins and manufacture of chocolate.
- Lessons will also involve aspects of art, design and ICT in creating new chocolate wrappers and video advertisements.

## Preparation

At least one copy of *Charlie and the Chocolate Factory* by Roald Dahl will be needed, and a wide range of books about chocolate, its types, history and production are needed for some lessons. It is recommended that you use online videos and photographs to explore the making of chocolate, though you should check these before using them in class.

### You will also need:

Dictionaries; the internet; a globe or atlas; range of information books (real or digital) that exemplify good layout; word cards (optional); structured writing frames (optional); access to a large indoor space; video camera (optional); percussion instruments (optional); A5 paper; coloured pens and pencils; a selection of televised adverts (these can be sourced from the internet); naturally, you will need access to real chocolate on more than one occasion!

### On the CD-ROM you will find:

Media resources 'Chocolate production', 'Emotions', 'Chocolate packaging'; interactive activity 'Correcting work'; photocopiable pages 'Roald Dahl biography', 'Willy Wonka's invitation', 'Oompa-Loompa song', 'Sweets poems', 'Chocolate poems'

# Chapter at a glance

An overview of the chapter. For curriculum objective codes, please see pages 8–10.

| Week | Lesson | Curriculum objectives | Summary of activities | Outcomes |
|------|--------|----------------------|----------------------|----------|
| 1 | 1 | RC: 10, 13 | Prepare to research chocolate, working in groups to plan questions and tasks. | • Can ask questions about a text and to prepare for intended research. |
| | 2 | RWR: 1 RC: 13, 15 | Research and present summarised information to their groups, identifying and explaining new words. | • Can research information for a specified topic. |
| | 3 | WC: 3, 4 | Prepare a presentation using text, images and oral delivery. | • Can prepare a presentation for a specific topic. |
| | 4 | WT: 6 | Consolidate understanding of words ending in '-sure' and '-ture'. | • Can understand, classify and spell new words in context. |
| | 5 | WC: 10 | Deliver and assess each other's presentations. | • Can research and present on a topic. |
| 2 | 1 | RC: 4, 13 | Discuss and summarise the opening chapters of *Charlie and the Chocolate Factory*, considering Roald Dahl's range, style, characters and situations. | • Can recognise the themes and style of an author. |
| | 2 | RC: 11 | Infer traits of characters from the story and predict how this will manifest itself in later chapters. | • Can infer character attributes and suggest consequences. |
| | 3 | RC: 11 WC: 3, 19 | Investigate the way that the different characters speak and write an imagined dialogue for them. | • Can infer character traits through speech and invent new speech for them. |
| | 4 | RC: 7, 9 WC: 1 | Explore and discuss Willy Wonka's invitation, and then write a reply. | • Can adapt writing style to suit purpose and occasion. |
| | 5 | RC: 11, 13 | Explore the chapters about entering the chocolate factory and improvise mimes to convey character emotions. | • Can interpret character actions and emotions in different scenarios. |
| 3 | 1 | RC: 6, 9, 13 | Continue reading and discussing the story, taking time to practise recitals of parts of an Oompa-Loompa rhyme. | • Can summarise events and recite passages with appropriate tone and intonation. |
| | 2 | RC: 3, 7 WT: 5 | Discovering and creating confectionery-related vocabulary for use in their own writing. | • Can acquire new vocabulary and investigate its meaning. |
| | 3 | RWR: 1 WT: 3, 6 WC: 16 | Revise and practise techniques for learning to spell harder words. | • Can use a range of spelling strategies. |
| | 4 | RC: 1, 11 | Debate the moral of the story and consider whether the outcomes for the five children are reasonable. | • Can reference a text to illustrate their views. |
| | 5 | RC: 5 | Compare *Charlie and the Chocolate Factory* with *George's Marvellous Medicine*, identifying similarities and differences. | • Can compare themes and conventions in books by the same and different authors. |
| 4 | 1 | RC: 13, 15 WC: 3 | Learn about how chocolate is made and research different types of chocolate, creating mini presentations. | • Can adapt research and presentation techniques for smaller tasks. |
| | 2 | RWR: 1 RC: 3 | Research dictionary entries for chocolate-related vocabulary, simplifying and paraphrasing them. | • Can understand the structure and style of a dictionary entry. |
| | 3 | RC: 3 WC: 1 | Analyse the names, wrappers and ingredients of a range of chocolate products. | • Can understand styles of writing used on product wrappers. |
| | 4 | WC: 2, 6 | Plan their own unique chocolate products, thinking about name, slogan, colours, description, ingredients, nutrients, and so on, moving on to design a suitable wrapper. | • Can be creative. |
| | 5 | WC: 9 | Review and finalise their chocolate wrapper designs. | • Can create a design that includes text and can present work to a high standard. |

## Chapter at a glance

| Week | Lesson | Curriculum objectives | Summary of activities | Outcomes |
|------|--------|----------------------|----------------------|----------|
| 5 | 1 | WC: 1, 2 | Looking at a range of adverts. | • Can understand persuasive language. |
| | 2 | WC: 2, 6 | Use vocabulary to plan an advert for a new chocolate product. | • Can plan and organise a short text. |
| | 3 | WC: 3 | Create a script of a TV advert for their chocolate product. | • Can create texts in a given style from a planned structure. |
| | 4 | RC: 6 WC: 7 | Share and discuss their adverts and make suggestions for how the structure and language might be improved. | • Can review writing and suggest meaningful improvements to vocabulary and structure. |
| | 5 | WC: 7, 8 | Perform and evaluate each other's chocolate product adverts. | • Can critically analyse each other's work. |
| 6 | 1 | RC: 7, 8 WC: 1 | Explore the features of poems about confectionery and consider how they have been created. | • Can identify and discuss different poetic forms. |
| | 2 | RC: 15 | Study and respond to information about a poet. | • Can find information in a text. |
| | 3 | RC: 8, 14 WC: 3 | Write a chocolate acrostic poem, then conduct peer and self-reviews, noting effective vocabulary choices and suggesting improvements. | • Can improve their work. |
| | 4 | WT: 7, 8 WC: 7 | Finalise their poems then write them in presentation form. | • Can use cursive script to write legibly. |
| | 5 | WC: 10 | Read or recite their chocolate poems. | • Can deliver a poem using their voice effectively. |

## Background knowledge

**Adjective**: A word used to describe a quality or characteristic. It modifies nouns and complements verbs.

**Direct speech**: The recording of spoken words in a text, typically using inverted commas.

**Morphology**: The make-up of a word, usually its root plus any changes.

**Prefix**: An addition to the start of a root word to make a new word.

**Root word**: The word that is not made up of any other root words, prefixes or suffixes.

**Suffix**: An ending that can be added to a word to modify its class and meaning.

# Week 1 lesson plans

With the focus of this chapter being 'chocolate', the opening week's lessons help children to research and create presentations on the history, trade and manufacture of chocolate at a level suitable to their learning. Developing their research skills, as well as historical and geographical knowledge, children work in groups to develop presentations on how the chocolate we all enjoy today came to be, using books and the internet to aid their research.

A brief overview of the story of chocolate introduces the topic, with activities aimed at reinforcing children's ability to summarise texts, as well as preparing to research the chosen topic. Subsequent lessons are structured to help the class plan, prepare and deliver presentations, with a discrete lesson on spelling words ending in '-sure' and '-ture'.

## Expected outcomes
● All children will research chocolate, creating questions and presenting their findings in a structured manner.
● Most children will represent their research in an interesting and accessible format.
● Some children will develop presentations that present the information an engaging and original way.

## Curriculum objectives
● To identify main ideas drawn from more than one paragraph and summarise these.
● To ask questions to improve their understanding of a text.

## Resources
Large bar of chocolate; photocopiable page 168 'The story of chocolate'; media resource 'Chocolate production' on the CD-ROM; globe or map

## 1: The story of chocolate

### Introduction
● Start as you mean to go on, and bring (ideally) a large bar of chocolate into class. Explaining that incorrect answers do not matter, pose a range of questions to the class about what chocolate is, what it is made of, where it came from, and how it is made. Ask also about the history of chocolate, where it came from originally and for how long it has been eaten.
● Note down suggestions and display them for reference during the week, explaining that by the end of the week we will know the real facts.

### Whole-class work
● Read photocopiable page 168 'The story of chocolate' with the class, initially spotting facts that confirm or correct suggestions made at the start of the lesson. In addition, elicit any words that need clarification and explain them. Using a globe or map, look at the places referenced in the text.
● Next, work through the text carefully and, through discussion, summarise each paragraph. If possible create a single sentence for each one.
● Load the media resource 'Chocolate production' from the CD-ROM and discuss the images in this.
● Finally, return to the text and ask for volunteers to ask questions that have their answer within the text and challenge peers to answer them.

### Group work
● In groups of four, explain that they will be working together to develop a presentation on chocolate. They will need to research information that will help them, as well as plan appropriate tasks for each member of the group.
● Write on the board the categories that groups can research: *The history of chocolate, Where chocolate comes from*. Ask them to research one or both of these categories, allowing groups to choose a focus or instruct them to research particular areas as desired.
● Ask each group to nominate a scribe and come up with a list of questions that they want to find answers to, reminding them of the overview provided by the photocopiable sheet. Explain also that in developing their questions they should allocate research tasks to each member of their group.

---
**Differentiation**
● Support children by organising groups appropriately and ensuring that realistic research tasks are distributed amongst the members.
● Challenge more confident children to research both areas and to use digital technologies for their presentation.
---

### Review
● Gather the groups together again and share research questions, ensuring that they are sticking to the research brief.

## Curriculum objectives
• To retrieve and record information from non-fiction.
• To identify main ideas drawn from more than one paragraph and summarise these.
• To apply their growing knowledge of root words, prefixes and suffixes (etymology and morphology) as listed in Appendix 1, both to read aloud and to understand the meaning of new words they meet.

## Resources
Completed research questions and group task lists (from week 1, lesson 1); range of information books on the history and manufacture of chocolate; internet access; dictionaries; photocopiable page 168 'The story of chocolate' (optional)

# 2: Researching chocolate

## Introduction
• Begin the lesson by using starter activity 3 'Vocabulary builder', including the words *cacao, chocolatl, equator, Montezuma* and *Aztecs*.
• Recap on the intended areas of research as outlined in lesson 1:
  • *The history of chocolate*
  • *Where chocolate comes from*

## Group work
• Explain that in preparation for their presentation, each group has to research their chosen lines of interest, divided up as per their lists. You can use popular websites such as Cadbury or The Story of Chocolate, but always check content before allowing children to access websites. (If you have limited books or internet access this may have to be done as a carousel activity.)
• Request, in particular, that children note and look up new vocabulary as they go, building a list of words beneath their research notes.
• When children are satisfied they have fulfilled their tasks, ask the groups to reconvene and report back to each other on any research they've done, ask questions of each other and clarify words and content as necessary.

> **Differentiation**
> • Children who need support can be guided to specific texts, including photocopiable page 168 'The story of chocolate' and/or be given cloze texts to complete via research.

## Review
• Gather groups together and discuss successes and difficulties, allowing class members to help each other out with missing information. List and clarify any new vocabulary encountered, and consider their next steps.

## Curriculum objectives
• To organise paragraphs around a theme.
• To compose and rehearse sentences orally (including dialogue), progressively building a varied and rich vocabulary and an increasing range of sentence structures (see Appendix 2).

## Resources
Media resource 'Chocolate production' on the CD-ROM; completed research work (from week 1, lesson 2); range of information books (real or digital) that exemplify good layout; internet access; computer access (optional)

# 3: Preparing a presentation

## Introduction
• Using two or three images (such as the media resource 'Chocolate production' on the CD-ROM), model a very short presentation to the class. Show how images and bullet points provide interest for the audience, while also prompting speakers as to what to say next.
• Briefly discuss what might make presentations memorable and hold an audience's attention. Can children cite examples from real or televised presentations that have interested them?

## Group work
• Ask the groups to plan a structure for a clear presentation of their research, and then create and rehearse their presentations about chocolate.
• Challenge the class to find interesting images for their presentations and talk about what might be a good caption for each image. Also remind them to clarify the meaning of any new or unusual vocabulary.
• Suggest that groups practise their presentations as they go, reminding them that short and snappy is best.

> **Differentiation**
> • To ensure equal participation, provide a range of tasks for children: typing, summarising text, collating images, and so on.
> • To extend groups, challenge them to consider using digital, multimodal texts with hyperlinks to different sections.

## Review
• Work with each group to check their work and organisation, providing support where needed and advice for areas to improve on and practise.

**Curriculum objectives**
● To write from memory simple sentences, dictated by the teacher, that include words and punctuation taught so far.

**Resources**
Dictionaries; word cards to trace over (optional, not provided)

# 4: Spelling words ending with '-sure' and '-ture'

## Introduction
● Read out a range of words that end with '-ture' or '-sure' and ask the class to sort the words according to the endings.
● Use dictionaries to confirm the spelling and meaning of words as required.

## Whole-class work
● Focus on the '-sure' and '-ture' endings of the words, clarifying the pronunciation of each.
● Explain that '-ture' words should not be confused with certain root words that have a '(t)ch' ending with 'er' added, such as *teacher*, *catcher*, and *richer*.
● Closing the interactive activity, dictate a small range of sentences for the children to write, containing some of the words covered, or introduce new ones adhering to these patterns, such as *leisure* and *feature*. At your discretion, include some of the '-tcher' words too.
● Ask children to review their own work, considering corrections as necessary.

> **Differentiation**
> ● Support children by providing them with word cards to study. Trace over and cover letters to help reinforce the patterns.
> ● Challenge more confident spellers to find new words, such as *capture* or *vulture*, and/or create word families, such as *adventurous* and *adventurer*.

## Review
● Repeat the introduction activity. Then, writing on the board or using strips of card, introduce new '-sure' and '-ture' words orally (such as *ensure*, *unsure*, *future*, *capture*), asking the children to identify letter patterns and spellings.

**Curriculum objectives**
● To read aloud their own writing, to a group or the whole class, using appropriate intonation and controlling the tone and volume so that the meaning is clear.

**Resources**
Completed presentations and speaking notes from earlier in the week; photocopiable page 169 'Presentation evaluation template'; computer access (optional)

# 5: Delivering presentations

## Introduction
● Display photocopiable page 169 'Presentation evaluation template' and provide a brief presentation on the subject of your choice, asking children to note what rating they would give you for each aspect.
● Discuss children's evaluations and list pertinent points. Focus on oral delivery and remind the class of the related aspects of tone, intonation and volume.
● Repeat your presentation with advice and adjustments incorporated.

## Group work
● Allow groups to finalise their presentations with one last run-through, checking that they all know their cues, and have their notes ready.

## Whole-class work
● Either have each group deliver their presentation to the class, or split the class in half to avoid repetition, with groups presenting within their half.
● Explain to the class that when they give their presentations their peers will have the opportunity to offer constructive advice to them. Distribute the photocopiable sheet, and allocate children to evaluate particular groups' presentations (ideally children will each evaluate two other groups).

## Review
● Gather the class and discuss both the presentations and the evaluations. Ask: *Were there any common difficulties or strong points?*
● If time permits, allow groups to amend and improve their presentations.

# Week 2 lesson plans

The focus of this and the next week's lessons is *Charlie and the Chocolate Factory* – this week covers Chapters 1 to 15. Please note that most of the lessons require a reading of between three and five chapters of the book.

Lesson 1 introduces the book and its themes, relating them to Roald Dahl's other books. Lesson 2 looks at the people from the book, with lesson 3 exploring how their speech helps define their characters. Lesson 4 looks at Dahl's rich and exuberant style, and the week concludes with a group mime of all the characters entering the chocolate factory, showing their thoughts and emotions.

Note that there are several excellent audio recordings of this book available, including one by Roald Dahl himself. However, it is also suggested that you avoid showing children either of the films of the book, at least until the book and related work has been finished.

## Expected outcomes
● All children will listen to and comment on the story, consolidating their understanding of direct speech and responding to specific passages of text.
● Most children will create interesting texts using engaging vocabulary as well as direct speech.
● Some children will create their own texts mimicking Dahl's style.

## Curriculum objectives
● To increase their familiarity with a wide range of books, including fairy stories, myths and legends, and retell some of these orally.
● To identify main ideas drawn from more than one paragraph and summarise these.

## Resources
Source a video on chocolate production (although they are American, the Hershey's website contains videos that give a very clear impression of the processes and atmosphere of a real chocolate factory); photocopiable page 41 'Roald Dahl bibliography'; photocopiable page 'Roald Dahl biography' from the CD-ROM; Charlie and the Chocolate Factory by Roald Dahl (print and/or audio version)

# 1: Introducing *Charlie and the Chocolate Factory*

## Introduction
● Watch the video you have sourced. List the stages in chocolate production and recap on the work from week 1.

## Whole-class work
● Explain that this week the focus will shift to an imaginary chocolate factory.
● Display photocopiable page 41 'Roald Dahl bibliography' and, using a show of hands, elicit which of his books are popular with the class. Discuss how Roald Dahl's plots are often similar: characters are either good or bad, situations are absurd and naughty people get their comeuppance.
● Display photocopiable page 'Roald Dahl biography' from the CD-ROM and briefly recap his life and work. Explain to the class that he created *Charlie and the Chocolate Factory*, and how it came about, in his words, *in the usual way – it grew from being a bedtime story told to my children.*
● Write the chapter titles for the first five chapters on the board:
● Read the opening five chapters of the book to the class, asking the children simply to listen for pleasure and to make a mental note of any words or phrases that catch their attention.
● When finished, discuss each chapter in turn and elicit its content and purpose, making notes on the board. As you progress, discuss with the children what information is important to retain to help remember the story, and what can be discarded.

## Group work
● In small groups, challenge the children to orally prepare a retelling of the opening paragraphs. Invite them to consider how to make their retelling as engaging as possible by creating strong images of characters and settings.
● Allow the groups time to practise their retellings, ensuring they use the notes on the board to check that they have covered every chapter.

### Differentiation
● To ensure equal participation, suggest that groups divide the retelling between them.
● As a significant challenge, ask children to memorise snippets of dialogue and incorporate these in their retelling, and/or to retell the chapters from the point of view of Charlie.

## Review
● Ask groups to present their retelling to the class, rating them as per their presentations in week 1.

### Curriculum objectives
● To draw inferences such as inferring characters' feelings, thoughts and motives from their actions, and justify inferences with evidence.

### Resources
*Charlie and the Chocolate Factory* by Roald Dahl (print and/or audio version); photocopiable page 170 'The ticket finders'

# 2: Understanding characters

## Introduction
● Introduce the lesson with starter activity 3 'Vocabulary builder' for a range of words used for describing more extreme personality traits, such as *obnoxious, delightful, glutinous, arrogant, self-centred* and *warm-hearted*.

## Whole-class, independent, group or paired work
● Recap the themes and characters in the book, reminding the children that the characters in Roald Dahl's books are usually either completely good or completely bad. Point out that it is okay to enjoy the bad characters as they are normally more fun than Dahl's good characters.
● Display photocopiable page 170 'The ticket finders' and look at the five statements about the characters (taken from the start of the original book), then read Chapters 6 to 8, pausing to discuss each ticket winner as they appear, and briefly consider their character.

## Paired work
● Make the link for the children between being able to infer and being able to ask questions, and ask them to talk in pairs to consider the proof of the statements (if any) and predict what might happen to the characters, completing the photocopiable sheet together.

> **Differentiation**
> ● Pair the children appropriately and re-read parts of the book to support discussions.

## Review
● Bring pairs of children together and ask them to share their thoughts with each other, investigating each other's thoughts on the characters.

### Curriculum objectives
● To draw inferences such as inferring characters' feelings, thoughts and motives from their actions, and justifying inferences with evidence.
● To compose and rehearse sentences orally (including dialogue), progressively building a varied and rich vocabulary and an increasing range of sentence structures (see Appendix 2).
● To use and punctuate direct speech.

### Resources
*Charlie and the Chocolate Factory* by Roald Dahl (print and/or audio version); completed photocopiable page 170 'The ticket finders' (from week 2, lesson 2); photocopiable page 45 'Twit-talk'

# 3: The things people say

## Introduction
● Display photocopiable page 45 'Twit-talk' (or draw two speech bubbles with heads next to them) and write a question in the first speech bubble. Ask for suggestions for possible responses in the second bubble. Transcribe this as direct speech underneath, emphasising correct punctuation.

## Paired work
● Pairing children as in lesson 2 with their completed photocopiable page 170 'Ticket finders' work to hand, read selected quotes from Chapters 6 to 8, covering speech from as many of the characters as possible. Discuss how the author uses speech to emphasise personality. (You may wish to note that Augustus Gloop's mother does all the talking.)
● Next, ask the pairs to choose two characters from the book (one a finder, and one not), and explain that they must talk in role to create a small, imaginary dialogue to reveal the character of the ticket finder.
● After a while, ask the pairs to write down their dialogue using direct speech.

> **Differentiation**
> ● Provide a list of situations and adverbs to support children's thinking and writing, or allow children to use speech bubbles if they need to.

## Review
● Ask pairs to review each other's work for accurate use of punctuation.
● Have pairs perform their dialogues to the class, considering whether their words convey the characters appropriately.

## Curriculum objectives
● To check that the text makes sense to them, discussing their understanding and explaining the meaning of words in context.
● To discuss words and phrases that capture the reader's interest and imagination.
● To discuss writing similar to that which they are planning to write in order to understand and learn from its structure, grammar and vocabulary.

## Resources
Photocopiable page 'Willy Wonka's invitation' from the CD-ROM; *Charlie and the Chocolate Factory* by Roald Dahl (print and/or audio version); structured writing frame (optional, not provided)

# 4: Willy Wonka's invitation

## Introduction
● Read Chapters 9 to 12 to the class (now or before the lesson).
● Display or distribute photocopiable page 'Willy Wonka's invitation' from the CD-ROM. In discussion, look at new vocabulary and clarify meanings.
● Discuss what sort of person Willy Wonka might be. Ask: *What can we guess about him from this invitation?*

## Independent work
● The task in this session is to write a reply of acknowledgement and thanks to Willy Wonka for his invitation.
● Keeping the photocopiable sheet displayed, talk with the class to consider their reply, which can be based on the structure of the invitation:
    ● Greeting and introducing selves; delighted to have ticket; looking forward to the factory tour; thanking him for the promise of 'eatables'; explain who will be coming; "See you on..."; sign off.
● Encourage children to mimic the exuberant use of language, and reassure them that reusing Dahl's vocabulary is fine.

### Differentiation
● Provide a structured writing frame for those who need support.

## Review
● Share extracts of children's letters, asking for volunteers to read their favourite phrases, noting children who have adapted the style and vocabulary of the original invitation.

## Curriculum objectives
● To identify main ideas drawn from more than one paragraph and summarising these.
● To draw inferences such as inferring characters' feelings, thoughts and motives from their actions, and justifying inferences with evidence.

## Resources
*Charlie and the Chocolate Factory* by Roald Dahl (print and/or audio version); media resource 'Emotions' on the CD-ROM; access to a large space such as the school hall; video camera (optional)

# 5: In the factory

## Introduction
● Open the images 'Emotions' on the CD-ROM and describe each emotion, practising mimes and expressions with the class.

## Whole-class work
● Read Chapters 13 to 15 to the class, pausing to discuss the descriptions of the children and of Willy Wonka.
● When moving on to read about entering the factory and then the chocolate room, ask the children to close their eyes and try to envisage how the place looks, smells and sounds.
● In discussion, summarise the main events of the chapters on the board, asking the class to consider what different characters might be feeling and thinking at each stage.

## Group work
● Ideally, in a large enclosed space, divide the class into three large groups and explain to each of them that they are going to allocate roles and create a group mime for the chapters they have just heard.
● Remind the children about exaggerated and slowed-down movement, and the use of facial expression to express emotions.

### Differentiation
● Provide children with cue cards to note their reactions and emotions at different points.

## Review
● Watch each group's mime, asking the viewers to check that all the events have been covered and to guess who is playing which role.

# Week 3 lesson plans

This week concludes the second half of *Charlie and the Chocolate Factory* (Chapters 16 to 30, which need to be read to the class before lesson 4 is started). Initial lessons concentrate on the rhymes of the Oompa-Loompas and evocative language used to describe the sweets and chocolate, encouraging the use of dictionaries, and with a separate lesson on techniques for learning their spellings. The week concludes with a debate on the treatment of the different characters in the book, followed by a focused comparison of *Charlie and the Chocolate Factory* with *George's Marvellous Medicine* and a book by a different author of the children's or teacher's choice.

## 1: The songs of the Oompa-Loompas

### Introduction

● Begin the lesson with starter activity 1 'Word pairs', writing some or all of the following pairs of rhyming words on opposite sides of the board (note that these are all rhyming words from the Oompa-Loompa song about Augustus. Also, remember to jumble the order of the right-hand column): *beast/feast, brat/that, horse/course, taste/haste, alarmed/harmed, been/machine, round/pound, grace/place, before/shore, grudge/fudge.*
● Work through the activity connecting rhyming words through class suggestions, looking at which rhymes share letter patterns and which do not.

### Whole-class work

● Read Chapters 16 and 17 to the class, ensuring that the song of the Oompa-Loompas is read with rhythm and style.
● Briefly discuss the fate of Augustus Gloop.
● Look at the illustrations of the Oompa-Loompas in the book you have. In discussion, elicit the details of the story about how the Oompa-Loompas came to be in Willy Wonka's factory.
● Reminding the children that this is a fantasy book, consider whether this was a good thing to do, or not. Is Willy Wonka kind, or is he profiting from their work?

### Group work

● Remind the class of the rhymes encountered at the start of the lesson. Also, point out how Roald Dahl uses near-rhymes at times (*fun/anyone, more/sure, ear/everywhere*), briefly discussing why he does this.
● Display photocopiable page 'Oompa-Loompa song' from the CD-ROM and look at the first two lines together. Demonstrate by clapping that every line is eight syllables long, which lends well to chanting or a simple melody, and work with the whole class to develop a well-delivered chant or song for these first two lines, modelling good variation of tone, intonation and volume.
● Arranging the class in groups of four to eight, give each group a copy of the photocopiable sheet and explain that they must decide how to break it down and deliver it to the rest of the class. (Note that the song is around 50 lines long, so you may prefer to give each group a section of the rhyme to perform.)
● If desired, issue simple percussion instruments (ideally small drums) to groups to allow them to keep a steady beat.

> **Differentiation**
> ● Prompt groups to allow less confident children to chant or sing alongside peers.
> ● Challenge more confident children to learn lines by heart.

### Review

● Perform the song in groups or as a class depending on how you have arranged things, noting children who use intonation, tone and volume.

---

**Expected outcomes**
● All children will take part in a debate about the moral of the story and compare it to other books.
● Most children will recite sections of a rhyme, developing dictionary skills and spelling techniques.
● Some children will reference the text to illustrate their arguments.

**Curriculum objectives**
● To identify main ideas drawn from more than one paragraph and summarise these.
● To check that the text makes sense to them, discussing their understanding and explaining the meaning of words in context.
● To prepare poems and playscripts to read aloud and to perform, showing understanding through intonation, tone, volume and action.

**Resources**
*Charlie and the Chocolate Factory* by Roald Dahl (print and/or audio version); photocopiable page 'Oompa-Loompa song' from the CD-ROM; percussion instruments (optional)

### Curriculum objectives
● To discuss words and phrases that capture the reader's interest and imagination.
● To use dictionaries to check the meaning of words that they have read.
● To use the first two or three letters of a word to check its spelling in a dictionary.

### Resources
*Charlie and the Chocolate Factory* by Roald Dahl (print and/or audio version); photocopiable page 171 'Sweet vocabulary'; dictionaries

# 2: Sweet vocabulary

## Introduction
● Read Chapters 18 to 20 to the class, discussing the interesting and imaginative sweets that Willy Wonka has developed and elicit interesting vocabulary used to describe them.
● Talk about Roald Dahl's imagination and his unusual ideas and vocabulary.

## Independent work
● Distribute photocopiable page 171 'Sweet vocabulary' and explain that the object of this task is to list real and imaginary words that work well to evoke the wonderful tastes and smells of confectionery.
● Work through the first word together: *scrumptious*. In the 'notes' explain it is a real word and, using a dictionary, model effective skills in looking up its meaning, noting its class (adjective).
● Discuss other words as desired, then challenge the children to complete the sheet, creating some of their own words (real and imaginary).

> **Differentiation**
> ● Allow children who find dictionary use difficult to work with partners who can help them, and encourage them to use words that are within their grasp.
> ● To extend children, ask them to use existing root words to create new ones.

## Review
● Ask for volunteers to read words from their list and challenge their peers to decide whether they are real or invented, noting perceptive responses.

### Curriculum objectives
● To apply their growing knowledge of root words, prefixes and suffixes (etymology and morphology) as listed in Appendix 1, both to read aloud and to understand the meaning of new words they meet.
● To spell words that are often misspelled (Appendix 1).
● To write from memory simple sentences, dictated by the teacher, that include words and punctuation taught so far.
● To learn the grammar for Year 3 in Appendix 2.

### Resources
Completed photocopiable page 171 'Sweet vocabulary' (from week 3, lesson 2)

# 3: Spelling techniques

## Introduction
● Write the following words on the board and ask the class how many syllables is in each word: *gooey, crunchy, delicious, mouth-watering, lickable*.
● Discuss each word in turn, considering its composition, and explain that in this lesson you will be looking at techniques for learning how to spell these and other descriptive words.

## Whole-class work
● Work with the class to explain and practise the following techniques, explaining that different techniques work better for different people; all can work at different times for different words; and none are guaranteed to give you correct spellings:
- **Syllabification:** the breaking down of words into syllables.
- **Over-pronunciation:** stressing every sound in each syllable.
- **Analysing:** looking for familiar letter patterns, word families and root words.
- **Shape-watching:** looking at and tracing/writing the shape of the word.

## Independent work
● Ensuring that children have their completed photocopiable page 171 'Sweet vocabulary' ask them to try some of these techniques for learning some of the spellings they worked with in lesson 2.

## Whole-class work
● After a while, dictate a small range of sentences containing the words focused on in lesson 2.

## Review
● Ask children to check their own work and note difficulties and successes.

# 4: Fair or unfair?

**Curriculum objectives**
● To listen to and discuss a wide range of fiction, poetry, plays, non-fiction and reference books or textbooks.
● To draw inferences such as inferring characters' feelings, thoughts and motives from their actions, and justifying inferences with evidence.

**Resources**
Copy of *Charlie and the Chocolate Factory* (print and/or audio version); photocopiable page 170 'The ticket finders' or completed versions (from week 2, lesson 2)

## Introduction
● Finish reading the book to the class at the start of or before this lesson.
● Displaying photocopiable page 170 'The ticket finders', recap on their personalities as necessary.
● Recap on what happened to each of the characters, explaining the irony of each of their fates.

## Group work
● Divide the class into six groups, giving half of the groups the title 'fair' and the other half the title 'unfair'. Ask each group to discuss and justify why the outcomes for the five children were 'fair' or 'unfair', depending on their focus, referencing the text wherever possible.
● After a while, pair up opposite groups and initiate three small debates, ensuring that children appreciate the protocols for discussion, and reminding them that citing the text is important for giving weight to arguments.
● Finally, bring the whole class together and debate together, with the teacher acting as a scribe to write key points on the whiteboard. Conclude the debate with a vote: *Fair or unfair?*
● Set debating rules that allow for equal say.

## Review
● Ask which children voted differently to what their group had prepared arguments for, looking out for justifications that reference the text.

# 5: Comparing books

**Curriculum objectives**
● To identify themes and conventions in a wide range of books.

**Resources**
Photocopiable page 41 'Roald Dahl bibliography'; copy of *Charlie and the Chocolate Factory*; copy of *George's Marvellous Medicine*; copies of children's current or favourite reading books

## Introduction
● Using a visualiser or an image from the internet, display the cover of *George's Marvellous Medicine* on the board. Recap on its content and characters, if necessary reviving character work from Chapter 1.
● Next, recap the cover of *Charlie and the Chocolate Factory*.

## Whole-class work
● Draw a line down the centre of the board and write the titles of the two books at the top of each side.
● Remind the class of Roald Dahl's use of stereotyped characters and elicit these (such as *good* and *greedy*) and recurring themes (such as *comeuppance for bad behaviour*) for each book. Elicit the similarities and differences of the two books (such as *elements of fantasy*, *character motivations*, *plot*, *setting* and *morals*), noting pertinent points on the board.

## Independent work
● Ensuring that each member of the class has their own reading book to hand, or can identify a favourite novel, ask them to draw three columns on a piece of paper and (using the notes already made on the whiteboard to help them) compare and contrast the three texts.

> **Differentiation**
> ● Support children by providing appropriate lists of genres, themes and conventions.

## Review
● Gather the class and share notes and observations. Display photocopiable page 41 'Roald Dahl bibliography', and try to elicit what sort of genre the children think this belongs to, and note how their own books compare with this.

## Expected outcomes

- All children design their own chocolate product and design its packaging.
- Most children will research and analyse product ingredients before designing their own product.
- Some children will identify and explain the different stages in the manufacturing process and explain variations in types and ingredients.

## Curriculum objectives

- To retrieve and record information from non-fiction.
- To identify main ideas drawn from more than one paragraph and summarise these.
- To compose and rehearse sentences orally (including dialogue), progressively building a varied and rich vocabulary and an increasing range of sentence structures (see Appendix 2).

## Resources

Chocolate presentations (from week I); media resource 'Chocolate production' on the CD-ROM; photocopiable page 172 'Making chocolate'; range of information books on the history and manufacture of chocolate; internet access; photocopiable page 169 'Presentation evaluation template'

# Week 4 lesson plans

This week's work moves towards the real world, with further research on the processes for making chocolate and the different types available and creating user-friendly dictionary entries for chocolate-related vocabulary, moving on to analysing and understanding the text on chocolate product wrappers. The world of fantasy is not left behind totally however, as in the final two lessons children must invent their very own chocolate products. In true Wonka fashion they can have special properties, which must be reflected in the unique product wrappers that they design. Note: try to give advanced warning to the class to collect as many different chocolate wrappers as they can.

## I: Making chocolate

### Introduction

- Start the lesson with starter activity 2 'Getting technical', for the words *cacao, aroma, liquor* and *conch*.
- Work through the media resource 'Chocolate production' on the CD-ROM and discuss the images, considering the journey from bean to bar.

### Whole-class work

- Spend time reviewing the work covered on the history and geography of chocolate in week I, accessing children's work and/or relevant websites.
- Next, display photocopiable page 172 'Making chocolate' and read through it with the class; identify new words and consider their meaning in context.
- Work with the class to summarise the first paragraph as a single statement, such as *The cacao beans are carefully weighed and sorted at the factory.*
- In discussion, continue looking at the photocopiable sheet, and work with the class to summarise each paragraph into a single sentence.

### Group work

- Organising the class in groups of three to six, explain that their task is to research and create a small presentation on the different types of chocolate that are commonly available.
- Reminding the class of the research and presentation skills they developed in week I, ask them to spend five or ten minutes planning their work and their roles, considering how they will search for the information they need, and prompt them to consider how they will deliver the information they are researching: *a simple list, a mind map, images only,* and so on. (If resources are limited, this work may have to be done as a carousel activity.)
- Allow groups to finalise their presentations with one last run-through, checking that they know their place in the presentation, and have notes ready.

---

### Differentiation

- As this is a brief research task, allow children to show pictures from books or the internet alongside their presentations, ensuring that appropriate roles are assigned in each group to ensure equal participation, such as identifying images while another group member is talking.

---

### Review

- Either, ask each group to deliver their presentation to the class, or split the class in half to avoid repetition, with groups presenting within their half.
- Explain to the class that when they give their presentations their peers will have the opportunity to offer constructive advice to them. Display photocopiable page 169 'Presentation evaluation template' and ask the class to bear the criteria in mind when delivering and assessing each other's presentations.
- To conclude the lesson, review any new and key chocolate-related vocabulary that has arisen, in preparation for lesson 2.

**Curriculum objectives**
• To apply their growing knowledge of root words, prefixes and suffixes (etymology and morphology) as listed in Appendix 1, both to read aloud and to understand the meaning of new words they meet.
• To use dictionaries to check the meaning of words that they have read.

**Resources**
Photocopiable page 172 'Making chocolate'; range of information books on the history and manufacture of chocolate; internet access (optional); dictionaries

# 2: A dictionary of chocolate

## Introduction

• Write the word *praline* in large letters on the board and ask if anyone knows the meaning of the word.
• Modelling good dictionary skills, look up the word and write its exact meaning next to the word, forming a complete dictionary entry, and review the structure and terminology this contains.
• Next, with suggestions from the class, rewrite this definition in a more user-friendly way (such as *praline, noun, a sweet, nutty mixture that is sometimes used to fill chocolates.*)

## Paired work

• Display and review photocopiable page 172 'Making chocolate' and review the vocabulary and processes discussed yesterday. Also remind children of the brief work they did on types of chocolate.
• Explain that in preparation for the next stage of the topic you would like to get some clear definitions in place, and then, either assigning words to avoid repetition, or letting children choose, ask them to find and write down clear dictionary-style definitions of a range of chocolate-related words, ensuring that they use child-friendly language that their peers will understand.

> **Differentiation**
> • Pair children appropriately and suggest that they take turns to identify, look up and reword dictionary entries.

## Review

• Gather the class and share some of their definitions, noting word classes (nouns, verbs, adjectives, and so on) as they come up.

**Curriculum objectives**
• To discuss writing similar to that which they are planning to write in order to understand and learn from its structure, grammar and vocabulary.
• To use dictionaries to check the meaning of words that they have read.

**Resources**
Wide selection of chocolate products (just wrappers are sufficient); dictionaries; analysis template (optional, not provided)

# 3: The chocolate we eat

## Introduction

• Start the lesson by showing a selection of well-known chocolate products, writing the name for each on our whiteboard and asking the class to describe both their taste and the appearance of the wrapper.
• Discuss ingredients and ask if children know what is in some of the products.

## Paired-work

• Organising the class appropriately, ask each pair to take two chocolate product wrappers and analyse every bit of text on them. Explain that for the moment it does not matter if they do not understand aspects of it.
• Choosing a wrapper that no one else will use, model how you want the children to copy each section, showing how to break down the information on a sheet of A4 paper, listing the name, ingredients, health information, and so on.
• Ask the class to highlight any new words (there will be several in the ingredients), and if possible to use a dictionary to find the meanings of these words.

> **Differentiation**
> • Provide a simple analysis template for those who need greater guidance with structuring their work and, if necessary, allow children to cut out and stick relevant parts onto the template.

## Review

• Ask the children to share their work with partners, in particular sharing information on new vocabulary. Ask: *Do any of the ingredients surprise you?*

## Curriculum objectives
● To discuss and record ideas.
● In non-narrative material, to use simple organisational devices.

## Resources
Completed work on chocolate packaging (from week 4, lesson 3); media resource 'Chocolate packaging' on the CD-ROM; photocopiable page 173 'Chocolate packaging plan'

# 4: A brand-new chocolate product

## Introduction
● Show the media resource 'Chocolate packaging' on the CD-ROM, asking for suggestions as to what each product might contain. Ask: *In what way do the shapes, colours, names and other details suggest what sort of product each one is?*
● Discuss which 'brands' appeal to the class and which do not. Ask why.

## Paired work
● Ask the children to imagine that they are chocolate manufacturers (or if you are game, Oompa-Loompas) and that Willy Wonka has asked them to develop a new chocolate product for him. Their ideas can be as wild and wacky as they like: perhaps healthy chocolate treats, a never-ending chocolate bar that re-grows itself, or maybe a strange new flavour. As such, their ingredients may be a mixture of the real and the fabulous.
● Distribute photocopiable page 173 'Chocolate packaging plan' and explain that once they have developed their idea they must consider the packaging for it and all the text that will go on it, thinking about name, slogan, colours, description, ingredients, nutrients, and so on; moving on to planning a suitable wrapper.

### Differentiation
● Ensure that children have their work from the previous lesson to support them.

## Review
● Organise the children in small discussion groups and ask each member in turn to present their plans, noting positive suggestions and highlighting errors in preparation for their presentation versions.

## Curriculum objectives
● To proofread for spelling and punctuation errors.

## Resources
Media resource 'Chocolate packaging' on the CD-ROM; completed photocopiable page 173 'Chocolate packaging plan' (from week 4, lesson 4); A5 paper and coloured pencils and pens

# 5: Perfect packaging

## Introduction
● Show the media resource 'Chocolate packaging' on the CD-ROM one more time, reminding the class that they should feel free to use any new ideas to modify their plans from the previous lesson.

## Paired work
● Explain that children will be creating presentation versions of their proposed chocolate product wrappers. The wrapper can be created larger than it would be in reality, and they should plan the different sides of the packaging on separate pieces of A5 paper, to be joined when they are finished.
● Distribute children's completed photocopiable page 173 'Chocolate packaging plan' work from the previous lesson, and ask them to spend ten minutes or so reviewing and improving these before moving on to produce their finished packaging.
● Remind everyone to begin by planning the layout of their work, ensuring that they leave plenty space to write ingredients and avoid cramped text.

### Differentiation
● Ensure that children distribute tasks appropriately, but also that they review each other's work to ensure engagement with their texts.

## Review
● Reminding the class of their previous analysis of chocolate bar wrappers, ask them to display their work on their desks and to circulate and evaluate, considering how well their peers have included the relevant aspects.

# Week 5 lesson plans

This week focuses on advertising, allowing children to understand the essence of persuasive writing, with opportunities to respond to and create their own adverts. Initially children examine a range of paper and video-based adverts, considering their purpose, honesty and effectiveness, then looking in more detail at the language used. Children then move on to working collaboratively to create their own advertisements for the new chocolate products they created in week 4, working up concepts into storyboards and scripts, culminating in producing (and hopefully videoing) their adverts.

Note that preparation for this chapter includes sourcing a small range of televised adverts suitable for showing to your class. Try to ensure that the adverts have differing qualities, including one or two humorous ones.

## I: Looking at adverts

### Introduction
● Without explaining yourself, start the lesson by miming the eating of the ultimate chocolate bar. Once finished, collect words to describe the experience, taste and overall enjoyment.

### Whole-class work
● Explain that the focus of this week's lessons is advertising: the attempt to persuade people to buy, use or do something using words and images.
● Show the class one or two video adverts and discuss their length, structure and content.
● Select one advert to review again and focus on the clarity of speech, the clarity of information provided, and the overall 'flow' of the advert. Also note any interesting vocabulary it contains.
● Display photocopiable page 174 'Advert analysis' and work with the class to complete it for the advert you have just watched, replaying the advert several times to really get across its structure and intent. Model effective comments in each section of the photocopiable sheet, reiterating that bland comments, such as *it was fun*, have little meaning.

### Paired work
● Arrange the children with partners and distribute the photocopiable sheet. Play one or more new adverts, and then ask the pairs to select a particular advert that interests them (or assign adverts as preferred).
● Note on the board aspects of their chosen advert that they should also be considering: clarity of people's speech, clarity of information provided, and the overall 'flow' of the advert.

### Whole class work
● Gathering the class together, ask pairs to share their work with their peers, ideally children who have analysed the same advertisement. Do they concur on points? Have they spotted anything that others did not?
● Next, ask: *What makes an advert successful?* Discuss this openly for a while, encouraging children to refer to their completed photocopiable sheets.
● Explore the difference between persuasive words and persuasive images, eliciting responses based on the adverts watched. Extend this discussion to cover advertisements that children have encountered out of school.
● Ask what the class perceives as the benefit of advertisements, and any hindrances.
● What would be the benefits of having no adverts, and what would be lost?

### Review
● Look at one or two adverts, with children using analysis skills to consider why they use the imagery and language they do.

---

### Expected outcomes
● All children will write, create and evaluate their own adverts, using appropriate language.
● Most children will critically evaluate their work and comment on its quality and suitability.
● Some children will show a good understanding of persuasive language, using and countering it effectively in their speech and writing.

### Curriculum objectives
● To discuss writing similar to that which they are planning to write in order to understand and learn from its structure, grammar and vocabulary.
● To discuss and record ideas.

### Resources
Selection of televised adverts (some humorous if possible); photocopiable page 174 'Advert analysis'

---

**Curriculum objectives**
● To discuss and record ideas.
● In non-narrative material, to use simple organisational devices.

**Resources**
Completed chocolate product wrapping work (from week 4); completed photocopiable page 174 'Advert analysis' (from week 5, lesson 1)

# 2: Planning adverts

## Introduction

● Display one or more of the class's completed photocopiable page 174 'Advert analysis' work. Discuss the adverts they are looking at and remind the class of the main aspects and functions of adverts: namely to persuade people to buy their products without telling lies.

## Group work

● Explain that everyone is going to create humorous adverts for their chocolate products, and since they are advertising special chocolates for Willy Wonka they can be as imaginative and wacky as they wish.
● Arranging the children in groups of four to eight, ask them to decide between them which of their new chocolate products they will create an advertisement for (teachers may need to adjudicate here).
● Remind them of the adverts studied in lesson 1, and also ask them to think of other adverts they like. Then allow groups time to brainstorm ideas until they reach one they are happy with.
● Groups then work to create a plan and/or storyboard for a TV advert for their chocolate product.

> **Differentiation**
> ● To support this task provide a template to help groups to equally allocate roles and plan their work.

## Review

● Gather the class and review progress, discussing difficulties and possible solutions. Ensure that children have enough time to complete their work before starting the next lesson.

**Curriculum objectives**
● To compose and rehearse sentences orally (including dialogue), progressively building a varied and rich vocabulary and an increasing range of sentence structures (See Appendix 2).

**Resources**
Completed advert plans and/or storyboards (from week 5, lesson 2); selection of televised adverts (optional)

# 3: Writing adverts

## Introduction

● Begin the lesson with starter activity 10 'Being descriptive', focusing on language used to evoke the sight, taste and smell of delicious chocolate.

## Whole-class work

● Explain that in this lesson, groups will be creating scripts for the adverts they started planning in lesson 2, honing down the language to a fine level of detail.
● Discuss the 'rules' of adverts: honesty, clarity and the 'key message'. Also remind children of the essence of this task – they are creating adverts for Willy Wonka chocolate, and so the tone of their advert can match the 'amazing' nature of their chocolate bars.
● Ask: *Will they have songs? Will they all speak? Will they tell a story?* And crucially: *What will persuade people to buy their chocolate bar rather than anyone else's?*

## Group work

● Ask the groups to review their plans from lesson 2, and to collaborate to produce a completed script for their advert, composing orally initially, with one of the group acting as a scribe.

## Review

● Review each group's work in 'private' with them to avoid letting others see too much before the final adverts are produced. Check language used and flow, suggesting and trying improvements with each group.

# 4: Making adverts

## Introduction

● Start the lesson with some voice work as a reminder of the importance of clear speaking, and the use of tone, intonation and volume in moderating speech. Use photocopiable page 'Oompa-Loompa song' from the CD-ROM to have a whole-class rendition of part of the Oompa-Loompas rhyme.

## Group work

● Divide the lesson roughly into two halves, the first half being rehearsal and improvement of groups' plans and scripts, the second being their enactment, ideally videoing each one for evaluation in lesson 5.
● Remind the class that the aim of the task is to produce extravagant, Wonka-style adverts for a new chocolate product. Ask groups to review their plans and scripts and consider any final tweaks and to gather any resources they need to make their adverts. In particular, ask them to focus on vocabulary – do their choices of words do their product justice?
● When ready, each group should rehearse their advertisement together, focusing on each other's delivery and providing constructive feedback.

> **Differentiation**
> ● Challenge children to learn their lines by heart to deliver a tight, crisp performance.

## Review

● It is not necessary to review each group's work at this stage, though letting individual groups reflect on their performances is fine, allowing them to reshoot if time permits.

## Curriculum objectives

● To prepare poems and playscripts to read aloud and to perform, showing understanding through intonation, tone, volume and action.
● To assess the effectiveness of their own and other's writing and suggest improvements.

## Resources

Photocopiable page 'Oompa-Loompa song' from the CD-ROM; video camera (preferable, but not essential); a large space such as the school hall may be an easier working environment

# 5: Evaluating children's work

## Introduction

● Show one or two of the adverts as encountered in lesson 1, focusing on the language used.

## Paired work

● Arrange the class in pairs and distribute photocopiable page 174 'Advert analysis'.
● Explain that they will be watching videos (or performances) of each other's chocolate promotional videos, and assessing them as with other adverts, in particular looking for language that can be improved on. You may find it beneficial to assign different videos to different pairs to ensure that everyone is covered and will receive feedback.
● Watch the videos and ensure that pairs complete the photocopiable sheet.
● Next, work through the list of adverts and allow children to offer feedback.

## Group work

● Moving children back into their original groups, ask them to discuss the feedback they have received and add their own reflections, listing four to six changes to language that would improve the effectiveness of their work.

> **Differentiation**
> ● Pair children appropriately so that one of the pair can offer comments orally to allow equal participation.

## Review

● Invite groups to present their self-reviews, noting groups that have successfully identified meaningful improvements.

## Curriculum objectives

● To assess the effectiveness of their own and other's writing and suggest improvements.
● To propose changes to grammar and vocabulary to improve consistency.

## Resources

Selection of televised adverts (as used in week 5, lesson 1); photocopiable page 174 'Advert analysis'; completed adverts, ideally on video (from week 5, lesson 4)

# Week 6 lesson plans

The final week moves on to poetry, with children encountering a range of confectionery-related poems in different forms, giving them the opportunity to plan and create their own poems, which they then edit, improve and present to their highest standards, finishing off with well-delivered readings or recitals.

## I: Sweet poetry

### Introduction
● Display photocopiable page 'Sweets poems' from the CD-ROM and read them to the class, modelling good use of exaggerated intonation and tone. Discuss each poem, allowing children to understand the form, style and intention.

### Whole class work
● Work with the children to create a whole-class recital of 'Pick 'n' Mix Zoo'.
● Look again at 'Gingerbread Man', and help the class to see the repetition of statements leading in a complete circle. Discuss the effect of each verse ending in a rhyme (or at least a near-rhyme) except for the very last verse. Ask: *Does this help or hinder the poet's intentions?*
● Display photocopiable page 'Chocolate poems' from the CD-ROM and discuss each poem in turn, considering the poet's intent (do the children appreciate the fact that the first poem is a play on *chocolate box*?), and the style of each poem, pointing out the internal rhyme in *I'd Do Anything for Chocolate*.

### Group work
● Arrange the class in groups of three and distribute photocopiable page 'Chocolate poems' from the CD-ROM. Ask the children to work together to read through them, noting words and expressions they like.
● Ask the children to allocate the three poems between them (drawing lots if necessary), and then plan and prepare individual readings or recitals of each of the poems. Remind them to consider tone, intonation and style.
● Allow groups plenty of time to rehearse and practise with one another, encouraging supportive advice and suggestions.

### Whole class work
● Ask for volunteers to deliver the chocolate poems they have practised and discuss their delivery, reminding the class to focus on intonation, tone and volume in assessing each other. Constructive comments might also be accompanied by suggested delivery of particular lines.
● Also ask if others have developed a delivery for a particular poem that is different to what you have already heard. If so, compare and discuss readings.

### Group work
● Organise the class into three large groups according to which poem they have been practising: 'Chocolate Box', 'I'd Do Anything for Chocolate', or 'An Easter Wish'. Explain that each group is to work together to plan a group reading. Remind the class of techniques for synchronising voices (counting in, keeping a beat, assigning a lead voice, and so on).

> **Differentiation**
> ● For those who find reading harder, assign shorter poems to ensure equal participation.
> ● Challenge confident children to develop a recital for at least some of their poem.

### Review
● Ask the groups to do their readings/recitals, and discuss difficulties and successes. Display the poems and remind them of the key features of each.

**Curriculum objectives**
● To retrieve and record information from non-fiction.

**Resources**
Photocopiable page 175 'Celia Warren: A chocolate poet'

# 2: A chocolate poet

## Introduction
● Begin the lesson with starter activity 1 'Word pairs', focusing on the rhyming words from all of Celia Warren's poems from lesson 1, remembering to jumble the order on the right-hand-side: *drops/lollipops, bears/hares, kangaroo/zoo, man/marzipan, said/gingerbread, lid/skid, bite/delight, wall/all, chocolate/omelette.*

## Paired work
● Distribute photocopiable page 175 'Celia Warren: A chocolate poet' and read through it with the class.
● Work together to summarise the first paragraph as a single sentence to reveal its focus, for example: *Celia gets her ideas for poems from things she sees, hears or thinks about.*
● Next, ask the children to try and summarise each paragraph in a single sentence, and to rewrite each of the writing tips in their own words.
● To conclude, ask them to write one question that they would ask Celia, given the opportunity.

> **Differentiation**
> ● For a more challenging task, ask children to work in pairs to conduct a mock interview, with one taking the role of Celia, and one the interviewer.

## Review
● Ask the class to review each other's summaries and questions, allowing them time to correct and alter each other's writing. If time permits, ask for contributions, pointing out strong answers and correcting any confusion.

**Curriculum objectives**
● To recognise some different forms of poetry.
● To compose and rehearse sentences orally (including dialogue), progressively building a varied and rich vocabulary and an increasing range of sentence structures (see Appendix 2).
● To identify how language, structure, and presentation contribute to meaning.

**Resources**
Completed sweet vocabulary work (from week 3) (optional); photocopiable page 79 'Poetry planner' (optional)

# 3: Planning chocolate poems

## Introduction
● Begin the lesson by writing *CHOCOLATE* vertically down the left-hand side of the board, and using the letter 'C', write *Creamy and soft, good enough to eat.* Eliciting contributions from the class, compile a simple acrostic poem.

## Whole class work
● Also demonstrate a list poem to the class, writing something fairly bland on the board, such as: *Selection boxes at Christmas,* or *Lunchbox snacks.*
● Work with the class to improve on what is written, extending sentences and using stronger vocabulary, as well as adding new lines.

## Independent work
● Remind the class of the different work they have done on confectionery-related vocabulary and the different forms of poetry they have encountered. Ask them to plan a chocolate or confectionery-themed poem.
● Stress that it is acceptable for children to plan their work orally and, if desired, distribute photocopiable page 79 'Poetry planner'.

> **Differentiation**
> ● To support learners, encourage them to adapt the acrostic or list poem formats exemplified in the lesson.
> ● Prompt more confident writers to try selecting different forms and metaphors.

## Review
● Ask children to share their plans and initial drafts with partners, reminding them that the immediate reactions of readers, positive and negative, are often valuable in assessing their work.

**Curriculum objectives**
● To assess the effectiveness of their own and other's writing and suggest improvements.
● To use the diagonal and horizontal strokes that are needed to join letters and understand which letters, when adjacent to one another, are best left unjoined.
● To increase the legibility, consistency and quality of their handwriting.

**Resources**
Completed draft poems and plans (from week 6, lesson 3); dictionaries

# 4: Reviewing and rewriting finished poems

## Introduction
● Begin the lesson with a review of handwriting techniques as desired, and remind children of the expectations you have for presentation-level work. (Ideally all of their poems will be collated for a class book.)

## Group work
● Arranging the children in small groups, ask them to review their plans together and consider further changes, then move on to completing their drafts.
● Circulate and provide feedback as appropriate, moving children on to final drafts, encouraging them to check their spellings independently.

## Independent work
● With their poems finalised, ask the children to write presentation copies of their poems, using the usual materials (guidelines, pens, and so on). (Note that this may require extra time outside of the lesson.)

## Review
● Organising the children back in groups, allow them to look at each other's poems (save reading and reciting until the next lesson).
● For each poem they look at, ask them to consider its form, style and meaning. Ask: *Is it enjoyable? Is it funny? Does it tell a story? Does it make good use of words?*

**Curriculum objectives**
● To read aloud their own writing, to a group or the whole class, using appropriate intonation and controlling the tone and volume so that the meaning is clear.

**Resources**
'Chocolate cake' by Michael Rosen or similar (not provided); video camera (optional); completed poems (from week 6, lesson 4)

# 5: A confectionery poetry day

## Introduction
● Get the class into the mood with a reading of 'Chocolate cake' by Michael Rosen, or any other confectionery-related poem of your choice.

## Group work
● Ask the children to work together to practise their poems with each other. Stress that it is enough to practise only a few lines of recital: the main purpose is to improve delivery.

## Individual work
● Have children read or recite a part of or their entire poem to the class.
● Depending on how you structure child-interaction, this is a good opportunity to allow for constructive feedback to be given peer-to-peer, as in the discussions of other poems earlier in the week.
● You can also take this opportunity to reinforce knowledge and understanding of poetry forms.

> **Differentiation**
> ● Allowing children to read only a part of their poem will help with equal participation, reminding them it is how they deliver their words, rather than the quantity that is important.
> ● Demanding a recital rather than a reading will provide a challenge to those who want or need it.

## Review
● To conclude, remind children of the different forms of poems they have encountered, and discuss what makes an effective poem – it is not just the poem, but how it is delivered.

**Curriculum objectives**
- To assess the effectiveness of their own and other's writing and suggest improvements.
- To propose changes to grammar and vocabulary to improve consistency.

**Resources**
Interactive activity 'Correcting work' on the CD-ROM

# Grammar and punctuation: Proposing changes to grammar and vocabulary

## Revise

- Sometimes it is better to separate improving the content and intent of a text from checking and correcting the grammar and vocabulary (although the two are often interconnected). As such, try to develop short, specific grammar and punctuation checklists to support children as they check specific work. For example:

| Grammar | Punctuation |
| --- | --- |
| Have I used pronouns correctly? | Have I used full stops and capital letters? |
| Have I started paragraphs in the right places? | Are my inverted commas in the right places? |
| Have I used clauses to improve sentences? | Do all of my commas need to be there? |

- Rotate children through the interactive activity 'Correcting work' on the CD-ROM.
- Use model texts from Summer 1 and consider them only in terms of specific aspects of punctuation and grammar.
- Rewrite some of the Summer 1 texts, or create your own, with a range of errors in them, and have children annotate and correct them.

## Assess

- In addition, provide a sample text similar to the one in the interactive activity and ask children to annotate and correct it.
- Also make assessments by reviewing children's own editing and improvement of their texts.

## Further practice

- Develop good classroom routines for children to develop their skills in reviewing, annotating and improving texts, using their own and peers' work.

**Curriculum objectives**
- To spell words that are often misspelled (Appendix 1).
- To write from memory simple sentences, dictated by the teacher, that include words and punctuation taught so far.

**Resources**
Dictionaries

# Spelling: Words ending with '-sure' and '-ture'

## Revise

- Distribute dictionaries and ask children to find the meanings of a range of '-sure' and '-ture' words.
- Create a display with each word written in unjoined and cursive writing.
- Create sets of cue cards with individual '-sure' and '-ture' words written on strips of card. Use these to play 'Endings snap', 'Kim's game', and so on.
- Have children trace words with a pen or finger while pronouncing them.
- Break down words into syllables and focus on the endings.

## Assess

- Dictate a range of sentences including words covered and new ones with the '-sure' and '-ture' endings, allowing children to write them in context.
- Also look out for use of these words in children's independent writing.

## Further practice

- If children are still having difficulties with these spellings, it is important that they encounter the words as much as possible in a range of contexts. Ask children to identify them in passages of text, invent and read specific passages using the target words.
- Use starter activity 12 'Word displays'.

**Curriculum objectives**
● To check that the text makes sense to them, discussing their understanding and explaining the meaning of words in context.
● To ask questions to improve their understanding of a text.

**Resources**
Completed work from week 1; photocopiable page 168 'The story of chocolate'; photocopiable page 172 'Making chocolate'; photocopiable page 175 'Celia Warren: A chocolate poet'

# Reading: Asking questions to improve understanding of a text

## Revise

● Remind children that the essence of 'controlling' their use of texts is to come to them with preconceived questions in mind. This is a hard skill for children to learn (and it ultimately needs to be accompanied by higher-level reading skills such as scanning), but they need to develop skills in rapidly evaluating and selecting texts as they move through the latter years of primary school.
● For non-fiction, work with one of the texts that accompany this chapter (photocopiable pages 168 'The story of chocolate', 172 'Making chocolate', and 175 'Celia Warren: A chocolate poet') to model questions that might help to guide their reading, such as: *What are the three main facts? Does the text mention any dates or names?* Also use more user-specific questions oriented around research, such as: *Where does chocolate come from?* Then, reviewing the text purely with these questions in mind, ask whether the text is useful to them or not, writing knowledge gained from the text under each question.
● Repeat this exercise with a range of non-fiction texts, defining research questions in advance and asking children to select the most appropriate texts to answer each one.
● For revising children's ability to understand fiction, working with short stories can be much easier for developing these skills as there is less ambiguity. That said, the type of questions asked will often be different, such as: *Who are the main characters? Where is it set? What is the focus or moral of the story?*
● To support and revise how children understand words in context, they need good routines for trying to pronounce and understand unfamiliar words, such as looking for letter patterns and sounding them out, as well as considering the meaning of the sentence and ultimately using dictionaries.

## Assess

● Remembering that accurate assessment requires knowledge, skills and understanding to be used in different contexts, try to find texts about subjects other than chocolate. (If you want to use texts available with this book, try photocopiable pages 'Roald Dahl biography', 'King Midas and the Golden Touch', or '*King of the Cloud Forests* extract' from the CD-ROM.
● Having chosen a suitable text, identify a suitable task related to the overall purpose of the text, such as summarising or reviewing it. Ideally, the text will contain several words that children should be asked to clarify the meaning of.
● Before distributing the text, explain its broad focus and clarify the task(s).
● Dedicate a fixed proportion of the time for children to finalise their questions before they start working, and encourage them to write answers to these questions on the same page.
● Also, as well as asking children to find the meanings of specific words, ask them to identify any others that they are unsure of the meaning of and try to consider what it might be.
● In assessing this work, look for children who have asked appropriate questions, as well as those who have modified their questions subsequent to discovering new information.

## Further practice

● Look at as wide a range of text types as possible, from age-appropriate newspapers and websites to children's favourite non-fiction.
● Apply the procedure of listing questions relevant to the task before starting any new non-fiction text and, similarly for fiction, before writing reviews or summarising them.
● Ensure that children know the routines for dealing with new words, and encourage this by having a class dictionary that they can add to as and when they encounter new words in their reading.

## Curriculum objectives

● To use the diagonal and horizontal strokes that are needed to join letters and understand which letters, when adjacent to one another, are best left unjoined.
● To increase the legibility, consistency and quality of their handwriting.
● To proofread for spelling and punctuation errors.

## Resources

Handwriting guides and pens as per your school policy

# Writing: Handwriting

## Revise

● Ultimately, the work to improve children's own presentation of their writing is a personal and ongoing task. Handwriting styles differ significantly between children and, of course, their aptitudes develop at different rates.
● Nevertheless, there are various activities and habits that are good to go through with children on a regular basis to help ensure that as they become more confident writers they are not hampered by the illegibility of their own work. These are typically covered in handwriting schemes and school policies.
● Introduce methods for children to rate their own work when proofreading it, scoring themselves out of five for handwriting, spelling and punctuation. There are other categories too of course, but those mentioned are enough for considering presentation.
● Look at model handwritten texts and discuss letter formation and joining, as well as spacing and individual quirks and styles.

## Assess

● Teachers need to decide in advance the focus of the assessments they plan and carry out. If you are very specifically looking at children's handwriting you may want to avoid other 'cognitive loads' that might limit their concentration. As such, ask children to write small passages of given text, such as a published poem or a short passage from a book.
● Alternatively, you may feel that handwriting assessed 'in context' is the most meaningful approach. The truth probably lies somewhere in between, and looking at children's handwriting in both presentation and everyday contexts is important to get a rounded picture.
● When assessing children's handwriting, look closely for recurring errors and problems, providing focused practice to correct these.
● For the assessment of children's ability to proofread and correct their own work, set limits that make it manageable for them, such as finding three spelling errors, and making three improvements to vocabulary or sentence structure, as well as punctuation of course. (Remember that reading their work aloud can make it easier for children to spot errors.)
● Once children have corrected their work ensure that their alterations are correct and meaningful.
● The above points regarding the assessment of handwriting and improving work can be assessed on any of the following written tasks that relate to this chapter, or you may prefer to use tasks of your own choice:
    ● Write a letter to one of the five golden ticket winners, congratulating them on their trip to the factory and asking them what it was like.
    ● Write a diary entry as one of the ticket winners, talking about their experience.
    ● Recount the stages of manufacturing chocolate.
    ● Write an email to Celia Warren, telling her about your recent poetry work and asking about hers.
    ● Write three further entries for a 'chocolate dictionary'.

## Further practice

● Of course, the development of handwriting and self-correction or amendment are ongoing skills, but focused practise, little and often, is just as important for children as writing, editing and redrafting larger passages to high standards.
● Try to show children's work that models good practice, as well as modelling reviewing for errors and improvement.
● Bear in mind that for a small number of children writing is a very difficult affair from which they need respite. Dictating work, using word-processors and text-to-speech software can all be a welcome relief and help to sustain a belief that those with specific problems can still create meaningful texts.

# The story of chocolate

Do you like chocolate? If you said 'no' to that question you are unusual! Chocolate is one of the most popular snacks or treats in the world. But where does chocolate come from, who invented it, and how is it made? The truth will take you halfway around the world and back again.

Chocolate is made from the fruit of the cacao tree. These trees are found in countries that are near the equator, where the climate is warm. We call their seeds 'cocoa beans'. The first people to make chocolate were the ancient tribes of Mexico and Central America, such as the Incas and Aztecs. They ground cacao seeds and then mixed them with seasoning to make a spicy, frothy drink.

The Spanish explorer Christopher Columbus was probably the first person to bring cocoa beans to Europe, more than 500 years ago. Unfortunately, everyone was more interested in the gold and treasure he brought back, so they were not too interested in the cocoa beans. But another explorer called Hernando Cortez noticed that the Aztec Indians used cocoa beans to make a drink for their leader, King Montezuma, called 'chocolatl', which means 'warm liquid'. It was said that Montezuma drank 50 or more cups of chocolatl a day, and served it to his Spanish guests in golden goblets, treating it like a food for the gods. Chocolatl was very bitter and the Spanish did not like its taste, so they sweetened it with sugar.

It is believed that the first solid chocolate bars were made in Britain more than 150 years ago using cocoa powder, cocoa butter and sugar. The chocolate bars were quite popular, but then someone had the idea of adding milk to make the bars sweeter and creamier. This was really popular and soon companies such as Fry and Cadbury were producing dozens of different chocolate bars with different fillings and flavours. These days, chocolate is made and eaten all over the world – millions and millions of bars and boxes of it!

Name: _____    Date: _____

## Presentation evaluation template

- Use this template to provide constructive advice to people after their presentations. Rate each of the areas below by colouring stars, and then provide an overall comment.

Visual resources (what was shown)

Clarity of speaking

Quality of information

Interest level

Organisation of group

Quality of vocabulary

Overall comment:

_____

_____

_____

_____

I can evaluate a presentation.

How did you do?

## The ticket finders

- Complete the chart below with your thoughts on the five children.

**Augustus Gloop:** A greedy boy

Proof: _____

_____

What will Mr Wonka think of him? _____

_____

---

**Veruca Salt:** A girl who is spoiled by her parents

Proof: _____

_____

What will Mr Wonka think of her? _____

_____

---

**Violet Beauregard:** A girl who chews gum all day long

Proof: _____

_____

What will Mr Wonka think of her? _____

_____

---

**Mike Teavee:** A boy who does nothing but watch television

Proof: _____

_____

What will Mr Wonka think of him? _____

_____

---

**Charlie Bucket:** The hero

Proof: _____

_____

What will Mr Wonka think of him? _____

_____

---

I can infer things about characters from a book.

How did you do?

## Sweet vocabulary

- Use the chart below to build up interesting vocabulary for describing confectionery.

| Word | Notes | Meaning |
|---|---|---|
| scrumptious | | |
| galumptious | | |
| crunchiferous | | |
| delectable | | |
| juicetastic | | |
| lickable | | |
| mouth-watering | | |
| | | |
| | | |
| | | |
| | | |
| | | |
| | | |
| | | |

I can identify, explain and create interesting adjectives.

How did you do?

# Making chocolate

The cacao beans are cut from the trees, then sorted and weighed at the factory. Some manufacturers use up to 12 types of cacao beans in their chocolate, so they must choose their beans carefully so that the flavour is always the same.

Next, the cacao beans are roasted in large, very hot ovens, for between 30 minutes and two hours. The heat improves the flavour and aroma, and it dries and darkens the beans.

Then the cacao beans are cracked and their shells are blown away, leaving the crushed and broken pieces of cacao beans, called 'nibs'. Nibs do taste of chocolate, but they are also very bitter.

The cacao nibs are then crushed until they make a thick paste called 'chocolate liquor'. Some of this is then squashed down to remove the fat, or cocoa butter. The leftover bits are very dry and are used to make cocoa.

The rest of the chocolate liquor has to be made sweeter and creamier, so ingredients such as sugar, vanilla and milk are added. It is now starting to look and taste like chocolate, but it is still a bit rough and bumpy.

To make the texture smoother and to really bring out the flavour, cocoa butter is added and the mixture is put through a chocolate making machine called a 'conch' that mixes, mashes, and swirls the chocolate (it is called a conch because it looks like a conch shell). 'Conching' can last a few hours for cheaper chocolates, and up to six days for the expensive stuff.

Finally, the chocolate is then stirred, cooled and heated back up again. This is done several times to give the chocolate a nice glossy look and to help it melt properly. Once it is ready, it can be put into moulds to make chocolate bars, or used to make other types of chocolate products.

## Chocolate packaging plan

- Use this template to plan your new chocolate product.

Name:

Slogan:

Why it will be popular:

Ingredients:

Packaging ideas:

I can create a new, interesting product.

How did you do?

## Advert analysis

■ Use this template to analyse an advertisement.

Product:

How long was the advert?

What happened in the advert?

Did you spot any persuasive or interesting words or images? What were they?

What did you like about it?

What didn't you like about it?

Overall rating:

I can analyse and comment on an advertisement.

How did you do?

**PHOTOCOPIABLE**

Name: _____     Date: _____

## Celia Warren: A chocolate poet

- Celia Warren has been writing poetry for many years. Here she talks about how she works and offers tips to young writers.

"A poem does not begin when I sit down to write. It starts much earlier, with a feeling, a thought, and a few words rattling round my head. Something I see or taste or hear sparks an idea or triggers a memory.

"I enjoy playing with words. Before I wrote 'The Chocolate Box', I had been mixing other odd words. I wrote 'The Wooden Dog' and 'The Water Dragon'. Then, I visited a school where there was a new girl. Later, I wrote a poem about the 'new' girl – all clean and shiny with her label still attached!

"Writing 'The Chocolate Box' was fun. Normally, it means 'a box *containing* chocolates'. I made it mean 'a box *made of* chocolate'. Lots of my poems are about sweets, as I have what's called 'a sweet tooth'. That means I like eating sugary things. I'm planning to write a poem called 'My Sweet Tooth', when I've decided what flavour it is. One day, I'll write about 'My Kind Toothbrush'!

"When my children were little they liked choosing pick 'n' mix sweets. Lots of the sweets were animals – jelly elephants and strawberry snakes. Writing my poem, I made up more. I chose 'red' for the elephants, as I liked the repeated /e/ sounds. Try saying 'orange jelly elephants'; now 'red jelly elephants'. See what I mean?"

### Writing tips

Write the sort of poem that you enjoy reading.

Read aloud as you write. Listen for bumpy bits. Change words to improve the rhythm.

Leave your poem for a while and then return to it. Can you replace any boring words? (See how I chose 'nibble' instead of 'eat').

Poems are so short that every word must work hard. Remove any that add nothing.

Keep your early efforts. As you write more, look back and see how your poems have improved.

# Superheroes

The concluding chapter moves children on to detailed consideration of characters and their role in stories. Week 1 focuses on known superheroes, based on those the children may have encountered in films and books, contrasting them with the villains they come up against. This culminates in verbally exploring an encounter between the two. Week 2 moves back in time to Greek mythology, looking closely at Heracles and pondering if he was the first ever superhero, before allowing children to explore and retell a myth of their choice. The chapter then moves back to the present to consider a real-life hero, with an opportunity to write and present news reports, as well as a focused lesson revising various aspects of grammar. Weeks 4 and 5 look at the creation of children's own superheroes (and villains), placing them in their own comic-book story. The chapter concludes with superhero poetry in week 6, including lessons revising homophones and introducing compound adjectives.

## Expected prior learning
- Can understand how characters are developed.
- Know the features of a myth.
- Know the features of a recount.
- Understand how a character can be described by what he/she does or says.
- Understand the use of time words to create flow in stories.
- Know the features of rhyme.
- Know what homophones are.
- Know what compound words are.

## Overview of progression
- There is a strong focus on spelling and dictionary skills throughout the chapter, including words of Greek origin, as well as reading and replicating different text-types.
- Most of the language skills covered in the rest of the book are revised and consolidated, including direct speech, the perfect form, possessive apostrophes, and time and cause words.
- In addition, there are many opportunities for children to develop and improve their ability to compose and present stories and information orally.

## Creative context
- There are two main cross-curricular opportunities, with Ancient Greece allowing aspects of the history and geography curriculum to be introduced, and graphic design through studying and creating comic strips.

## Preparation
It is essential to collate (with your class' help) as many relevant resources as possible – a wide variety of books, comics, models and images of superheroes, and age-appropriate versions of Greek myths. Newspaper cuttings that present articles on everyday heroes would also be very useful.

### You will also need:
Atlases; real-life news reports; dictionaries; atlases; large indoor space; video camera (optional); pre-recorded television news reports; a range of poems of your choice; internet access is preferable.

### On the CD-ROM you will find:
Media resources 'Map of Greece', 'Superhero comic strip'; interactive activities 'Good and evil words', 'Direct speech', Correcting work', 'Homophones', 'Compound adjectives'; photocopiable pages 'The story of Heracles', 'A real-life hero', 'The Really Cool Adventures of Captain Underpants', Superhero story planner', 'Superhero poems'

# Chapter at a glance

An overview of the chapter. For curriculum objective codes, please see pages 8–10.

| Week | Lesson | Curriculum objectives | Summary of activities | Outcomes |
|------|--------|----------------------|----------------------|----------|
| 1 | 1 | RC: 2, 5, 7 | Identify and describe the characteristics of different superheroes. | Can identify themes and character traits. |
| | 2 | RC: 2, 5, 7 | Identify and describe the characteristics of different villains. | Can identify themes and character traits. |
| | 3 | RC: 5 WC: 2 | Describe a superhero and a villain to ensure a balanced contrast between them. | Can develop characters. |
| | 4 | RC: 7 | Create a verbal retelling of an episode between their chosen superhero and villain. | Can retell scenes using engaging, appropriate language. |
| | 5 | WT: 5, 6 | Study a range of words with 'y' in them and learn their spellings. | Can spell a range of /i/ words. |
| 2 | 1 | RC: 4, 5 | Listen to and discuss the story of Heracles. | Can listen attentively and identify information in a story. |
| | 2 | WT: 5, 6 | Study a range of 'ch' words of Greek origin and learn their spellings. | Can spell a range of 'ch' words of Greek origins. |
| | 3 | RC: 4, 5, 13 | Understand the different components of a Greek myth and identify them in a story. | Can recognise and identify elements of a Greek myth. |
| | 4 | WC: 2, 3 | Plan the retelling of a myth in their own voice or style. | Can identify the essential points and elements of a myth. |
| | 5 | RC: 4 WC: 3 | Refine and retell a myth to an audience. | Can retell a myth in their own voice. |
| 3 | 1 | RC: 2, 10, 13 WC: 1 | Read, discuss and summarise a newspaper report about a real-life hero. | Can ask questions about and identify key information in a non-fiction news report. |
| | 2 | WC: 11, 12, 13 | Revise the meaning and use of pronouns, conjunctions and the perfect form. | Can identify and use appropriate grammatical terms and structures. |
| | 3 | WC: 2 | Plan a news story, incorporating key features. | Can dramatically capture the main events in a story. |
| | 4 | WC: 4, 6, 7, 8 | Write, review and edit a short news story. | Can review and improve non-fiction texts. |
| | 5 | WC: 3 | Prepare and perform televised-style coverage of their news reports. | Can adapt and present news reports orally. |
| 4 | 1 | WC: 1, 20 | Read and discuss a superhero comic strip. | Can understand how text is used in comic strips. |
| | 2 | WC: 19 | Rewrite the comic strip as a narrative story. | Can use direct speech correctly in a narrative. |
| | 3 | WT: 5, 6 | Learn a range of words ending in '-sion'. | Can spell words with '-sion' endings. |
| | 4 | WC: 2 | Plan a comic strip for a superhero. | Can convert narrative to a comic-book format. |
| | 5 | WC: 3, 7 | Review and improve their comic-strip work. | Can review and edit their work to improve it. |
| 5 | 1 | WC: 5, 13, 18 WT: 4 | Revise aspects of grammar and punctuation; create superheroes and write sentences for them. | • Can create characters. |
| | 2 | WT: 5, 6 | Learn a range of words using 'ou', as in *young*. | • Can spell words with vowel digraphs. |
| | 3 | WC: 5 | Plan an adventure story for their superhero. | • Can plan a story. |
| | 4 | WC: 2 | Write an adventure story for their superhero. | • Can write an adventure story for a specific character. |
| | 5 | WC: 7, 8, 9 | Review each other's work; edit their stories and present them for publication. | • Can improve writing through review and editing. |

# Chapter at a glance

| Week | Lesson | Curriculum objectives | Summary of activities | Outcomes |
|------|--------|----------------------|----------------------|----------|
| 6 | 1 | RC: 1, 6, 8 | Read and listen to a range of superhero poems: discuss styles and expression and consider improvements. | • Can understand different forms of poetry, and how approaches to reading aloud can change their style. |
| | 2 | WT: 2 WC: 3 | Revisit work on homophones, considering how to use them for rhymes. | • Can understand what homophones are, and know the different spellings for a range of homophones. |
| | 3 | WC: 3 | Learn about compound adjectives, predicting meanings and using them in simple sentences. | • Can understand how to form and use a compound adjective. |
| | 4 | WC1 WC2 | Plan a poem about a superhero. | • Can plan a poem, choosing subject and style to suit their needs. |
| | 5 | RC: 6 WC: 2 WT: 7, 8 | Edit, present and recite a poem. | • Can create a poem using relevant vocabulary and style. |

## Background knowledge

**Compound adjective**: An adjective made by joining two words with a hyphen, such as *hard-nosed*.

**Free verse**: Poetry that tends to follow the rhythm of natural speech, with no set rhythm or rhyme.

**Form**: The type of poem, such as free verse, rhyming, and so on.

**Homophone**: Words that would sound the same but are spelled differently and have different meanings.

**Myth**: A story that reflects aspects of a culture, often related to gods, which sometimes offers explanations for how things exist.

**Rhyme**: When words end with the same sound as each other.

**Rhythm**: In poetry, the 'beat' of a poem, often presented through syllables.

**Structure**: In poetry, how a poem is arranged.

**Voice**: In poetry, 'who' is telling a poem, or the speaker if it is in the third person.

**Vowel digraph**: Two vowel letters that make a single sound, such as 'ou'.

# Week 1 lesson plans

The opening section of this chapter looks at known superheroes and considers their traits and characteristics. Discussion about superheroes in popular culture leads to creation of a 'superhero checklist' for both known heroes and villains. In lesson 3 children must compare and contrast a superhero with an arch-enemy, leading to creating a dialogue between the two in lesson 4. The week finishes with a focused lesson on spelling words with 'y' in the middle (pronounced /i/) and using dictionaries to check their meanings.

## 1: Superheroes we know

### Introduction

- If possible, display an image of a well-known superhero on the board and write the word *SUPERHERO* in large letters below it.
- Write the appropriate dictionary definitions for 'super' and 'hero' elsewhere on the board. Review and explain these, and discuss what the class thinks a superhero is.

### Whole-class work

- Discuss TV and film superheroes that the children know. Brainstorm and note pertinent facts about them on the board.
- Discuss the sort of plots that the superheroes become part of. Ask: *Why do they exist? What do they do?*
- Discuss the themes of two or three typical superhero stories (such as good versus evil) and consider variations between the chosen ones.
- Point out that not all superheroes fit in with stereotypes, and try to elicit suggestions for superheroes of both genders, animals and robots, as well as comical characters and themes.
- Display photocopiable page 200 'Superhero checklist' and, choosing a very familiar superhero, work through the sections with the class, modelling appropriate comments and discussing suitable ratings, and finishing with an overall rating and a suitable conclusion.

### Group work

- Ideally, the following task will be completed by referencing a range of comics and books based around superheroes. If you have a limited range of these available you may need to arrange this as a carousel activity. If there are no published materials available, a range of superheroes will need to be introduced using internet-based images and materials. While not ideal, this can at least provide a range of starting points for children's discussions.
- Arrange the class in groups of three to six and give them access to a small range of comics and books with superhero characters. Allow time for them to look and share aspects with each other.
- Distribute the photocopiable sheet, and explain that you would like each group to select a different superhero that they all agree on and ensure that they all understand the character's background and so on. Through consensus, complete the checklist and assign appropriate ratings.

> **Differentiation**
> - It is very possible that some children will choose a superhero that others may have limited awareness of. This is fine, but they must clearly inform their group members of everything they know about the chosen superhero.

### Review

- Gather the class together and ask groups to share their work with the class, discussing disagreements as appropriate. Note well-identified characteristics and clarify misconceptions or unclear statements.
- Can the class agree on the 'top' superhero according to the ratings given?

---

### Expected outcomes
- All children will use the characteristics of superheroes to create character profiles.
- Most children will use appropriate language to summarise a character.
- Some children will create detailed character profiles, using descriptive words, and showing an understanding of antonyms.

### Curriculum objectives
- To identify themes and conventions in a wide range of books.
- To read books that are structured in different ways and reading for a range of purposes.
- To discuss words and phrases that capture the reader's interest and imagination.

### Resources
Images of superheroes (not provided); selection of books and comics containing superheroes; photocopiable page 200 'Superhero checklist'

**Curriculum objectives**
● To identify themes and conventions in a wide range of books.
● To read books that are structured in different ways and reading for a range of purposes.
● To discuss words and phrases that capture the reader's interest and imagination.

**Resources**
Selection of books and comics containing superheroes; completed superhero ratings (from week 1, lesson 1); photocopiable page 200 'Superhero checklist'

# 2: Villains

## Introduction

● Reminding the class about work from lesson 1 on superheroes, explain that you will now be looking at their enemies. Elicit words for these, such as *arch-enemy, villain, baddy*, and so on, exploring and explaining each term as appropriate.
● Briefly discuss a range of villains that the class know of. Focus in on one of them, showing how photocopiable page 200 'Superhero checklist' from lesson 1 can be easily adapted (or defaced, as a true villain would) to make it suitable for providing a rating of 'evilness'.

## Group work

● Arrange the class in the same groups as in lesson 1, and ensure that they have their original superhero checklists to hand, as well as distributing fresh sheets for them to create a 'villain checklist'.
● Repeat the group-work exercise from lesson 1, focusing instead on the villains of the stories. Stress that groups do not have to choose a villain from the same story as their superhero.
● Also point out that where aspects on the ratings list cannot be found (such as 'catchphrase') that it is acceptable for this exercise to invent one.

### Differentiation
● As in lesson 1, remind the class that ratings can only be given with group consensus.

## Review

● Gather the class together and ask groups to share work. Can the class agree on a 'top' villain according to the ratings given?

**Curriculum objectives**
● To identify themes and conventions in a wide range of books.
● To discuss and record ideas.

**Resources**
Photocopiable page 201 'Good and evil'; selection of books and comics containing superheroes; completed superhero and villain ratings (from week 1, lessons 1 and 2)

# 3: Character traits

## Introduction

● Draw a simple balancing scale on the board with a 'balance point' in the middle, explaining that these are the scales of good and evil. Label each side appropriately. (You could label each side of the scale from 1 to 10, ideally making the evil side negative numbers.)
● Brainstorm public acts and deeds of good and evil, gaining agreement on where these sit on the scales, positioning them appropriately in order of magnitude on your scales. Challenge the class to provide enough contributions to balance the scales.

## Paired work

● Distribute photocopiable page 201 'Good and evil' and explain that children must work in pairs to describe a superhero and their arch-enemy who are well balanced against each other. Stress that they do not have to be extreme.
● Use your own discretion as to whether children base their work on characters already studied in lessons 1 and 2, on different characters, or on characters of their own invention. (Note that subsequent weeks include work on this, though these would not be affected.)

### Differentiation
● To really challenge children, explain the meaning of *antonyms*, and insist that any descriptive words for their arch-enemy are antonyms of their superheroes words.

## Review

● Invite children to share their work, asking them to consider the balance between characters. Have they achieved it in their descriptions?

## Curriculum objectives
● To discuss words and phrases that capture the reader's interest and imagination.

## Resources
Interactive activity 'Good and evil words' on the CD-ROM; selection of books and comics containing superheroes; completed photocopiable page 201 'Good and evil' (from week 1, lesson 3)

# 4: Superhero dialogues

## Introduction
● Open the interactive activity 'Good and evil words' on the CD-ROM, and work with the class to categorise the words according to their relevance to a superhero or a villain, explaining meanings where appropriate.

## Paired work
● Arranging the children in the same pairs as the previous lesson, ask them to consider a known scene between their two chosen characters or to invent a new one. They must then work orally to plan and rehearse a scene between the two characters, ensuring that the dialogue reveals their identities, rather than explicitly stating them. Encourage them to use their completed work on photocopiable page 201 'Good and evil'.
● State that the scene must not be a fight, although it could include one or other of the characters having trapped the other. The main thing is that it is a dialogue that reveals something about them and their situation. If the dialogue can include one or more catchphrases, so much the better.

### Differentiation
● Provide greater structure for those who need it, suggesting scenarios and dilemmas as appropriate.
● Challenge children to include some of the good and evil words from the introduction in their dialogue.

## Review
● Time permitting, have pairs present their work to the class, challenging everyone to identify which is the superhero and which is the villain, and to rate them on the good and evil scale, as used in previous lessons.

## Curriculum objectives
● To use the first two or three letters of a word to check its spelling in a dictionary.
● To write from memory simple sentences, dictated by the teacher, that include words and punctuation taught so far.

## Resources
Dictionaries

# 5: 'y' words

## Introduction
● Write a reasonable selection of words containing the letter 'y' on the board, explaining that it can make different sounds, depending on where it is located in a word, and what other letters surround it. Words might include: *my*, *fly*, *you*, *year*, *gym*, *myth*.
● Categorise the words according to the sounds 'y' makes in them, and raise children's awareness of the different sounds it makes without going into too much detail.

## Independent or paired work
● Write a range of words using the focus 'y' spelling on the board. Words should include: *myth*, *mythical*, *gym*, *gymnasium*, *Egypt*, *Egyptian*, *pyramid*. Ask the class to write them down and then locate them in a dictionary, noting their meanings.
● Dictate a range of sentences including these words, asking children to spell them correctly and to highlight the words including 'y' that make an /i/ sound.

### Differentiation
● Provide the focus words on cue cards and allow children who find spelling difficult to practise them with a range of techniques as per your school spelling policy.
● Challenge children to find more words with this sound, spelling them out and checking their meanings.

## Review
● Check children's spellings and dictionary work, ensuring they understand the use of 'y' as the second letter to find the word's listing.

# Week 2 lesson plans

This week's lessons sustain a focus on Ancient Greece, not as a topic but as a stimulus for hero-like stories. The lessons aim to broaden children's appreciation of the contexts for superheroes, considering the story of Heracles and debating whether he can be classified as a superhero or not. As well as a one-off lesson on words of Greek origin with the /k/ sound, children have the opportunity to study and understand a range of Greek myths, identifying key elements that define the genre, while looking out for superheroes. The week concludes with children preparing and delivering a retelling of a Greek myth in its original, or a modern context.

## 1: Heracles

### Introduction
● Display media resource 'Map of Greece' on the CD-ROM and discuss the country's location and importance to the history of our culture and language. Elicit what the class already know about it – where it is, the origins of the Olympics, and so on.
● Explain that Ancient Greece had a thriving culture over 3000 years ago, and that many stories and events from that period were written down and survive to this day. Explain also that in Ancient Greece, mythology was a popular part of their culture and was used to explain their religion, their history, and the origins of various places and features in the world, such as The Pillars of Heracles (Gibraltar).
● Clarify also that who the Greeks called 'Heracles', the Romans adopted as 'Hercules'.
● Read photocopiable page 'The story of Heracles' from the CD-ROM.
● Discuss the story and note the 12 labours on the board.
● Ponder his superhero status: *What are his powers? Who was his arch-enemy?*

### Whole-class work
● Gathering the class together again, display photocopiable page 202 'Looking at myths', and complete it based on the story of Heracles, modelling effective summary skills as you go.
● Once complete, discuss how the completed template could be used to support work on a retelling of the story.

### Group work
● Arranging children in groups, ask them to debate whether Heracles is a superhero, or not. Assign half the groups as 'yes', and the other groups as 'no'.
● Give each group a copy of the story, and ask them to work together to develop an argument to support their position, referring to the text as necessary.
● Circulate between groups, clarifying as needed and prompting further discussion as appropriate.
● When enough time has passed, pair each 'yes' group with a 'no' group, and ask them to debate the issue, reminding them of the polite rules of etiquette and participation.

### Review
● Gather the class together and have groups present their arguments, ensuring that everyone has an opportunity to participate. Allow debate as appropriate and then end with a vote. Note children who have changed their mind and ask them to elaborate on why.
● To supply an additional challenge, issue children with a copy of the map of Greece, and ask them to locate and label the different places of Heracles' labours using an atlas or the internet to help them.

# 2: Greek words

## Introduction

● Display the media resource 'Map of Greece' on the CD-ROM and play a quick quiz with the class, asking them to point out the location of key cities, features and neighbours.
● Explain how the Greek language had an influence over our own, with some words coming directly, and others through Latin, as spread by the Romans.

## Independent or paired work

● Write a selection of words of Greek origin containing 'ch' on the board, demonstrating their /k/ sound. Words should include: *chorus*, *chemist*, *scheme*, *echo*, *character*, *chaos*, *choir*, and *choreography*. Adapting starter activity 4 'Hard-to-spell words', ask the class to write them down, then locate them in a dictionary and note their meanings.
● Next, dictate a small range of sentences including these words.

> **Differentiation**
> ● Provide the focus words on cue cards and allow children who find spelling difficult to practise them with a range of techniques, as per your school spelling policy.
> ● Challenge children to find more words with this sound, or of Greek origin, spelling them out and checking their meanings.

## Review

● Check children's spellings and dictionary work, ensuring they understand the use and sound of 'ch' in Greek-derived words.
● If you have internet access, go to an online translation site, type in some of the words and have them translated to Greek. (Some sites will even let you hear the words.)

# 3: Understanding Greek myths

## Introduction

● Write *What is a myth?* on the board, and discuss this with the class. Elicit that it is a story set in our world, but often with mythical figures and creatures (including gods), which provides reasons why things exist or are so.
● Display media resource 'Map of Greece' on the CD-ROM and recap on the country's history and significance to our own culture.

## Group work

● Arranging the children as desired, ask them to read a selection of Greek myths and discuss them with their partners or group members. Before they start reading, explain that their task is to find a myth they all like, and to use photocopiable page 202 'Looking at myths' to break down the myth into its different elements. (Note that if the resources available to you are limited you may have to arrange this as a carousel activity. You may also wish to avoid any groups tackling the same myth.)

> **Differentiation**
> ● It may help to photocopy myths that children are interested in (if your school has permission) and allow children to highlight different elements.
> ● As a challenge, more confident children might compare two myths.

## Review

● Gather the class together and review their work. Ask them to share their work in small groups, and allow them time to adjust their work if necessary.

## Curriculum objectives
● To compose and rehearse sentences orally (including dialogue), progressively building a varied and rich vocabulary and an increasing range of sentence structures (see Appendix 2).
● To discuss and record ideas.

## Resources
Good selection of books containing Greek myths; completed photocopiable page 202 'Looking at myths' (from week 2, lesson 3); photocopiable page 142 'Play planning template' (optional)

# 4: Planning a retelling

## Introduction
● Model the retelling of one of the labours of Heracles, using your own words and style, as a model for the type of work you want the class to achieve in this lesson. Discuss your retelling as appropriate.

## Group work
● Arranging groups as per lesson 3 and ensuring that they have their completed work on photocopiable page 202 'Looking at myths' to hand, ask the children to plan a retelling of their Greek myth.
● Explain that a retelling can take various forms – from a straight narration to a dramatic performance – and guide them according to your wishes as well as the time and resources available to you.
● Also explain that they do not need to write anything down, unless they wish to. Their summary from lesson 3 should provide a series of cue points.
● Point out that they will need to assign roles, and consider any props they might wish to use (photocopiable page 142 'Play planning template' may be useful).

> **Differentiation**
> ● To create a significantly more challenging exercise, ask groups to retell the story in a modern context.

## Review
● Try to review work with groups away from the rest of the class to make the actual retellings more engaging. Provide pointers as necessary, encouraging effective use of voice and body, as well as monitoring participation levels to ensure everyone is challenged and takes part.

## Curriculum objectives
● To increase their familiarity with a wide range of books, including fairy stories, myths and legends, and retell some of these orally.
● To compose and rehearse sentences orally (including dialogue), progressively building a varied and rich vocabulary and an increasing range of sentence structures (see Appendix 2).

## Resources
Completed work (from week 2, lessons 3 and 4); large space such as the school hall; video camera (optional)

# 5: Retelling myths

## Introduction
● Start the lesson with a voice exercise of your choice to loosen up the class's vocal chords and free up any inhibitions. Singing a well-known song will suffice.

## Group work
● Allow groups some time for a final run-through of their retelling, reminding them that the use of voice and body are critical for effective delivery.
● Remind the class that as this is a retelling they should feel free to develop their lines as they wish, and that rich, expressive vocabulary will help to create stronger images in their audience's minds.
● Organise a rota for the retellings and video performances if possible, then ask each group to deliver their myth to the class.

> **Differentiation**
> ● Ensure equal participation, let children have access to notes or only take on acting or miming parts as desired.

## Review
● If possible, use the video recordings to facilitate a more substantial review session, looking at each performance in turn and asking children to initially evaluate themselves for use of voice and body, and then to evaluate each retelling as a complete piece.
● If any groups have chosen to place their myth in a contemporary context, take time to compare it to the original and consider the difficulties they have faced and how they overcame them.

# Week 3 lesson plans

This week moves on to working with news reports. The first lesson looks at a report about a real-life hero, considering both the content and structure of the text. Lesson 2 is a one-off revision of the perfect form, conjunctions and pronouns. Lessons 3 to 5 allow for much creativity, with children planning and creating news reports for true or fictional events or characters, concluding with oral adaptations to create televised news reports. Please note that in lesson 1 you will need a small selection of newspaper pages and website articles that are suitable for children. Note also that the plans use the word 'hero' irrespective of gender. Teachers can use the term 'heroine' at their discretion.

## 1: A real-life hero

### Introduction

● Show the class a small selection of newspaper pages and/or website articles, discussing the nature of the text they include, such as headlines, captions and subheadings.

### Whole-class work

● Explain to the class that heroes also exist in real life, in all sorts of ways. Elicit if the class have any heroes and, using their contributions and other examples, discuss the differences between the following:
  ● Role models (people whose behaviour and attitudes are in some way exemplary)
  ● Heroes as people we may choose to look up to (such as sports or music personalities)
  ● Heroes as people who have been brave or helpful, often putting their own welfare below that of other people, animals or the environment
● Display photocopiable page 'A real-life hero' from the CD-ROM and read through the article with the class. Discuss the style of writing for the headlines, and then for the article as a whole. Focus on the events of the report while encouraging the children to develop their familiarity with the article by asking questions of each other.

### Paired work

● Organising the children as desired, distribute copies of the newspaper report and ask them to discuss and agree on the following aspects of the story:
  ● **Who** is the article about?
  ● **What** is the article about? What happened?
  ● **Where** did the events happen?
  ● **When** did it happen?
● Explain that for each of the categories the children must identify a suitable quote from the text, either writing it down or highlighting it on the photocopiable sheet.
● To conclude, ask each pair to try and summarise the article in a single sentence.

### Whole-class work

● After a while, gather the class and work through the four W's of the article, checking that everyone concurs with the answers to these points. Ask for volunteers to share their single-sentence summaries of the article, and ask for others to offer praise or constructive criticism as appropriate.

### Review

● Gather the class and ask for suggestions for questions that the journalist may have asked the characters in the story, challenging the rest of the class to identify the relevant part of the text that has come from the answer to each question.

## Expected outcomes
● All children will read and discuss a news report, before planning and creating their own news feature.
● Most children will make correct use of text structure and quotes in their articles.
● Some children will correctly use quotation, pronouns, conjunctions and the perfect form in their articles.

## Curriculum objectives
● To identify main ideas drawn from more than one paragraph and summarise these.
● To read books that are structured in different ways and read for a range of purposes.
● To ask questions to improve their understanding of a text.
● To discuss writing similar to that which they are planning to write in order to understand and learn from its structure, grammar and vocabulary.

## Resources
Selection of newspaper front pages or website articles that are suitable to show to children; photocopiable page 'A real-life hero' from the CD-ROM

**Curriculum objectives**
● To choose nouns or pronouns appropriately to avoid repetition.
● To extend the range of sentences with more than one clause by using a wider range of conjunctions.
● To use the present perfect form of verbs in contrast to the past tense.

**Resources**
Photocopiable page 'A real-life hero' from the CD-ROM; photocopiable page 108 'Perfect sentences'

# 2: Revising grammar

## Introduction

● Begin the lesson with starter activity 2 'Getting technical', for the terms *pronoun*, *conjunction* and *perfect form*, and stress that this activity is a revision of these aspects of grammar.

## Independent or paired work

● Using photocopiable page 108 'Perfect sentences', either write the same sentences on the board or create your own variations. Start with one complete example to recap and discuss the three elements under consideration (*pronoun*, *conjunction* and *perfect form*).
● Next, provide sentence starters for children to offer verbal completions, challenging their peers to confirm if they are correct as well as point out the different grammatical aspects.
● Dictate two or three sentences to the class and ask them to highlight the different aspects.

> **Differentiation**
> ● Allow those who need support to focus only on pronouns and/or conjunctions, encouraging contributions when appropriate.

## Review

● Recap on pronouns and discuss how they can be used to avoid repetition and how we need to get the balance of pronouns to nouns correct.
● Display photocopiable page 'A real-life hero' from the CD-ROM and work through it with the class, asking them to identify pronouns in it. Exemplify the importance of pronouns for flowing text and speech by replacing them with the proper nouns they represent. Discuss the 'clumsiness' of the amended text.

**Curriculum objectives**
● To discuss and record ideas.

**Resources**
Photocopiable page 203 'News scenarios'; photocopiable page 'A real-life hero' from the CD-ROM

# 3: Planning a news report

## Introduction

● Display photocopiable page 203 'News scenarios' and look at the first one together, discussing the five categories and visualising the events of the story.
● Work as a class to develop a coherent plan for the story that could be used to write a coherent newspaper article, including headline, image and caption, subheadings and good quotes.
● Remind children that photocopiable page 'A real-life hero' from the CD-ROM included quotes from people, and ask who these may be in the new article.

## Paired work

● Challenge the children to create and write a news report for an event involving a 'a real-life hero'. Children can invent their own or choose from one of the six options available on photocopiable page 203 'News scenarios'.
● Remind the children that this is only a planning exercise. As the explanations for *who*, *what*, *where*, *when*, and *how* have already been done for them, they should plan good headlines, an image with a caption, good quotes, and a simple structure for their report.

> **Differentiation**
> ● To extend the challenge, ask children invent a new story or report on a real-life event.

## Review

● Gather the class and ask them to share their plans with one another, providing each other with advice as to the thoroughness of their plan. How does it compare to the one created at the start of the lesson?

## Curriculum objectives
- To organise paragraphs around a theme.
- In non-narrative material, to use simple organisational devices.
- To assess the effectiveness of their own and other's writing and suggest improvements.
- To propose changes to grammar and vocabulary to improve consistency.

## Resources
Selection of newspaper front pages or website articles that are suitable to show to children; completed news report plans (from week 3, lesson 3); news report templates (optional, not provided)

# 4: Writing a news report

## Introduction
- Begin the lesson with starter activity 7 'Conjunction challenge', reinforcing that extended sentences allow more information and explanations in a text – essential for news reports.

## Independent work
- Remind the children about the essentials of news reports, showing them newspapers and websites as necessary, and considering the similarities and differences between the two.
- Next, ask the class to work independently to write a news report.

## Paired work
- After a while, ask the children to work again with their planning partners from lesson 3, looking at each other's work to provide constructive feedback regarding the report itself. Have they covered all the areas (*headline*, *who*, *what*, *where*, *when*, *how*, *quotes*, *image* and *caption*)?
- Allow further time to ensure all areas are covered, then ask them to review and edit their own grammar and punctuation, assessing their own use of sentences, pronouns, inverted commas, connectives and time and cause words.

### Differentiation
- Provide structured templates for those who need support, with space for a headline and an image with a caption, using subheadings to appropriately structure their text.

## Review
- Allow children to share their work in pairs, offering constructive feedback. If time permits, allow them to review and improve their work before the final lesson of the week.

## Curriculum objectives
- To compose and rehearse sentences orally (including dialogue), progressively building a varied and rich vocabulary and an increasing range of sentence structures (see Appendix 2).

## Resources
Completed news reports (from week 3, lesson 4); pre-recorded TV news reports (optional); video camera (optional)

# 5: From print to screen – live news reports and interviews

## Introduction
- Select one or two of the finished news reports to read to the class, modelling good use of voice to capture the essence of the piece. As you read, ask children to mentally check if you have covered all areas of the report (*who*, *what*, *where*, *when*, *how*), and request constructive comments that identify good use of language and/or suggestions for improvement.
- Briefly discuss television news reports (watching some if desired), explaining that these essentially cover the same information, but also provide more spontaneity for interviews and have less need for physical description.

## Group work
- Arrange the children in groups of three or four and ask them to agree which of the news scenarios they will enact as a TV report. Explain that as well as a presenter they will need to select individuals as the 'hero' figure and others who might have been involved or who want to speak highly of the hero.
- Ask the groups to work together to orally plan and rehearse the reporter's introduction and questions and answers from the people involved, followed by a final summary from the reporter.

## Review
- Either invite groups to perform their reports or watch the videos, again discussing thoroughness of the report and aspects that hold viewers' attention.

# Week 4 lesson plans

The chapter now returns to fiction with a rather unusual superhero – Captain Underpants. Initially, children consider a comic-book format short story, looking carefully at the language used and style of presentation. Then, to consolidate children's understanding and use of inverted commas, they must rewrite the comic-book story as prose. Lesson 3 is a discrete spelling lesson for words ending in '-sion' (pronounced /zhun/). Children use them in a text and have an opportunity to consolidate dictionary skills. The final two lessons move on to collaborative planning and writing, to create their own comic strips.

## 1: Meet Captain Underpants

### Introduction
● Open the interactive activity 'Direct speech' on the CD-ROM and work through it with the class, reinforcing the correct use of inverted commas and the associated language of recording speech.
● Explain that over the next few lessons children will be consolidating their understanding of direct speech and its punctuation, grammar and vocabulary.

### Whole-class work
● Examine the cartoon strip in Chapter 3 of *The Adventures of Captain Underpants* by Dav Pilkey, considering the cover, blurb and author profile.
● If you have limited access to the book, hand out photocopiable page 'The Really Cool Adventures of Captain Underpants' from the CD-ROM and read it with the class.
● Recap on the difference between the spoken and written word, reminding the class how the sense of the spoken word can be captured in speech bubbles. Discuss how the speech bubble takes on the job of inverted commas, and that these are not needed in comic strips.
● Look at the different styles of speech bubbles when groups of children are speaking or shouting, and consider why the author has created 'jagged' bubbles. Also consider thought bubbles, and how these are illustrated.
● Clarify any difficult language, considering non-standard English as appropriate, and also discuss the author's use of incorrect spelling and capital letters. Spend time identifying deliberate errors only if desired, but be sure to stress that this way of writing is not appropriate for children's schoolwork.
● To conclude the whole-class work, display photocopiable page 200 'Superhero checklist' and, in discussion, ask groups to create a superhero rating for Captain Underpants.

### Group work
● Ask each group to choose superheroes they know of, and compare them with Captain Underpants. Consider justifications for their preferred character.
● Ask groups to prepare a one-minute presentation, comparing and contrasting their superhero with Captain Underpants, emphasising that they can use mime as well as oral explanations to create a humorous presentation.

> **Differentiation**
> ● Arrange groups appropriately, and encourage children to nominate two members to create accompanying mimes to ensure equal participation.

### Review
● Ask each group to deliver their presentation in turn, noting down on the board the various superheroes that Captain Underpants is compared to. Allow the class time to raise points or questions about each presentation.
● To conclude, in discussion consider how effective the concept of a humorous superhero is – what are the pros and cons compared to more serious characters? Do the children know of any other fun superheroes?

## Curriculum objectives
● To use and punctuate direct speech.

## Resources
Media resource 'Superhero comic strip' on the CD-ROM; photocopiable page 'The Really Cool Adventures of Captain Underpants' from the CD-ROM

# 2: Rewriting *Captain Underpants*

## Introduction
● Open the media resource 'Superhero comic strip' on the CD-ROM and work through it with the class. Discuss what 'G' and 'E' might stand for (good and evil), and invent a story to give the opening frames a meaning.
● Work collaboratively with the class to write a brief narrative for the opening frames, including direct speech. Once written, discuss the punctuation and grammar involved.

## Whole-class work
● Opening the first spread of photocopiable page 'The Really Cool Adventures of Captain Underpants' from the CD-ROM, discuss how to convert this into prose, considering how the descriptive text almost tells a complete story, but that without the pictures and text in speech bubbles it is not complete.

## Independent or paired work
● Display or distribute the remaining two spreads of the photocopiable sheet and explain that the task for this session is to rewrite the Captain Underpants comic strip as a story, using direct speech where necessary.

### Differentiation
● To avoid children being daunted, allow them to focus just on one spread.
● Encourage children to use adverbs to describe how people are speaking.

## Review
● Focus initially on the correct use of punctuation and grammar, and if desired allow further time for children to complete their stories.

## Curriculum objectives
● To use the first two or three letters of a word to check its spelling in a dictionary.
● To write from memory simple sentences, dictated by the teacher, that include words and punctuation taught so far.

## Resources
Photocopiable page 204 '-sion' words'

# 3: '-sion' words, pronounced /zhun/

## Introduction
● Write a selection of words containing the '-sion' ending on the board, demonstrating their /zhun/ sound. Words should include: *division, invasion, confusion, decision, collision* and *television*.

## Independent or paired work
● Adapting starter activity 4 'Hard-to-spell words', ask the class to write down the words from the introduction then locate them in a dictionary and note their meanings. As children work, circulate and discuss their findings, looking at root words and consider how they are changed, looking for common patterns concerning spelling and pronunciation.
● As children complete their work, distribute photocopiable page 204 '-sion words' and ask children to complete it.

### Differentiation
● Provide the focus words on cue cards and allow children who find spelling difficult to practise them with a range of techniques as per your school spelling policy.
● Challenge children to find more words with this sound, spelling them out and checking their meanings (such as *erosion, occasion, persuasion*).

## Review
● Check children's worksheet and dictionary work, ensuring they understand the use and sound of words ending with the /zhun/ sound.
● If appropriate, explain the pronunciation rules, contrasting the sound made for words such as *expression* ('-ssion' is used if the root word ends in 'ss' or '-mit'), *tension* and *expansion* ('-sion' is used if the root word ends in 'd' or 'se').

**Curriculum objectives**
● To discuss and record ideas.

**Resources**
Media resource 'Superhero comic strip' on the CD-ROM; photocopiable page 'The Really Cool Adventures of Captain Underpants' from the CD-ROM; photocopiable page 'The story of Heracles' from the CD-ROM; completed work on myths from week 2 (optional)

# 4: Planning a comic strip

## Introduction
● Open the media resource 'Superhero comic strip' on the CD-ROM and, in discussion, summarise the purpose of each frame (*superhero uses x-ray vision, villain admits defeat*, and so on).

## Whole-class work
● Display photocopiable page 'The Really Cool Adventures of Captain Underpants' from the CD-ROM and briefly recap the work from lessons 1 and 2, looking at images, speech bubbles and additional text for conveying a story.
● Next, work with the class to summarise some of the frames to explain the content or purpose of each one, such as: *Opening shot of cafeteria to set the scene, Captain Underpants flushes monster down the loo*, and so on.

## Paired work
● Remind the class of the work covered in week 2 looking at Greek myths. If appropriate, it may be productive for children to base their work in this lesson around the Greek myth they analysed in week 2. If not, using photocopiable page 'The story of Heracles' from the CD-ROM is fine.
● Ask the children to plan a comic strip for all or part of a Greek myth – either the one they analysed in week 2, or one of the labours of Heracles. Explaining that they do not have to draw the comic strip, merely identify how they might structure each frame.

## Review
● Ask children to share their plans and offer constructive comments, checking that their plans flow logically.

**Curriculum objectives**
● To compose and rehearse sentences orally (including dialogue), progressively building a varied and rich vocabulary and an increasing range of sentence structures (see Appendix 2).
● To assess the effectiveness of their own and other's writing and suggest improvements.

**Resources**
Completed comic strip plans from week 4, lesson 4

# 5: Creating comic strips

## Introduction
● Choosing one or more pieces of children's work from lesson 4, look at comic strip plans and discuss what sort of comic-strip frames these plans might give rise to. Use this opportunity to model effective oral composition, perhaps starting with a boring frame and reviewing and improving it through discussion.
● Also, remind the class of the three components of a comic strip: images, narrative text and speech bubbles.

## Paired work
● Ensuring that each pair's plans from the previous lesson are completed, ask them to create a comic strip from them, composing their text orally to begin with, then transcribing their text once they are happy with it. Stress that drawing detailed pictures should come later.
● It is more important to produce two or three comic book frames that are engaging and flow well than to create a finished piece. Stress to children the importance of discussing options for dialogue and accompanying text, as well as considering what information the images convey.

> **Differentiation**
> ● Allow children to alternate frames to allow equal participation. (This also challenges thinking to sustain a coherent plot.)

## Review
● Ask the class to review and edit their comic strips with partners, check for sense, best vocabulary, spellings, and so on, and discuss improvements. If desired, allow more time to improve and complete their work.

# Week 5 lesson plans

This week returns children to fictional superheroes. New characters are created in lesson 1, which also revises a small range of grammar and punctuation. This is followed by discrete spelling pattern work (focusing on the /ou/ sound as in *young*) in lesson 2. Lesson 3 returns to the superheroes, working on strong plans for a short story with lesson 4 used for drafting and lesson 5 editing and writing for presentation.

## 1: Brand-new superheroes

### Expected outcomes
● All children will plan a well-rounded character, before planning, drafting, editing and writing a short story.
● Most children will write an engaging story, logically aligned to the character's traits.
● Some children will create a unique character in an engaging story.

### Curriculum objectives
● In narratives, to create settings, characters and plot.
● To indicate possession by using the possessive apostrophe with plural nouns.
● To choose nouns or pronouns appropriately to avoid repetition.
● To place the apostrophe accurately in words with regular plurals and in words with irregular plurals.

### Resources
Photocopiable page 205 'Superhero planning sheet'; image of a well-known superhero

### Introduction
● Begin by adapting starter activity 2 'Getting technical' to cover the following terms (remember to jumble up the order):
  ● **Personal information:** details about the person that could identify them.
  ● **Alter ego:** a separate personality that someone uses some of the time.
  ● **Unique attributes:** abilities that only this person has.
  ● **Back story:** an explanation as to why someone is the way they are.
  ● **Motivation:** what makes a person want to do what they do.

### Whole-class work
● Display the image of a well-known superhero, and use them to complete the aspects of their persona explained in the introduction (personal info, alter ego, unique attributes, back story and motivation).

### Independent or paired work
● Distribute photocopiable page 205 'Superhero planning sheet' and ask children to carefully consider and develop their own superhero. Ensure they work in pencil and encourage them to reconsider and amend ideas as they go. Allow half the lesson to complete this task.

### Whole-class work
● Focusing attention on you and the board, revise the possessive apostrophe and personal pronouns through a range of suitable sentences around the appearance and attributes of a superhero.
For example: *Captain Underpants has an alter ego called Mr Krupp. Mr Krupp is a head teacher.* would become: *Captain Underpants' alter ego is called Mr Krupp. He is a head teacher.*
Or: *Captain Underpants has no hair on his head. His head is very round.* would become: *Captain Underpants' head is bald. It is very round.*
● Stress the use of the possessive apostrophes and the pronouns.

### Independent or paired work
● Ask children to write five sentences about their superhero using possessive apostrophes and pronouns on the reverse of their photocopiable sheet.

---

**Differentiation**
● For children who find the sentences difficult to copy, encourage them to use the example sentences, substituting information for their own superhero.
● To make the task more challenging, ask the children to write a coherent introductory paragraph rather than discrete sentences.

---

### Review
● Arrange the children with review partners and allow them time to look at each other's work, discussing the content of their superhero information, and checking the quality of their superhero sentences.
● If possible, allow further time for them to improve and correct these before they start on their story planning in lesson 3 of this week.

**Curriculum objectives**
● To use the first two or three letters of a word to check its spelling in a dictionary.
● To write from memory simple sentences, dictated by the teacher, that include words and punctuation taught so far.

**Resources**
Dictionaries

# 2: The 'ou' letter pattern

## Introduction

● Begin with starter activity 2 'Getting technical', focusing on the words 'vowel' and 'digraph'. (A digraph is defined as a combination of two letters making one sound.)
● Write a selection of words containing the 'ou' digraph on the board: *group, soul, mouth, touch, could, thought* and *curious*, and ask the class to decide in which of the words shown will the 'ou' digraph make the same sound.
● Elicit through discussion that 'ou' makes a different sound in all of these words, and that learning specific spellings is a matter of practice.

## Independent or paired work

● Write a range of words using the focus 'ou' digraph on the board. Words should include: *couple, young, touch, double, trouble, country, southern.* Ask the class to write them down then locate them in a dictionary and note their meanings.
● Dictate a range of sentences including these words, asking children to spell them correctly and to highlight the focus words.

> **Differentiation**
> ● Provide the focus words on cue cards and allow children who find spelling difficult to practise them with a range of techniques, as per your school spelling policy.

## Review

● Check children's spellings and dictionary work, ensuring they understand the use of 'o' as the second or third letter to find the word's listing.

**Curriculum objectives**
● In narratives, to create settings, characters and plot.

**Resources**
Completed photocopiable page 205 'Superhero planning sheet' (from week 5, lesson 1); photocopiable page 206 'Superhero story planner'

# 3: Planning superhero stories

## Introduction

● Explain that over the next three lessons children will be aiming to produce a high-quality story, with their newly-invented superhero as the central character.
● Reminding children of a well-known superhero, run through an event from one of their films or stories, briefly listing the superhero, their sidekick, the villain, the setting and the dilemma (explaining that 'dilemma' is the term used as the central point or theme of the story, providing its purpose).

## Independent work

● Distribute the completed work on photocopiable page 205 'Superhero planning sheet' and photocopiable page 206 'Superhero story planner' and ask children to think through the details of a story they would like to create for their superhero.
● Before they start, encourage them to imagine the scenes from their story as a film to help create images in their minds, and encourage them to plan in pencil so that they can easily alter their work as ideas evolve.

> **Differentiation**
> ● In discussion with the whole class, brainstorm a range of interesting settings and dilemmas, leaving these available for children to reference if they wish.

## Review

● Ask children to share their plans with a review partner, questioning each other to ensure that their plot makes sense.
● Before they start writing, ask them to consider how they will create the atmosphere they imagine, noting useful vocabulary on the back of their plans.

## Curriculum objectives
● To discuss and record ideas.

## Resources
Photocopiable page 'The Really Cool Adventures of Captain Underpants' from the CD-ROM; completed photocopiable page 206 'Superhero story planner' (from week 5, lesson 3)

# 4: Drafting superhero stories

## Introduction
● Begin the lesson with starter activity 10 'Being descriptive', ideally basing this around a passage of text that models engaging writing, with sentences that are both descriptive and extended.
● Discuss the importance of evocative language within interesting sentences in creating engaging stories.

## Whole-class work
● Revisit photocopiable page 'The Really Cool Adventures of Captain Underpants' from the CD-ROM with the class, and consider how it might break down into sections (the three spreads of the book more or less fall neatly into the categories of beginning, middle and end).
● Ask the class to re-read their work on photocopiable page 'Superhero story planner', and consider whether they have enough information in place to develop an interesting story.

## Independent work
● Ask the children to start drafting stories with their superheroes as central characters, reminding them that in dialogue, new paragraphs are necessary for new speakers, as well as for changes of subject.

### Differentiation
● Support children by verifying their plans with them, then provide structured writing frames or allow them to compose orally, transcribing for them if possible.

## Review
● Ideally, try to allow an extended lesson, or two or three sessions, for children to complete their writing.
● Whatever way you structure the session(s), be sure to bring the children together from time to time and let them share progress.

## Curriculum objectives
● To proofread for spelling and punctuation errors.
● To assess the effectiveness of their own and other's writing and suggesting improvements.
● To propose changes to grammar and vocabulary to improve consistency.

## Resources
Interactive activity 'Correcting work' on the CD-ROM; story plans and drafts from previous lessons

# 5: Editing and presenting superhero stories

## Introduction
● Begin the lesson with interactive activity 'Correcting work', emphasising the importance of good grammar and punctuation.
● Emphasise that this activity is only about correcting punctuation and grammar, and that in reviewing their own work children should also be looking at spellings, but perhaps more importantly at the quality of their own writing.

## Independent work or paired work
● Organising the class as desired, ask the children to proofread their own and/ or other's work to check for spelling, punctuation and grammar in the first instance, using notation as per school policy and guidelines.
● Stress that this lesson is about two things: correcting the accuracy of their texts (proofreading), and reviewing and improving the quality of the text itself. Then have children read through again (preferably aloud) to help identify where the text does not flow well or where language could be improved.
● Allow time for everyone to edit and improve their texts accordingly.

## Review
● Have the children read their stories to their peers. Try to follow this up with personal and peer evaluations.

# Week 6 lesson plans

As with other chapters, the final week is focused on poetry. Children are introduced to a range of superhero poetry to read and enjoy, with time to practise their control of volume, tone and intonation to enhance reading or recital. This is followed by lessons revising homophones and introducing compound words to provide strong descriptions. Children then move on to create their own poetry, leading to presentation copies and readings.

## 1: Superhero poetry

### Introduction
● Read a small selection of poems of your choice to the class, modelling good intonation, tone and volume.
● After each poem, encourage the class to comment on its meaning and how it was delivered. Also encourage comments on how the poem is structured, its vocabulary and use of rhyme, and so on.

### Whole-class work
● Read 'Steve the Superhero' from photocopiable page 'Superhero poems' from the CD-ROM, or watch the animated song 'Steve the Superhero' that is available online, and discuss whether it is a song or a poem.
● Recap the terms *voice*, *structure* and *style* for understanding poetry:
  ● **Voice:** 'who' is telling the poem, or the speaker if it is in the third person.
  ● **Form:** the form of the poem – free verse, rhyming, acrostic, and so on.
  ● **Structure:** how it will be arranged.
● Ask how these are addressed in the song or poem.
● Watch the animation again and consider whether it would work just as well without the backing music.

### Group work
● Arranging the class in groups of four to six, give each group photocopiable page 'Superhero poems' from the CD-ROM, and then ask them to compare and contrast their differing styles, with questions such as: *Do they rhyme, and if so how? Do they tell a story? Are they funny? What are their strengths and weaknesses?*
● Ask groups to prepare to read or recite their favourite poem to the class. They should also be prepared to explain it, and their reasons for liking it.
● Give groups enough time to prepare their reading or recital, reminding them of the different ways they might present it.

### Whole-class work
● Have groups read or recite their poem and present their work to the class.
● After each reading, praise and reinforce effective delivery and presentations and then allow other groups to offer comments as appropriate, reminding them to focus on tone, intonation and volume.

> **Differentiation**
> ● Support less confident children by grouping the class appropriately and ensuring they are able to present poems and work that is manageable for them.
> ● The learning can be extended by asking children to categorise the poems by form or genre and to analyse rhythms.

### Review
● Gather the class together and work through the photocopiable sheets one more time, analysing the poems more thoroughly, initially through numbers (verses, lines per verse, syllables and so on) moving on to how the elements of voice, form and structure are addressed in each one. Reinforce strong vocabulary as appropriate. To conclude, discuss which poems are the most effective for reading aloud, and why.

## Curriculum objectives
● To spell further homophones.
● To compose and rehearse sentences orally (including dialogue), progressively building a varied and rich vocabulary and an increasing range of sentence structures (see Appendix 2).

## Resources
Interactive activity 'Homophones' on the CD-ROM; photocopiable page 136 'Homophones'

# 2: Rhymes with homophones

## Introduction
● Before the lesson starts, write a number of sentences on the board containing homophones, but using the incorrect spelling. Use some of these words (covered in Spring 2): *accept/except, affect/effect, ball/bawl, berry/bury, brake/break, fair/fare, grate/great, groan/grown, here/hear, heel/heal/he'll, knot/not, mail/male, main/mane, meat/meet, medal/meddle, missed/mist, peace/piece, plain/plane, rain/rein/reign, scene/seen, weather/whether* and *whose/who's*.
● Remind the class of the work they have previously done with homophones, and work through the sentences you have written, spotting errors and listing homophones for all words identified.

## Whole-class work
● Open the interactive activity 'Homophones' on the CD-ROM and work through it together.
● Next, orally deliver a range of sentences with a homophone, asking the class to identify which is the correct spelling, reinforcing letter patterns as you go.

## Paired work
● Challenge the children to collaborate orally to produce some rhyming couplets using homophones. Remind them that there should be the same number of syllables in each line.

> **Differentiation**
> ● For struggling spellers, make cue cards and allow them to match homophones against definitions (see photocopiable page 136 'Homophones').

## Review
● Gather the class and ask for successful rhymes to be shared. Stress to the children that this is a difficult activity, and discuss any difficulties – were they thinking more about sensible sentences, or choosing words to give the correct number of syllables?

## Curriculum objectives
● To compose and rehearse sentences orally (including dialogue), progressively building a varied and rich vocabulary and an increasing range of sentence structures (see Appendix 2).

## Resources
Interactive activity 'Compound adjectives' on the CD-ROM; photocopiable page 207 'Compound adjectives'; completed superhero story work (from week 5)

# 3: Compound adjectives

## Introduction
● Explain that children have encountered compound words before (such as *superhero*), but compound adjectives are a little different. They require the use of hyphens and often end in similar letter patterns.
● Open interactive activity 'Compound adjectives' on the CD-ROM and work through it with the class, pointing out the use of hyphens.
● If desired, discuss the structure of the words involved, considering their class and why they typically end in 'ing' or 'ed'.

## Independent or paired work
● Distribute photocopiable page 207 'Compound adjectives' and ask children to complete the task, offering meanings for the compound adjectives. Encourage them to work in pencil so that they might easily alter their work.
● After a while, gather everyone's attention and discuss the meanings of the compound adjectives on the photocopiable sheet. Ask children to consider their own interpretations and alter their work as necessary.
● Challenge the children to write sentences that describe a superhero or villain using words on the photocopiable sheet or try to create new ones.

## Review
● Ask the children to share their sentences with each other, checking to see if they are using the compound words correctly.

# 4: Planning superhero poems

## Introduction

● Display photocopiable page 'Superhero poems' from the CD-ROM and recap on the key elements discussed in lesson 1, reminding children of the voice, style and structure used in each one.
● Focusing on the poem 'Aunt Betty Thinks She's Batgirl', show children that short poems can be just as effective as longer poems.
● Recap on the superheroes discussed over the previous weeks, from the serious to the mythical (Heracles), not to mention the comical (Captain Underpants), as well as their own creations. Give the children time to consider who they want to write about, and in what style.

## Independent or paired work

● Using photocopiable page 79 'Poetry planner' if desired, ask the children to start preparing for their own superhero poem, reminding them of the compound adjectives and homophones revised this week.
● Those who wish to write about their own superheroes should access their previous work.

> **Differentiation**
> ● Challenge more confident children to write a rhyming couplet poem using homophones, or one using compound adjectives in every line.

## Review

● Gather the class together and ask children to share their work in pairs, discussing their reasons for choosing particular styles and vocabulary. Ask them to review vocabulary choices with each other and discuss alternatives.
● To conclude, share plans as appropriate and reinforce knowledge of poetry styles and strong vocabulary choices.

# 5: Writing superhero poems

## Introduction

● Begin the lesson with starter activity 3 'Vocabulary builder' for a small range of homophones and compound adjectives, preferably some of those used in lessons 2 and 3.

## Independent work

● Ask the children to each draft their own superhero poem, using their plans from lesson 4 to help them, encouraging them to avoid over-long poems.
● As work progresses circulate and discuss work with individuals. Where interesting work is emerging, stop the class briefly and share good words or lines, discussing why particular work seems effective.
● Allow time for children to review and check their work, supporting them as appropriate, before moving them on to rewriting their poems in their best handwriting for a display or class anthology.

> **Differentiation**
> ● Remind those who struggle with words that rhyming is not essential – the main purpose is for them to consider interesting, descriptive language.
> ● For children using rhyming couplets and homophones, give them support or leeway if they are struggling to find suitable language.

## Review

● Ideally, in a separate session, complete the chapter's work with readings and recitals, before combining all finished superhero poems in a class anthology.

**Curriculum objectives**
● To learn the grammar for Year 3 in Appendix 2.
● To use and understand the grammatical terminology in Appendix 2 accurately and appropriately when discussing their writing and reading.

**Resources**
Various photocopiable pages from across the book; many of the interactive activities on the CD-ROM

# Grammar and punctuation: Revising grammar and punctuation

## Revise

● In Year 3, children should be familiar with, and use, the following aspects of vocabulary, grammar and punctuation (see Appendix 2):
  ● Formation of nouns using a range of prefixes.
  ● Appropriate use of the forms 'a' or 'an'.
  ● Word families based on common words.
  ● Expressing time, place and cause using conjunctions, adverbs or prepositions.
  ● Using the present perfect form of verbs instead of the simple past.
  ● Inverted commas to punctuate speech.
  ● The following terminology: *adverb, preposition, conjunction, word family, prefix, clause, subordinate clause, direct speech, consonant, consonant letter, vowel, vowel letter, inverted commas (or speech marks).*
● Revision can be done using several of the photocopiable sheets and starter activities in this book, plus many of the interactive activities on the CD-ROM, working through them and using grammatical terms wherever possible.

## Assess

● Look at age-appropriate texts from a grammatical point of view, asking children to highlight and explain particular words or structures.
● Try to assess knowledge of grammar when talking to children about their writing – ask them to highlight and explain their use of certain aspects.

## Further practice

● Give children grammatical terms to learn each week at home.
● Have children create their own 'technical dictionaries' to develop all the way through school, listing key terms and adding definitions and examples.

**Curriculum objectives**
● To read further exception words, noting the unusual correspondences between spelling and sound, and where these occur in the word.
● To spell words that are often misspelled (Appendix 1).
● To write from memory simple sentences, dictated by the teacher, that include words and punctuation taught so far.

**Resources**
Dictionaries

# Spelling: Words including spelling patterns 'y', 'ou', 'ch' and 'sion'

## Revise

● This chapter has focused on a range of letters and spelling patterns that offer different pronunciations because of their location in words:
  ● 'y' as in *myth, mythical, gym, gymnasium, Egypt, Egyptian, pyramid*
  ● 'ch' as in *chorus, chemist, scheme, echo, chaos, choir, choreography*
  ● 'sion' as in *division, invasion, confusion, decision, collision, television*
  ● 'ou' as in *couple, young, touch, double, trouble, country, southern*
● The number of words in each of these categories is relatively small. As such, the main focus of any revision exercises should be to consolidate children's knowledge, taking the opportunity to develop their understanding of the different pronunciation in different word positions, and any exceptions.
● As well as your usual spelling routines, provide other words with the same letters but different pronunciations and sort them accordingly.

## Assess

● Dictate a range of sentences including some of the words covered, introducing new ones if possible. Allow children to spell them in context.
● Also look out for use of these words in children's independent writing.

## Further practice

● If are still having difficulties with these spellings, ask children to identify them in passages of text, invent and read specific passages using the target words.
● Use starter activity 12 'Word displays'.

**Curriculum objectives**
● To identify how language, structure, and presentation contribute to meaning.

**Resources**
Selection of books and comics containing superheroes; good selection of books containing Greek myths; photocopiable page 'A real-life hero' from the CD-ROM; photocopiable page 'Superhero poems' from the CD-ROM

# Reading: Understanding texts

## Revise

● Staying with the focus of this chapter initially, over time review the different texts encountered: comics, myths, news reports and poems.
● Try to develop discussions about why the structure of poems can be effective, but would be inadequate for a news report, and so on.
● Consider the differences between standard and non-standard English, and consider why some texts are well suited to their presentation whereas others are not, and how much this is a matter of personal taste.
● For all the texts you encounter, spend a short time considering each from the separate perspectives of language, structure and presentation:
  ● **Language:** Identify, note and explain effective words and phrases. Look for hidden meanings from what characters say and how they say it.
  ● **Structure:** Take a paragraph and cut it into sentences, then ask children to arrange them for sense.
  ● **Presentation:** Display and look at a variety of text types, including those covered in Summer 2. Ask the class to identify the different elements in each, such as speech bubbles or photos with captions, and consider how these affect our understanding and enjoyment, as well as the meaning the texts convey.

## Assess

● Remembering that accurate assessment requires knowledge, skills and understanding to be used in different contexts, try to find texts about subjects other than superheroes (there are several texts on the CD-ROM that you may find useful).
● The difficult part is crafting a range of questions that will allow you to assess children's understanding of the roles of language, structure and presentation. As a guideline, try the following approaches (they can all be presented in the same assessment):
  ● **Language:** Choose questions that encourage children to focus on words or expressions, such as: *Can you find five words or phrases that create an image of the main character? Explain your choices. What does the way in which character X talks tell you about him/her as a person?*
  ● **Structure:** Ask children to summarise each paragraph in a piece, and then ask the more difficult question: *What is the purpose of each paragraph?*
  ● **Presentation:** Ask children to comment on the way the text is presented, asking them to suggest what they would do to improve this, not so much from the aspect of making the text more accessible, but richer. This might include varying fonts, moving or adding images, adding subheadings, a contents list or even an introduction.
● In assessing children's responses to these challenges, look for children who are using the appropriate 'meta-language' (such as *metaphor, heading, paragraph* and *bullet point*), as well as those who can justify their choices and offer alternatives.

## Further practice

● Continue to introduce a wide range of text types, in particular those that can be covered in a single lesson, and try to embed the ideas and routines mentioned above.
● Continue encouraging the children to consider each aspect carefully when creating their own texts, covering them when reviewing their work.
● Try rewriting narrative texts as non-fiction, and vice versa, and even applying the same treatment to poetry.

## Curriculum objectives

● In narratives, to create characters, settings and plot.

## Resources

Photocopiable page 205 'Superhero planning sheet'; photocopiable page 206 'Superhero story planner'; video or audio recording devices

# Writing: In narratives, creating characters, settings and plot

## Revise

● To increase children's knowledge of text structure and styles while avoiding disinterest and reducing stories to mere words and techniques, provide them with a broad range of fiction, particularly short stories from as many different genres and styles as possible. Encourage them to read freely of the styles that they like, and try to use more neutral texts for analysing and 'deconstructing' texts.

● Encourage a critical eye for text, allowing children to compare, contrast and criticise texts that they do not like. Ask: *Are they too slow? Are the descriptions over the top? Are the characters too obvious?*

● Character:
  ● Remind children of work in Chapters 1 and 5, which focused on the characters of Roald Dahl, where the essence of different characters is created quickly through what they say, rather than over-long descriptions.
  ● Remind children of the compound adjectives they have learned about in this chapter. Often these are metaphorical (*hard-nosed*, *tight-fisted*), and can create a strong feel for a character.

● Setting:
  ● Build up children's vocabulary banks, including similes and metaphors for settings to help them describe places.
  ● Display this vocabulary prominently in your classroom, perhaps around a range of photographs of interesting locations.
  ● Use and adapt starter activity 10 'Being descriptive' regularly – reminding children that a description of any setting can involve more than one of the senses.

● Plot:
  ● Encourage children to read a range of genres and styles, looking at chapter listings to compare their structures.
  ● Read a wide range of short stories to the class, especially those of a similar length to that expected of children (under 1000 words). Discuss what is omitted and included, as well as the way authors often 'jump' straight into the action, leaving characterisation and even setting to reveal itself through incidental details and dialogue.

## Assess

● Photocopiable pages 205 'Superhero planning sheet' and 206 'Superhero story planner' can be reused for an entirely different genre, or to challenge children to write a new story for their hero, perhaps by providing details of a new villain and/or scenario that they have to adapt their hero for.

● Allowing children to compose orally may reveal the extent of their skills as well as any issues they might have in recording ideas.

## Further practice

● Organise storytelling events at school, with children working alone or in pairs to tell stories to their classmates or younger children.

● Some children take instinctively to story writing, whereas others need ongoing, structured support. Try to differentiate between the two so as not to stifle creativity, while ensuring that those who struggle receive support to keep ideas flowing. Speech-to-text software is improving all the time, as are virtual puppet shows. These provide alternative ways to let children freely construct stories and, used alongside guidance on structure and vocabulary, they can help develop story skills without letting the mechanics of writing slow children down.

Name: _____                    Date: _____

## Superhero checklist

■ Superheroes come in all shapes and sizes, but they often have special characteristics or traits, such as an interesting name or special powers.

■ Use the chart below to list the different characteristics for the superhero of your choice. Give them a rating out of 10 for each characteristic, and decide just how super your hero really is.

| Features | Description | Rating |
|---|---|---|
| Name | | |
| Costume | | |
| Special powers | | |
| Special possessions | | |
| Catchphrase | | |
| Sidekick | | |
| | Total rating | |

■ You can now calculate an average Superhero rating for your chosen character by dividing your total by 6. So, 32 would give you a superhero rating of 5 (ignore the remainder). 10 is obviously the maximum possible rating.

Superhero rating for _____

Conclusion: _____

_____

I can describe elements of a character.

How did you do?

■SCHOLASTIC www.scholastic.co.uk

Name: _____

Date: _____

# Good and evil

■ Compare and contrast a superhero with an arch-enemy.

## Good

Name: _____

Appearance: _____

Superhuman powers: _____

Morality: _____

Weaknesses: _____

Catchphrase: _____

## Evil

Name: _____

Appearance: _____

Superhuman powers: _____

Morality: _____

Weaknesses: _____

Catchphrase: _____

I can use descriptive words for good and evil characters.

How did you do?

## Looking at myths

■ Use this template to help you summarise a well-known myth.

| Myth: |
| --- |
| Characters: |
| Locations: |
| Gods: |
| Main problem: |
| Is there a superhero? |
| Is there an arch-enemy? |
| Summary of the story: |

I can identify elements and summarise a myth.

How did you do?

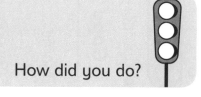

**PHOTOCOPIABLE**

Name: _____     Date: _____

## News scenarios

■ Choose or adapt one of the scenarios below to write a news story.

**1.**
**Who:** Young boy
**What:** Rescued dog
**Where:** Down a cliff
**When:** Last weekend
**How:** Called the coastguard and waited

**2.**
**Who:** Mother of three
**What:** Stopped a burglar
**Where:** In her house
**When:** In the middle of the night
**How:** Used a pram and nappies

**3.**
**Who:** Elderly man
**What:** Saved a speeding bus
**Where:** Town centre
**When:** Saturday afternoon
**How:** Drove it when driver fainted

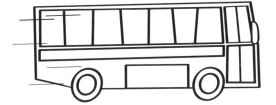

**4.**
**Who:** Two-year-old toddler
**What:** Helped mum after fall
**Where:** In the house
**When:** Monday morning
**How:** Called 999

**5.**
**Who:** Smudge the cat
**What:** Found owner's valuable ring
**Where:** In the garden
**When:** Monday evening
**How:** Digging a hole

**6.**
**Who:** Teenage girl
**What:** Stopped school burning down
**Where:** In school
**When:** Last Friday afternoon
**How:** Waved a flag from a window

I can write a news story.

How did you do?

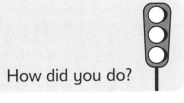

## '-sion' words

■ Complete the text below by inserting the correct words. All of them end in '-sion'.

**Maths Girl Defeats the Aliens**

The alien _____ took the whole world by

surprise. The huge spaceship had crash-landed in Mexico after a

_____ with the moon. Since then, everyone had been

watching _____ , and they saw that aliens were

escaping. There was _____ everywhere, because

nobody knew what powers the aliens had.

Someone had to make a _____ , and that fearful

task fell to Maths Girl, the World's only number-crunching superhero. Using her

extraordinary skills of multiplication and _____ ,

she devised a new potion to destroy the aliens forever. All over the world

everyone was pleased, and a party was organised for Maths Girl. There was

singing and dancing, and it was a very happy _____ .

I can use and spell words ending in '-sion' correctly.

How did you do?

**PHOTOCOPIABLE**

**SCHOLASTIC**
www.scholastic.co.uk

Name: _____          Date: _____

## Superhero planning sheet

■ Use this sheet to prepare a well-rounded portrait of your superhero. Use a pencil, and do not be afraid to change your ideas as you work.

**My superhero**

| Personal information | Alter ego | Unique attributes |
|---|---|---|
| | | |
| Portrait | Back story | Motivation |
| | | |

I can create a new character.

How did you do?

## Superhero story planner

■ Use this sheet to plan your superhero story.

| Superhero | | |
|---|---|---|
| **Sidekick (optional)** | **Villain** | **Setting and dilemma** |
| **Scene 1: setting** | | |
| **Scene 2: main action** | | |
| **Scene 3: conclusion** | | |

I can plan a short story.

How did you do?

## Compound adjectives

■ Can you decide what these adjectives mean? Write the meanings below.

| Compound adjective | Meaning |
|---|---|
| sharp-eyed | |
| tight-fisted | |
| sure-footed | |
| mean-spirited | |
| broken-hearted | |
| open-minded | |
| tongue-tied | |
| cold-blooded | |
| fast-moving | |
| eye-popping | |
| never-ending | |
| record-breaking | |
| fast-thinking | |
| hard-hitting | |
| mouth-watering | |
| ever-lasting | |

I can interpret and suggest meanings for compound adjectives.

How did you do?